HOLMAN *New* *Testament* *Commentary*

I & II *Peter,* I, II & III *John, Jude*

GENERAL EDITOR

Max Anders

AUTHORS

David Walls and Max Anders

HOLMAN REFERENCE

Nashville, Tennessee

Holman New Testament Commentary
© 1999 Broadman & Holman Publishers
Nashville, Tennessee
All rights reserved

ISBN 0–8054–0210–1

Dewey Decimal Classification 226.6
Subject Heading: BIBLE.N.T. 1, 2 PETER; 1, 2, 3, JOHN; JUDE
Library of Congress Card Catalog Number: 98-39365

Walls, David H.
     1, 2 Peter, 1, 2,3, John, Jude / by David Walls.
        p.   cm. — (Holman New Testament commentary)
     Includes bibliographical references.
     ISBN 0–8054–0210–1
     1. Bible. N.T. 1, 2 Peter, 1, 2,3 John, Jude—Commentaries.   I. Title.
II. Series
BS2625.3.G36   1999   98–39365
226.6'07—dc21   CIP

1 2 3 4 5 6 02 01 00 99
D

No aspect of ministry that I have been privileged to be a part of can in any measure be credited to only myself. In fact, alone I would have long ago moved on to other things. Thankfully, I am not alone and it is with the deepest love and gratitude that I applaud my cherished wife Patricia—for her enduring love and encouragement, and our two sons, Jeremy and Kent, for their unending support and enthusiasm. Without these three, my life and ministry would echo with emptiness. But with them, I have been enriched beyond measure and consider my family a rare treasure indeed.

- *David Walls* -
May 1999

Contents

Editorial Preface

Today's church hungers for Bible teaching and Bible teachers hunger for resources to guide them in teaching God's Word. The Holman New Testament Commentary provides the church with the food to feed the spiritually hungry in an easily digestible format. The result: new spiritual vitality that the church can readily use.

Bible teaching should result in new interest in the Scriptures, expanded Bible knowledge, discovery of specific Scriptural principles, relevant applications, and exciting living. The unique format of the Holman New Testament Commentary includes sections to achieve these results for every New Testament book.

Opening quotations from some of the church's best writers lead to an introductory illustration and discussion that draw individuals and study groups into the Word of God. "In a Nutshell" summarizes the content and teaching of the chapter. Verse-by-verse commentary answers the church's questions rather than raising issues scholars usually admit they cannot adequately solve. Bible principles and specific contemporary applications encourage students to move from Bible to contemporary times. A specific modern illustration then ties application vividly to present life. A brief prayer aids the student to commit his or her daily life to the principles and applications found in the Bible chapter being studied. For those still hungry for more, "Deeper Discoveries" take the student into a more personal, deeper study of the words, phrases, and themes of God's Word. Finally, a teaching outline provides transitional statements and conclusions along with an outline to assist the teacher in group Bible studies.

It is the editors' prayer that this new resource for local church Bible teaching will enrich the ministry of group, as well as individual, Bible study, and that it will lead God's people to truly be people of the Book, living out what God calls us to be.

Contributors

Vol. 1 Matthew

Stuart Weber
Pastor
Good Shepherd Community Church
Boring, Oregon

Vol. 2 Mark

Rod Cooper
Professor
Denver Theological Seminary
Denver, Colorado

Vol. 3 Luke

Trent C. Butler
Editor, Bibles
Broadman & Holman Publishers
Nashville, Tennessee

Vol. 4 John

Kenneth Gangel
Professor of Practical Theology and Ministry
Toccoa Falls College
Toccoa Falls, Georgia

Vol. 5 Acts

Kenneth Gangel
Professor of Practical Theology and Ministry
Toccoa Falls College
Toccoa Falls, Georgia

Vol. 6 Romans

Kenneth Boa
President
Reflections Ministry
Atlanta, Georgia

Vol. 7 1 & 2 Corinthians

Richard Pratt
Professor of New Testament
Reformed Theological Seminary
Maitland, Florida

Vol. 8 Galatians, Ephesians, Philippians, Colossians

Max Anders
Senior Pastor
Castleview Baptist Church
Indianapolis, Indiana

Vol. 9 1 & 2 Thessalonians, 1 & 2 Timothy, Titus, Philemon

Knute Larson
Senior Pastor
The Chapel
Akron, Ohio

Vol. 10 Hebrews, James

Thomas Lea
Dean, School of Theology
Southwestern Baptist Theological Seminary
Fort Worth, Texas

Vol. 11 1 & 2 Peter, 1, 2, 3 John, Jude

David Walls & Max Anders
Pastor
Church of the Open Door
Elyria, Ohio

Vol. 12 Revelation

Kendell Easley
Professor of New Testament
Mid-America Baptist Theological Seminary
Memphis, Tennessee

Holman New Testament Commentary

Twelve volumes designed for Bible study and teaching to enrich the local church and God's people.

Series Editor	Max Anders
Managing Editors	Trent C. Butler & Steve Bond
Project Editor	Lloyd W. Mullens
Marketing Manager	Wendell Overstreet
Product Manager	David Shepherd
Typesetter	TF Designs, Mt. Juliet, TN

1 Peter 1

Suffering Strengthens

"*Hope is not a sedative; it is a shot of adrenaline, a blood transfusion. Like an anchor, our hope in Christ stabilizes us in the storms of life; but unlike an anchor, our hope moves us forward, it does not hold us back.*"

W a r r e n   W i e r s b e

BOOK PROFILE: 1 PETER

- A circulating letter to first-century Christians scattered over the northern part of modern Turkey
- Delivered or recorded by Silas (5:12), a friend and coworker of the apostle Peter
- Sent from Rome identified by the code name Babylon (5:13)
- Written shortly before the outbreak of the Neronian persecution in A.D. 64
- Addressed an audience made up of both Jewish and Gentile Christians, with the majority Gentile
- Written during a time of political, social, and personal persecution
- Emphasizes the reality of suffering in the lives of Christians, but also offers words of encouragement and challenge
- Has suffering as a primary theme, mentioning it sixteen times by using eight different Greek terms

AUTHOR PROFILE: PETER

- Simon, a fisherman, who followed John the Baptist until his brother Andrew introduced him to Jesus
- Name changed to Peter by Jesus, signifying the rock-like character that would ultimately dominate Peter's personality
- Natural leader and spokesperson for the disciples
- Impulsive, sometimes selfish, and short-tempered
- Emerged as primary figure in the early church after the day of Pentecost

- Traveled widely in ministry
- Tradition indicates he was crucified upside down in Rome during the persecution by the emperor Nero, around A.D. 68

IN A NUTSHELL

In chapter 1 Peter greets God's chosen people, calling them to praise God. Although you are experiencing trials of great pain, he told them, through Christ you have a new life. These temporary detours of suffering will actually strengthen your commitment to Christ and your testimony for him. Don't allow the trauma of the present to blur your vision of your glorious future with Christ in heaven. Don't allow the trials of the moment to distract you from living a life of obedience to God. Demonstrate this life by reaching out to one another in love.

Suffering Strengthens

I. INTRODUCTION

The Lord Deals in Futures

A man wrote this letter to a pastor friend of mine:

Eighteen years ago the Lord blessed my wife and me with a child born with multiple birth defects. When he was born, the doctor came to me and said, "Don't hope, he will not live out the day." I got on my knees and said, "God, I don't know why you sent me this little boy with so many problems—three and one half pounds, three months premature, only a portion of a left leg, malformed right hand, possible lung damage, etc.; but please don't take him back now." That evening when I came to the hospital the doctor greeted me by saying, "I just examined your son again. I don't believe it's the same boy. I think he's going to make it." My son stayed five weeks in that hospital. He came home and then for years, it was in and out of hospitals for one operation after another. Each time his little stump would grow the bone would push through the tip of his stump and would have to be sawed off. Seeing the pain that boy went through, I thought I was going insane. I cursed God and turned my back on him.

I crawled into a bourbon bottle for fifteen years. The more I drank, the deeper into hell I went. Sometimes, waking up hungover, I would be confronted with horrible things I had done that I didn't even remember doing. One morning I awoke with a broken right hand and discovered twenty-two holes in my wall that I had punched. I didn't remember doing it.

One Sunday morning I laid in bed and reflected on what a lousy husband and father I was and decided I would take one of my shotguns and stick it in my mouth and pull the trigger. The radio was on, and you were speaking. I had never heard you before. You said that Jesus loved me. It had no impact because I had heard it all before. Only then you said, "THE LORD DEALS IN FUTURES." I don't know, to this day, why that phrase hit me like a ton of bricks. It saved my life. I started crying and said, "God, if you deal in futures, then take this wretched life and make something of it before I give it to Satan." Of course, God answered.

And my boy? In the eighth grade he was third on the east coast in a math competition and received a certificate from our governor and a mini scholarship from John Hopkins University in Baltimore. In his freshman year of high school, he was the number one world geography student in the nation. Today he is a junior in high school and continues to astound us with his brilliance. My lovely wife stayed with me through all the hell I put her through. When I asked her why, she just said, "The Lord deals in futures, and so do I."

If anyone in the world could identify with the Lord who deals in futures, it would be the apostle Peter. Everyone remembers Peter. What we remember most vividly about him is his denial of Jesus Christ. Mention the name Peter, and even those who don't know much about the Bible seem to be able to recall a rooster and a guy named Peter who swore he didn't know who Jesus was. That same Peter—the one who struck out badly, who didn't get to home plate, let alone limp around the bases, the one person everybody figured was all washed up—that Peter spent the bulk of his adult life speaking *for* Christ. Some thirty years later and thousands of miles after warranty, Peter sat down in Rome and wrote this letter. If anybody understood that the Lord deals in futures, it was Peter.

First Peter is preeminently a letter of hope, of second and third chances. In the midst of suffering and pain that would attempt to derail us, Peter provides an epistle of triumphant faith. He strengthens and encourages his readers, whose troubles are in the background of virtually every paragraph and who, as a result, felt like they had no future.

Chapter 1 helps us see the true nature of our suffering. It reminds us that as believers in Jesus Christ we have not been abandoned simply because difficult times have assaulted us. Our future in Christ is not in jeopardy. Rather than allowing our pain to derail our Christian living, our hope and trust must remain with God, who loves us and will use even the suffering in our lives to grow us into better people.

II. COMMENTARY

Suffering Strengthens

MAIN IDEA: *God, in his mercy and through the resurrection of Jesus Christ, has given Christians a living hope that cannot be taken away, even though our lives may be excruciatingly painful. In him we have the resources to continue living holy lives.*

A Greeting (vv. 1–2)

SUPPORTING IDEA: *God's plan has always been to choose us to be sanctified by Jesus' death and to live obedient lives.*

1:1. The author identifies himself as **an apostle of Jesus Christ**. He distinguishes himself from the many false apostles who visited the churches in that day. An *apostle* is "one who is sent out with a message."

The letter is addressed to **God's elect**, and to those **who have been chosen** (v. 2). These two expressions—mirror images of each other—are inserted early on, to provide comfort. In his greeting Peter's primary purpose was to strengthen Christian faith in the midst of suffering, not to teach the intricacies of doctrine. In themselves, believers are just ordinary people, but the gracious choice of God makes us what we are—the ones whom God favors and loves.

Peter describes the believers to whom he wrote as being **strangers** who are **scattered**. They included both Jewish and Gentile people who had become followers of Jesus Christ. They did not live in the heartland of God's people Israel. Neither did they live close to the mother church of Christianity, also in Jerusalem. Rather, they formed the Diaspora (which derives from the Greek word for "strangers"). That is, they had been dispersed or scattered to other cities and countries all over the world. Specifically, he wrote to believers living in what is now northern Turkey, some five hundred to eight hundred miles from the hometown of God's people and God's church. They could easily have felt isolated and insignificant. Peter says to these people, "Take courage. Wherever you live geographically, in Christ you are part of God's elect. He chose you."

1:2. Peter's initial desire was to give the believers a lift, an encouraging word. His emphasis in these first two verses should most likely be translated: "To the chosen ones who are strangers in the world, scattered . . . according to the foreknowledge of God the Father."

Peter linked their scattering to the foreknowledge of God. In other words, the difficulties God's people face do not surprise God. God the Father knows about everything his chosen people face. He works it all out as part of his plan. **According to the foreknowledge of God the Father** also suggests that all we go through is "according to God's fatherly care." God knew our circumstances of pain before the world began and cares for us in accordance with his fatherly care.

This occurs **through the sanctifying work of the Spirit.** Even in the midst of pain, the Holy Spirit is molding, shaping, and growing believers. The Holy Spirit is turning every circumstance, every sorrow, every hardship into a tool of spiritual maturing.

In the same sentence Peter spoke of being obedient to Jesus Christ. **Obedience** conveys the idea of listening and submitting to what is heard. It involves a change of attitude in the believer. In the midst of pain, it is difficult to listen to God, let alone obey him. Yet, since we are chosen of God and are objects of his fatherly care, we are never out of his plan. He is designing our sanctification, our spiritual growth. Knowing that, we can continue, with the assistance of the Holy Spirit, to obey the commands of Jesus Christ. That obedience begins with accepting Jesus as personal Lord and Savior and continues by living life each day just as Jesus told us and leads us to live it. We obey the call of Jesus to salvation, the word of Jesus in the Bible, and the encouragement of Jesus found in personal relationship with him each day.

Sprinkling by his blood reflects the language of Numbers 19 and the red heifer purification rites (cf. Exod. 24:4–8; Heb. 9:13–21; 10:22,29). For Christians, the blood of Christ on the cross covers our sins and brings us salvation.

To people sprinkled with Christ's blood and obedient to Christ, Peter gave the typical Christian greeting. Peace reflects the Hebrew greeting *shalom,* wishing wholeness and meaningful life. Grace is the explicitly Christian greeting, placing believers under the blood of Christ to receive God's free, undeserved grace and hope for living each day.

B Hope for the Disenfranchised (vv. 3–12)

> **SUPPORTING IDEA:** *God the Father has given us who believe a living hope as a result of the resurrection of Jesus Christ.*

1:3. Peter piled up expressions in verses 3–5 to talk about a believer's relationship with God through salvation. His opening words are those of worship and praise, reminding us that salvation did not come because of who we are or because of what we have accomplished. Salvation came as a gift of mercy. Salvation represents a new birth (see John 1:13), a changing of who we are. Salvation makes us dead to sin and alive to righteousness in Christ.

Peter linked our salvation relationship to what he termed "a living hope." Peter is without question the apostle of hope. The hope that he had in mind is the eager, confident expectation of life to come in eternity. Hope in the New Testament always relates to a future good! Amid present and difficult dangers we are justified in viewing the future with optimism because we are securely attached to the God who deals in futures. Furthermore, our hope is a

living hope because it finds its focus in **the resurrection of Jesus Christ from the dead.** Our living hope comes from a living, resurrected Christ.

1:4. Peter used the word *inheritance* to describe our relationship with God through Jesus Christ. **Inheritance** emphasizes the believer's eternal home in heaven. Peter used a triple word picture to describe this inheritance. Our inheritance can **never perish, spoil or fade.** These three verbal adjectives indicate that the inheritance is untouched by death, unstained by evil, and unimpaired by time. Our inheritance is death-proof, sin-proof, and time-proof. This inheritance is **kept in heaven,** for believers. *Kept* means "to guard or reserve." The tense of the verb emphasizes the state or condition and underlines the fact that the inheritance already exists and is being preserved. God himself has reserved this inheritance in heaven for believers, and it continues to be there, still reserved for us. The difficulties we experience cannot undermine the certainty of our coming inheritance.

1:5. **The salvation that is ready to be revealed** is synonymous with the inheritance described in verse 4. Believers are cared for by God the Father. We are **shielded by God's power.** *Shielded* means "to guard" or to "watch over." This military term describes how soldiers guard someone. The present tense emphasizes the continual nature of this shielding. It does not suggest that believers are shielded from pain, difficulty, or anguish. It means that God himself guards and watches over our salvation, our inheritance. Our relationship with God now as we grow more like Christ is a foretaste of that salvation which will be revealed when Christ returns.

1:6. This kind of care from God the Father suggests a response of great rejoicing. Verse 8 repeats this emphasis on joy, calling it **an inexpressible and glorious joy.** Such joy springs from the contemplation of God and of the salvation that comes to us from God.

This joyous response occurs even in the midst of grief caused by suffering through all kinds of trials. **Suffer grief** forms a metaphor derived from a military expression for being harassed. It includes the inner mental distress or sadness that comes because of painful circumstances. **All kinds of trials** literally means "varied, multicolored, or diversified" trials. This takes on a depth of meaning against the background of the ghastly persecution led by the Roman emperor Nero. In that persecution, Christians were wrapped in freshly slaughtered animal skins and fed to dogs and wild animals. They were dipped in pitch or tar and set on fire as torches to light Nero's gardens at night. This persecution was the first of nine that took place under the Roman Empire during the next 250 years. Peter himself very likely died during this first persecution.

All of this sheds some light on the expression Peter used to describe these varied trials: **a little while.** Suffering here is brief in light of our inheritance that lasts for eternity. Regardless of how long our trials last, that length of time is nothing in light of eternity.

1:7. Why does God allow this suffering to occur? Faith is being proved **genuine** through the trials. One purpose of trials is to sift out what is genuine in a person's faith. Followers of God, in both the Old and New Testaments, know that God uses trying circumstances to test the hearts and lives of his people in order to mature them spiritually. Through difficulties God often tests whether our faith is genuine.

Peter cemented his point with the illustration of a goldsmith. To form a useful object, raw gold must be cast into a mold. For that to occur, the solid ore must be melted, requiring a temperature of 1,900 degrees Fahrenheit. When the gold is melted, the impurities rise to the surface, where they are skimmed off or burned off. A goldsmith knows the gold is ready to cast when the liquid gold becomes mirror-like and he can see his face reflected in the surface.

The parallel in a believer's life is obvious. Through the refining heat of trials, we as followers of Jesus Christ grow spiritually and thus reflect more of Christ's character in our lives. The language of this illustration may also refer to the first-century process of making pottery. Potters baked clay pots to give them strength. The process sometimes cracked pots that had flaws, but the ones that survived the process were then marked with the same Greek word that Peter used here (*dokimos*) for "genuine."

Warren Wiersbe reminds us, "The trials of life test our faith to prove its sincerity. A faith that cannot be tested cannot be trusted. A person who abandons his/her faith when the going gets tough is only proving that he/she really had no faith at all" (Warren W. Wiersbe, *Be Hopeful* [Wheaton, Illinois: Victor Books, 1982], p. 25.)

Peter moved his focus from our present life to look forward to the day of the second coming of Christ and the testimony our approved faith will declare on that day. The faith of these first-century Christians met with scoffing, rejection, and persecution on earth. When the Lord returns, the scene will be reversed. Gold is certainly valuable, Peter said, but it is not as valuable as our proven faith. Gold is temporary, but out proven faith is eternal. The fact that our faith in Jesus is tested and has been proven genuine results in **praise, glory and honor when Jesus Christ is revealed.**

God's purposes in present grief may not be completely known in a week, a year, or even a lifetime. In fact, some of God's purposes will not even be known when believers die and go to be with the Lord. Some will only be discovered when Christ is revealed to everyone at the Second Coming.

1:8. How could these Christians face their suffering? They chose to **love** Christ and to **believe in him** even though they had not actually seen him in the past and had not encountered him visibly in the present. Most of Peter's readers had no personal contact with Christ while he lived on earth. They were a generation removed from the time of his earthly ministry. This did not become an excuse. Instead, by accepting the testimony of those, like Peter, who had seen Christ, they entered into a personal relationship with Christ marked by love and belief.

"Believe," as used here, means "to trust or rest your confidence in someone, to depend on them." Having trusted Christ with present salvation from sin, you can also trust him with future salvation from pain and suffering. The result of this active trust is **an inexpressible and glorious joy** even in the midst of suffering. Peter repeated the theme of joy that he introduced in verse 6. This joy issues from gratitude to God for who he is and for what he has provided through salvation. Joy comes especially from our hope of seeing Christ one day. Although our trials may result in temporary grief, this need not extinguish our deep, abiding joy anchored in our hope in Jesus Christ.

Biblical joy does not depend on circumstances. Joy is inseparably connected to love and trust. Even during pain, the fullness of joy comes from a deep sense of the presence of God in our lives. We can experience joy in suffering when we believe our suffering has a redemptive or refining purpose.

1:9. Not only our joy but also the assurance of salvation is not contingent upon our circumstances. We are marching, even though in pain, toward the final goal of our faith—our place in eternity and in heaven. One day believers will enjoy salvation to the full in the presence of Jesus Christ. Pain and suffering will be no more.

1:10. The next three verses (vv. 10–12) attempt to increase our appreciation for the great salvation we enjoy in Jesus Christ. The spiritual blessings believers now experience are greater than anything the Old Testament prophets or even the angels imagined. The prophets longed to participate in this salvation and coming period of grace. They thought about it; they searched the subject out as best they could—all in an effort to comprehend more clearly what we seem to take for granted.

1:11. In their searching for more, they discovered that Jesus would first of all suffer and only then would glory follow. The pattern seen in the life of Christ is, in fact, the pattern of our lives. Our suffering is not a sign that Christ has betrayed us, or that he is no longer concerned about us, or that he has abdicated his throne. Our suffering is a sign of our fellowship with the resurrected Lord, who first suffered for us. Suffering, in some respects, becomes a sign of the glory that is to follow in our lives when we enter the presence of Christ in heaven.

1:12. Old Testament prophets did not understand the timing or calendar of dates surrounding the incarnation of Jesus Christ. They did understand that their words would have a dramatic impact on future generations. The prophets realized that what they wrote was not for themselves, but for those who would live later and who would hear the gospel and follow Christ (see also Heb. 11:32,36–39). For generations, the prophets faithfully recorded their prophecies about the coming Messiah, but they did not know who this Messiah would be, or when he would come to earth. Even the angels were looking intently to see if they could get a glimpse of the grace of God at work. New Testament believers had already received the grace that the prophets would have liked to seen and the angels would have liked to understood. We, too, in our day have received that same grace: it is Jesus Christ our Lord.

Believers in Christ are the heirs of the full message of the prophets. The least disciple of Jesus Christ is in a better position to understand Old Testament revelation than the greatest prophet before Christ came. Knowing Jesus gives us a clearer picture of salvation than the prophets ever knew. It reminds us that our pain and suffering do not diminish the living hope that has been given to us through the death and resurrection of Jesus Christ.

◪ Living Out Holiness in the Midst of Pain (vv. 13–25)

SUPPORTING IDEA: *Our living hope, our great salvation does not simply impact the future; it is to mark the way we live today, particularly when we experience suffering and pain.*

1:13. This verse sets the time line boundaries for our behavior. The first word, **therefore**, points back to the preceding discussion that focused on our salvation hope. We entered into that hope when we committed ourselves in faith to the death and resurrection of Jesus Christ. The last words in this verse, **when Jesus Christ is revealed**, point ahead to an undisclosed day in the future when Jesus Christ will come to earth the second time. Christians must not forget the first chapter of our salvation or ignore its final chapter. The first affects the second. The second affects the first. From the outset believers are to live each day for that great final day.

How do we do this? First, **prepare your minds for action.** In the first century, people who wanted to walk or run quickly faced a problem. Before they could quicken their pace, they had to gather up their loose flowing robes with a belt so they would not trip and fall flat on their face as they set off for their destination. Translating that into daily living, Peter said, "Pull your thoughts together. Don't let anything hinder your mind as you put it to work for God." In other words, have a disciplined mind.

Be self-controlled expresses the same idea. A loose paraphrase might be, "Stay on your toes spiritually." Be realistic about what you face in your life as a Christian. Be alert and ready in your whole spiritual and mental attitude, because it is so easy to slide, especially when you are suffering. In those moments it is very difficult to "pull your thoughts together," and to "be realistic" about your circumstances. The tendency of our mind is to scream exaggerations and denials. The inclination is to lean away from spiritual concerns.

That will be our fate unless we set [our] **hope fully on the grace to be given [us] when Jesus Christ is revealed**. The main emphasis is on putting one's hope completely in the final demonstration of the grace of God in Jesus Christ. At this moment, we enjoy only the beginning of that grace. What we have experienced of grace up to this point in our lives does not begin to compare with the grace that will be ours at the second coming of Christ. We must have the long view in mind, or the short run will kill us. Peter is really issuing a command: "Keep looking toward your final salvation, which will be fully experienced when Christ returns. You have been saved, you are being saved, and you will be saved, so don't get off course." Our future hope is not simply a theological doctrine with little or no practical application. It is, in fact, an ethical hope. It has behavioral consequences. If we really believe in the second coming of Christ, this belief must make a difference in the way we live.

1:14. The difference in the way we live is described by Peter's words, **as obedient children**. Obedience does not produce a believer in Jesus Christ, but true belief will always produce obedience in a believer in Jesus Christ. Part of this obedience is our nonconformity to evil desires. The verb *conformed* means "to be fashioned into something." The word describes the practice of adopting for oneself a pattern or mold of life that is changeable and unstable.

The emphasis of verse 14 helps us see that this conformity does not begin with outward actions, as much as it begins with our attitude, our mind-set, our character. Peter is referring to a conformity of thought and purpose. What God requires in us is a total change of purpose. Our outward life will change only as it is a natural outworking of an inner change. Conformity is a lack of obedience that adopts the attitudes, mind-sets, and purposes of the culture of which we are a part. Conformity belongs to the time of ignorance when we did not know Christ and so lived like the world.

One of the prevailing attitudes of our culture is, "I don't want any problems, any pain. I do not deserve to experience difficulties or trauma in any measure." As believers, we are not to adopt that mind-set. We are to conform to the example of Christ, the Suffering Servant.

1:15–16. The alternative to conformity is holiness. Among God's characteristics, as he has revealed himself, none is more significant than his holiness (see Lev. 11:44–45; 19:2; 20:7). Both the Old and New Testaments speak more about his holiness than any other attribute. The implication is that believers who cultivate Christian hope must also cultivate personal holiness. The root meaning of the word *holiness* could be expressed as "different or distinct." It describes a qualitative difference. Holiness includes a specific moral sense of separation from evil and a dedication to a life of right living. The lives and attitudes of Christians should be qualitatively different because of their relationship to God through Jesus Christ. Holiness produces in our lives a loving conformity to God's commands which ultimately produces the character of God in us.

1:17. God takes character development seriously, so Peter highlighted God's role as judge. Membership in God's family, although a great privilege, must not lead to the presumption that disobedience will pass unnoticed by God. Judging here may describe either God's present dealings with believers in the development of holiness in their lives or the time of judgment when Jesus Christ returns and each person will give an account of his/her works.

In any case, this judgment is done **impartially**, literally, "without receiving the face." God's judgment is not determined by outward appearance or pretense. Whatever faces or masks people try to hide behind, they remain transparent to God. God's judgment deals with a person's character, not simply one's actions, which can be faked. God is concerned with individual actions and the internal motivation behind these actions.

In light of this judgment, whether present or future, believers will not be quite so anchored to earth and time. Instead, we focus on the hope of eternity and view our life in this perspective. We view ourselves as **strangers** on earth. The term means that we have "temporary residency." It describes a person who visits for a short time in a country where he does not take out citizenship. This is the perspective of the believer who lives with pain in the light of hope. This is our viewpoint since we desire to see God forge his own holy character into our lives, even when this involves pain. We desire to be obedient to the commands of God even when it is difficult to believe because of the extremities of life. Thus, we live life in **reverent fear.**

Although some interpreters would suggest that this expression reflects the believer's fear of God's discipline, the flow of the chapter suggests a different emphasis. This expression does not refer to terror or even to the fear of judgment or the loss of reward. The expression could best be understood with the words "reverential awe." This is the kind of positive awe that a son or daughter has toward a respected and loved parent. This is the kind of positive awe that motivates a child to shrink from whatever would displease or grieve his or her parents.

Reverential awe surrounds the believer's desire to live a life of holiness and obedience even in the face of difficulties. Reverential awe forms the major backbone of the believer's life. As believers, we constantly set before ourselves the hope of the resurrection and the grace and mercy of God that has provided that hope. Peter returned to that theme in the next section of verses.

1:18–19. **Redeemed** is the dominant word used to describe our salvation hope. The word means "to release by paying a price or a ransom." For the Jews, the picture of redemption would be God's deliverance from Egypt. For the Gentiles, it would be the picture of a slave whose freedom was purchased. The message for both audiences is the same: before we can enter a relationship of faith with Jesus Christ, we must realize that we are slaves who need to be set free from our **empty way of life**.

An empty way of life is a life that has no real direction or purpose and leads to no good results (cf. Eph. 4:17). It is essentially a life of entrapment. Peter's readers were trapped in the lifestyle inherited from their pagan ancestors. We are too often trapped in the pagan materialism inherited from our culture. It is a life that has no escape from the futile and sinful behavior that will end in condemnation from the Eternal Judge. The only escape comes through the death of Jesus Christ, who is described in verse 19 as the perfect sacrifice. Christ's death was the ransom paid for our spiritual deliverance. The ransom was not paid with first-century currency, such as gold or silver. These commodities have no eternal value. Redemption was paid with the blood of Christ, upon which no value can be placed.

1:20–21. The death of Christ was not simply a panicked, emergency, plan-B approach. Nor was it an accident or twist of fate. The death of Christ (the ransom price) was planned before the cosmos appeared. Redemption salvation through the death of Jesus Christ was a plan made in eternity past, but demonstrated actually through the incarnation when Christ died and shed his blood on the cross. **Was revealed** focuses attention on the incarnation, but it also implies the preexistence of Christ.

The death of Jesus Christ, planned prior to creation, was **for your sake**. We should not view Christ's death as an isolated, distant, impersonal event. Peter personalized the death of Christ for each of us. It is as if the entire purpose of God was planned and implemented specifically for each of us alone.

God's gracious gift of salvation was planned before creation. It was accomplished two thousand years ago on Calvary. Still, it becomes real only through the active belief of individuals. Through Christ we believe in God. We confidently put our trust in God as the One who raised Jesus from the dead (Rom. 4:24) and gave him a share in his glory (1 Pet. 3:21–22; Acts 3:13).

The broader context of chapter 1 encourages us: Hang in there. Don't waste your lives in irresponsible living. The same God who allowed his son to suffer will also allow you to suffer. He raised Jesus to glory, and he will also raise you to glory. You are redeemed. The ransom price was the life of Jesus Christ. Because he was raised from the dead, you, too, can look forward with confidence to that hope.

1:22. Believers are people who **have purified** themselves. The perfect tense suggests a state that began in the past at our conversion to Jesus Christ and is still the case as we live out our salvation each day. When we placed our faith in Christ, God the Father cleansed us of our sin. He declared us pure in his eyes. Since that time we have begun to live out that purity or holiness in our daily behavior. We may not yet show all the characteristics of holy people, but the process has begun and will continue (cf. Phil. 1:6). It continues as we obey the truth of the gospel and its demands.

Peter insisted so firmly on this point that he doubled his instruction in this area. He repeated for emphasis one of the demands of the gospel: in our relationships we are to demonstrate a **sincere love** for each other, a love that emerges from the depths of our heart. Two Greek words for love—*phileo* and *agape*—appear here. Whether a major distinction is intended is not clear. Peter may have been recalling the language that Jesus used with him years earlier (see John 21:15–17). What is clear is that people of vertical faith know how to live with each other horizontally. God demands that we relate to one another with a self-sacrificing love. Our motive is not to get something out of the deal but to give to the other person. We are not attempting to manipulate others in order to benefit ourselves, but we are to extend ourselves for the sake of the other person.

The adverb **deeply** reinforces this point. It describes the intensity of our love for others. Drawn from the world of athletics, this word means "to exert oneself with all of one's energy." This kind of love is something that a person must work at, even when life is difficult. The love we extend to one another must be constant and enduring, unshaken by adversity or painful circumstances.

1:23–25. We can demonstrate this love in such fashion only because we have entered into a new way of life with Jesus Christ by faith. Everything in our lives turns on this axis, which explains Peter's constant reference to this subject. Verse 23 reminds us that we **have been born again.** We have been given a new start spiritually. Part of the demonstration of that new start appears in the way in which we relate to each other.

The new birth is brought about through the agency of the Word of God. The Word of God is the instrument for the communication of the new birth. The **word** here includes the Old Testament Scriptures, the New Testament apostolic proclamation, and the presentation of both in the message of the first-century evangelists.

Living suggests the power of the Word of God to awaken new life and to initiate change in our lives through the application of its teaching. **Enduring** reinforces the idea of the permanence of the new life that God's Word generates as well as the permanence of the Word itself.

This latter focus is emphasized in verses 24–25. The permanence of the Word is contrasted with the impermanence of people and vegetation. The focus of this section is the Word of God that endures or stands forever; it can never be made ineffective. It is an unchanging, vital, ever-present word of truth. It meets people's needs, providing them with a sense of direction and wholeness. This is of crucial importance when everything around us seems to be coming apart. The Word of God stands forever because the God who speaks it is the eternal, faithful, powerful one who always keeps his promises. This Word stands as the foundation for Christian preaching. Through it you may come to know Jesus Christ as Savior and receive the eternal, living hope.

> **MAIN IDEA REVIEW:** *God, in his mercy and through the resurrection of Jesus Christ, has given Christians a living hope that cannot be taken away, even though their lives may be excruciatingly painful. It is in him that we have the resources to continue living holy lives.*

III. CONCLUSION

Avoid the Detours

A single moment in this chapter convinces us that the heart of a true pastor beats inside Peter. His opening words show that he cared deeply for the people to whom he wrote. More than anything else, he wanted them to walk away from his words encouraged. Although they felt like strangers in their corner of the world, isolated from others and God because of their pain, God's Word brought exciting news: God the Father had especially and eternally chosen them as objects of his love. As a result, their future in heaven was assured. They could count on this living hope even in the midst of circumstances that promised only uncertainty.

We feel weak and anemic in faith, but God the Holy Spirit empowers us. He enables us and assists us in our spiritual journey and in our obedience to God the Son. God has done everything he can to assure us of his special love for us. Our pain does not prove we are spiritually inferior. Quite the opposite! God continues to use our circumstances of extremity to stretch us and to validate our faith. This stretching is necessary, because it isn't going to get any easier living the Christian life. Difficulty, opposition, and persecution are never out of the rearview mirror of our experience. We must remember this when the going continues to be rocky. The temptation to revert to a former way of life may be intense. Still, Peter encourages us to stay strong and avoid those detours.

Individually, as we rely on and trust in the hope that God has given us, we can be strong. Corporately, as we reach out to others in love, we can also draw strength from one another. Finally, we must never lose sight of the eternal Word of the Lord. When people fail us, our journey can find direction and assurance from the "enduring Word of God," which finds its character from the unchanging character of God himself.

PRINCIPLES

- Believers are chosen of God and are objects of his care, and therefore are never out of his plan, even when this plan includes difficulties and pain.
- The believer's eternal inheritance of heaven is reserved by God.
- The Christian life does not exempt a believer from experiencing difficulties.
- The trials of the Christian life are designed to produce Christlike character in the believer and to demonstrate the sincerity of our faith.
- The prophets of the Old Testament desperately wanted to experience the visible, historical presence of Jesus the Messiah, something all Christians are to appreciate and value.
- The doctrine of the second coming of Jesus Christ is to impact positively the behavior of Christians in the present moment.
- Obedience and holiness are to mark the believer's life in Christ.
- God is the final and ultimate judge of humankind.
- The death and resurrection of Jesus Christ form the bedrock of the believer's salvation.
- The Word of God is central in the life of the believer.

APPLICATIONS

- Whatever your past may include, God is in the business of giving you a future with a hope.
- Do not resist or resent the trials of your life, but view them as God-designed instruments of spiritual growth.
- Any sound theology of the Second Coming must emphasize the positive behavior that is to mark the Christian's way of life today.
- Continue to examine your life for true marks of holiness and obedience to Jesus Christ.
- Cultivate a "reverential awe" toward God.
- Regularly personalize the benefit of Christ's death for you.
- Consider ways that you can demonstrate a sincere and deep love for other Christians.

IV. LIFE APPLICATION

Only Because of Jesus

It was supposed to be like any other two-week period in my life. It turned out to be like no two weeks that I can remember. This brief time span began with the suicide of a prominent member of the church I was serving. Over six hundred people attended the funeral for this "successful businessman." These fourteen days also included:

The confession of a forty-three-year-old man who had murdered his father when he was thirteen and had never gotten over it.

A lunch with a dear friend who told me how he had made thirty million dollars in three and one-half years and had lost it all in the space of just a few weeks.

A Christian friend who had loaned seventy thousand dollars to another Christian—money that was to be paid back in seven days—but the guy walked.

A long-distance call from a pastor friend in another state letting me know that after just fourteen months in his new church, he had been fired that week.

In moments like these—the extreme moments of living—1 Peter 1 proves to be helpful. This chapter of hope and encouragement gives assurance when everything seems to be flying apart: God, in his grace, **has given us new birth into a living hope** (v. 3) and an eternal inheritance that is **kept in heaven** (v. 4) for us.

We as Christians, in light of our assured future, have the privilege, opportunity, and spiritual resources to model a response or reaction to trials, difficulties, and pain that will surprise and intrigue those who do not know Jesus Christ. Rather than feel rejected or abandoned by God in the midst of pain, we can reflect a positive, genuine joy to those around us (v. 8).

As believers, we have a perspective that others do not enjoy and one that others could only wish to experience (vv. 10–13). We can look back to the death and resurrection of Jesus Christ and bring his work for our salvation into our view of life and eternity. What he has started for us, he will finish at the Second Coming. In light of that assurance, our motivation for obedience is not fear of God but gratitude to God.

God is crazy about us. He loves us so much that not only did he send Jesus Christ to die for us—not only did he extend to us the gift of eternity and the forgiveness of all of our sin—he has also made an effort to demonstrate his continued interest in our future—in our growth—by allowing us to encounter trials in our lives. This does not mean for a moment there is something defective about our faith. It simply means that God is continuing to refine our character and behavior so the image of Christ will be positively reflected through us.

How encouraging to know that God has not left us alone, without his presence and care. He is involved in our continuing growth and maturity. He wants to see us become the best we can be, for his glory.

When we allow this truth to settle into our hearts, it encourages us to reflect to others around us—Christians and non-Christians alike—the character of Jesus. This includes a deliberate choice to extend the love of God to each other within the body of Christ. Whatever else the church is to be doing, it is to be demonstrating love through its members. How desperately anemic we have become at this point. We are prepared to divide and split apart for the smallest offense or infraction, rather than to travel obediently on the high road of love.

In our interpretation of "holiness" we sometimes substitute the words "separation, isolation, and alienation." We become critical, caustic, and cold toward others and actually convince ourselves that we are honoring the Lord as we do so. Peter emphasizes the necessity of moral purity and holiness, while at the same time reminding us to model lives that are positive and attractive and that offer hope, assurance, comfort, and love. The church should certainly avoid conforming to **the evil desires** (v. 14) of our culture. But in our pursuit of this goal, have we lost sight of our opportunity to impact a dying world with the love of Jesus Christ and the hope he provides when the extremities of life bombard us?

Several years ago I read an article by Sue Holtcamp. She told of having a life almost untouched by suffering. She credited this to the fact that God protects his people. Then her life started to cave in. She was hospitalized seven times, endured three back surgeries in three years, and developed a drug dependency problem as she took medicine for the pain. Her husband, after twenty years of building a business, lost it all.

"You know," she wrote, "one night I was talking to our seventeen-year-old daughter, Katie. Talking about Jesus, she ended with this statement, 'All I know, and I know it for certain, is that I love and I trust Jesus Christ.' Under her breath she said, 'I may never know anything more.'"

The next day Sue saw her daughter and her husband take off in a private plane. Shortly after it was out of sight, the plane disintegrated. "Half my family was dead," she observed, "and I wondered if I could bear it. By the grace of God I could, because of Jesus Christ."

V. PRAYER

Lord, allow us the ability to view our suffering in light of our salvation. May our outlook on life here on earth not be so clouded by our pain that we lose sight of you and your mercy. Allow our difficulties to draw us closer to you in obedience and holiness, recognizing that your character is being formed in us all the time. May we find strength in our future hope and in your present and enduring word to us. Amen.

VI. DEEPER DISCOVERIES

A. God's Elect (v. 1) . . . Chosen According to the Fore- knowledge of God (v. 2)

"Election" has been variously interpreted throughout church history. The limited scope of this commentary does not allow us to provide exhausting and detailed answers to such issues; however, a brief overview is appropriate.

Evangelicals primarily hold one of two major views of election:

1. *Arminianism.* The conditional choice of God by which he deter-mined who would believe based on his foreknowledge of who *will* exercise faith. It is the result of man's faith (House, 97). Another way to define this point of view is that God chose those whom he knew would believe in him of their own free will or choice. In this sense, election is conditional, based on man's response in faith (see Enns, 491).

2. *Calvinism.* The unconditional and loving choice of God by which he determines who *must* believe. It is the cause of man's faith (House, 97). Another way to define this point of view is that God uncondi-tionally, from eternity past, elected some people to be saved. Election is not based on man's future response (see Enns, 491).

The same differences of opinion overlap when a person specifically attempts to understand the foreknowledge of God in respect to election. The particular noun, translated as **foreknowledge** in verse 2, occurs only twice in the New Testament, here and in Acts 2:23. Some suggest that the word means "to know beforehand." It carries with it the idea of knowing with affection and with a resulting impact. This is, then, the foreknowledge of what people would do in response to the gospel and would most often be a definition con-nected with an Arminian view. The other point of reference, Calvinism, would teach that the term *foreknowledge,* when used in reference to God, has the added meaning of "choice" or "determined purpose." It refers, then, to that counsel of God in which, after deliberate judgment, certain people were designated to a certain position eternally.

B. Salvation That Is Ready to Be Revealed in the Last Time (v. 5)

When Christians talk about salvation, they generally do so in the past tense. Their understanding, which is correct, is that when a person embraces by faith the person and work of Jesus Christ, that person is "saved" or enters into **salvation** (Acts 16:30; 1 Cor. 15:2; Eph. 2:8). There is a sense through-out the New Testament, however, that our salvation, although completely effective, has not yet been fully appreciated by us or revealed to us. An aspect of our salvation is yet future. The revelation or appearance of Jesus Christ on the day of the Lord will complete this aspect of the believer's salvation (cf. 1 Thess. 4:16–17).

C. Be Holy Because I Am Holy (v. 16)

Holiness is an important part of the believer's life. Committed believers debate the extent or degree of that holiness. Generally, the New Testament perspective on holiness is that it belongs to all believers. A common term for all believers is *holy ones,* normally translated as "saints." "Saints" does not refer to people who have made more progress in holiness than others, but to believers in general. All true believers are holy through Jesus Christ (1 Cor. 1:30). Holiness is a reality for all who belong to Christ.

At the same time, the New Testament places a strong emphasis on holiness in the moral or ethical realm. In this sense, holiness refers to the transformation or change that occurs in the follower of Jesus (1 Thess. 5:23). Since God is totally holy, his concern is that his people become completely holy. Therefore, holiness is not simply an internal reality but also something that is to be perfected (2 Cor. 7:1; see Elwell, *Evangelical Dictionary of Theology,* 516).

According to Bockmuehl,

> Christians are called to sanctification. It is part of the purpose of their election and remains the indispensable condition of their communion with God. As the complement of their justification (forgiveness of sins) it is, in the first place, a work of God, more specifically of the Holy Spirit, both as a one-time act, valid for all time, imputing and imparting holiness, and as an ongoing, progressive work. In the latter sense, it also becomes a human work. It takes place in our earthly lives as a moral and spiritual cleansing and dedication of soul and body, harnessing and deploying all human faculties in the service of God, for the upbuilding of Christian fellowship and the implementation of God's will in the world (K. Bockmuehl, "Sanctification," in *New Dictionary of Theology,* 615).

Our moral condition and life are meant to reflect our standing in Jesus Christ. How far can we take this? John Wesley, founder of Methodism, taught that we can experience "perfect love." He suggested that believers, in their spiritual growth, can enjoy the experience of God's love dominating their lives. A follower of Christ, according to Wesley, will make mistakes or have faults, but the fount of his life is love. He can experience "moment by moment non-transgression of the known will of God." This position certainly has some difficulties; however, most Christians would agree that we can never know full perfection or holiness until we see Christ. Working toward the goal of complete maturity or holiness is still one of the primary forces of the Christian experience (see *Eerdmans Handbook*, 363).

VII. TEACHING OUTLINE

A. INTRODUCTION

1. Lead Story: The Lord Deals in Futures
2. Context: Peter's readers were feeling abandoned by God and battered by their difficulties, so Peter began his letter by addressing their fears and reassuring them of God's abiding care for them.
3. Transition: This chapter introduces us to the incredible encouragement and practical hope that the gospel of Jesus Christ brings to the believer. Even in the midst of pain and trials, believers can model a positive life of obedience to Jesus Christ out of gratitude for his grace.

B. COMMENTARY

1. Greeting (vv. 1–2)
   a. Author—Peter (v. 1)
   b. Recipients—Christians living in northern Turkey (v. 1)
   c. Greetings (v. 2)
2. Hope for the Disenfranchised (vv. 3–12)
   a. Praise for the Christian's eternal relationship with God through salvation (vv. 3–5)
   b. Rejoicing because of our salvation of hope (v. 6)
   c. Rejoicing in spite of our suffering (vv. 6–9)
   d. Appreciating the grace that has come to us (vv. 10–12)
3. Living Out Holiness in the Midst of Pain (vv. 13–25)
   a. Obedience and holiness in our lives (vv. 13–16)
   b. Reverent fear in our lives (v. 17)
   c. Appreciating our redemption (vv. 18–21)
   d. Demonstrating heartfelt love (v. 22)
   e. Remembering our new birth (vv. 23–25)

C. CONCLUSION: ONLY BECAUSE OF JESUS

VIII. ISSUES FOR DISCUSSION

1. How does your hope for eternal salvation in Christ help you get through the dark days of suffering and frustration?
2. How does being chosen by God's foreknowledge bring hope to your daily life?

3. How can you be shielded by God's power and still have to suffer grief and trials?
4. How do you find assurance that your faith in Christ is real?
5. Describe Christian joy. Do you have this joy? How can you know for sure that you have it?

1 Peter 2

God Is Building You

I. INTRODUCTION
I Am Still Growing

II. COMMENTARY
A verse-by-verse explanation of the chapter.

III. CONCLUSION
Spiritual Rigor Mortis

An overview of the principles and applications from the chapter.

IV. LIFE APPLICATION
Did You Do Your Best?

Melding the chapter to life.

V. PRAYER
Tying the chapter to life with God.

VI. DEEPER DISCOVERIES
Historical, geographical, and grammatical enrichment of the commentary.

VII. TEACHING OUTLINE
Suggested step-by-step group study of the chapter.

VIII. ISSUES FOR DISCUSSION
Zeroing the chapter in on daily life.

Quote

"*A*lthough it's great to be called a PGA Tour player, and

it's probably greater to be called a PGA Champion,

I don't think there's any greater gift than is mine,

to be called a child of God."

P a u l   A z i n g e r

1 Peter

I N   A   N U T S H E L L

*C*hapter 2 describes how God is building Christians. Live godly lives, Peter declared, for God is building you into a spiritual house through Christ. He has made you a royal priesthood to be a positive example and witness to others. Therefore, respond properly to human authorities as well as to unjust suffering in your lives. Remind yourselves that Jesus Christ himself suffered unjustly and is your example.

God Is Building You

I. INTRODUCTION

I Am Still Growing

*S*ir Edmund Hillary failed in several of his early attempts to climb Mount Everest, the tallest mountain in the world. On one occasion he had to leave five associates dead on the side of that great mountain. Still, the British parliament wanted to recognize these valiant efforts, so they invited Hillary into their chambers. They even placed a picture of Mount Everest at the front of the room.

When Sir Edmund Hillary entered the room, the members of Parliament rose to give him a standing ovation. When he saw these great legislators standing and applauding his good effort, tears filled his eyes. Many members of Parliament noticed the tears and thought, *Look, the tears of happiness that we are recognizing this good effort he has made.*

They were not tears of happiness and joy; they were tears of anger and frustration! Sir Edmund Hillary certainly had not set out to leave five associates dead on the side of that mountain, so he walked to the front of the room and literally pounded on the picture of Mount Everest. He screamed at the mountain: "You defeated me! But you won't defeat me again! Because you have grown all that you can, but I am still growing!"

As Hillary walked to the front of the room, he recognized something that many people never recognize: Certainly he had made a good effort to climb that mountain, but the greatest enemy of excellence is good! He had not set out to make a "good effort" at climbing Mount Everest, but to arrive at the top. Ultimately, he was the first person to climb Mount Everest. Why? Because he continued to grow and refused to be satisfied with the good.

Having worked for many years in Africa, David Livingstone returned to England briefly. Someone greeted him, "Well, Dr. Livingstone, where are you ready to go now?" Livingstone responded, "I am ready to go anywhere, provided it be forward."

Every Christian should find a moment of transparent honesty for spiritual life assessment. Are we, with Sir Edmund Hillary, still growing? Are we, with David Livingstone, moving forward? Or, has rigor mortis of the soul begun to set in?

First Peter 2 is about growing spiritually. The apostle Peter understood the danger of spiritual rigor mortis. He knew what it was like to yawn spiritually, to find yourself ankle deep in concrete with no forward movement or progress. Peter had spent enough time in the twilight zone of spiritual nothingness to be able to relate to it and warn against it. Chapter 2 will assist us in moving forward in our faith and growing up spiritually.

II. COMMENTARY

God Is Building You

MAIN IDEA: *Becoming a member of God's family initiates a life-long building program. Just as buildings under construction improve in appearance as they near completion, so, too, should the behavior and attitudes of believers improve as we get nearer our eternal reward.*

A Beginning to Grow Up (vv. 1–3)

SUPPORTING IDEA: *Spiritual growth is fueled by an apprecia-tion of God's grace.*

2:1–2. This section logically flows out of the previous chapter and is connected to it with the word **therefore** which draws the reader back to the subject of the Word of God. The Word of God was the content of Peter's preaching. The life-changing power of the Word must affect our lives as Christians. Reborn children of God should exhibit their new life in their day-to-day conduct. Believers ought to exhibit a different quality of life, marked by continuous growth (see v. 2c).

Newborn babies connects chapter 2 directly with the last section of chapter 1 with its reference to new birth (1:23). "Newborn babies" does not indicate that these readers were new Christians. Some were thirty years old in the faith. All believers need to long for the spiritual milk or nourishment of God's Word in the same way that a baby longs for milk. **Crave** refers to an intense and continuous desire. Spiritual growth begins and continues through the application of the Word of God (see 1:23–25).

These verses list five sins of attitude and speech that we must **rid** ourselves of if spiritual growth is to proceed. "Rid" is a forceful word that calls us to "cast off or aside" certain practices that are deterrents to spiritual growth. What needs to be cast off "is not the grosser vices of paganism, but community destroying vices that are often tolerated by the modern church. When a community is under pressure, there is a tendency to begin bickering and division, which only makes the community that much more vulnerable to outside pressure" (Davids, 80).

Malice, an attitude similar to hatred, is the desire to inflict pain, harm, or injury on another person. It includes the holding of grudges and acting out of these grudges against others.

Deceit refers to deliberate dishonesty, to speaking or acting with ulterior motives. Anything less than speaking the full and honest truth from the heart is deceit. This vice is the selfish, two-faced attitude that deceives and hurts others for personal gain.

Hypocrisy has an intriguing history. It comes from a verb meaning "to answer." A hypocrite originally was simply a person who answered. Then the word came to mean "an actor," a person who takes part in a stage drama, specifically the interactive narrative parts of question and answer in the play. From there, this word came to mean a person who is acting out a part and concealing his true motives.

Envy must also be cast aside. Envy begins with a desire to possess what belongs to someone else. But it is more than this. It is a resentful discontent. Envy is "the feeling of displeasure produced by witnessing or hearing of the advantage or prosperity of others" (Hiebert, 111).

Envy often finds expression through **slander of every kind**—the final behavior attitude that Peter mentions in verse 1. "Slander" (*katalaleo*) literally means "to speak against someone." It suggests running others down verbally. It is speech that deliberately assaults the character of other persons. It is any speech that harms another person's status or reputation.

None of these practices should have any place in those people who are born again. In obedience to the command of God, believers are to rid themselves of such attitudes and actions.

2:3. Believers in Jesus Christ have experienced a taste of God's grace in their lives. God's grace is no excuse for us to behave as we please. The goodness and grace of God should be our greatest incentives to spiritual growth and progress.

ⒷBeginning to Grow Up Together (vv. 4–10)

SUPPORTING IDEA: *Christians must grow together not just as individuals, but as living stones, which, when joined together with others, become integral parts in God's building of a spiritual house.*

2:4. We are coming to Christ, **the living Stone**. Christ is the living, resurrected, and life-giving God. Each person accepts or rejects this "living Stone." *Rejection* means "to examine and reject because of lack of value." This rejection refers to the people of the first century who ultimately crucified Christ and to anyone since that time who has not embraced him as personal Savior.

God the Father places infinite value upon Christ. **Precious** (*entimon*) describes our costly redemption through Christ, mentioned in 1:19 (*timio*).

2:5. The decision to believe in Jesus Christ admits an individual into a spiritual building program. When anyone comes to Christ, as the Living Stone, a new stone is added to God's spiritual building—Christ's church. As a

spiritual building, the church is to be influenced or dominated by the Holy Spirit. Christians are a new temple of God under the influence and power of the Holy Spirit. Together we function as **a holy priesthood**. All believers are priests. Every Christian has immediate and direct access to God through Jesus Christ and serves God personally by bringing others to God.

A priest offers **spiritual sacrifices acceptable to God**. What are spiritual sacrifices? The Old Testament speaks of spiritual sacrifices of prayer, thanksgiving, praise, and repentance. The New Testament goes even further by identifying spiritual sacrifices as (1) the offering of our bodies to God for his service; (2) the offerings of our financial gifts; and (3) practical, loving service to other people. Spiritual sacrifices in the New Testament involve our bodies, our money, and our time (Rom. 12:1–2). When you come to Christ as the Living Stone, you become a part of a building, the church. Your growth begins to speak for itself as you offer up spiritual sacrifices acceptable to God.

2:6–8. Peter wove together two strands of Old Testament prophecy to further illustrate the centrality of Jesus Christ in the life of the individual Christian and the corporate church. He drew the picture of the precious cornerstone from Isaiah 28:16 and the rejected capstone from Psalm 118:22. The cornerstone or foundation stone established the design and structure of the building. The capstone might describe a foundation stone or, more likely, the topmost piece, the finishing or crowning touch to the building. The point is that from beginning to end, the church is built on Jesus Christ. Jesus is both the foundation cornerstone on which his church is built and the capstone up to which it grows. Jesus Christ is always the foundation of all that the individual Christian—as well as the church as a whole—believes.

Of course, not everyone accepts this Living Stone (see 2:4). The **builders** of verse 7 picture anyone who rejects Jesus Christ. Such people continually **stumble** and **fall** over who Jesus Christ is. They refuse to acknowledge him as the cornerstone of their lives. They **disobey the message**. This word carries the strong sense of refusing to believe. Despite this kind of rejection, God, the chief architect, takes this rejected stone and lays it down as the foundation stone. God the Father honored Christ by giving him the preeminent position in the building of the church.

In the position of preeminence, Christ is unique. He is a fortress; he is a refuge or stronghold; he is the foundation for every generation; he is eternal. We should build our lives on this rock and continually turn to him—the one who holds us together during difficult times.

2:9–10. In the midst of a culture that stumbles over Jesus Christ, disobeys the message of Christ, and then persecutes any who embrace Christ, believers can easily become discouraged from continuing in the journey with Christ. The thought of further growing pains is certainly not attractive to everyone. So Peter laid out in ascending order some of the incredible spiritual riches that believers have in Christ. This encourages us and reminds us of the value God places on each of us. It also ties us to the Old Testament heritage of the people of God, since much of the language here comes from Exodus 19.

A chosen people emphasizes God's loving initiative in bringing people to himself and allowing us to be a part of his church. **A royal priesthood** reminds us as believers that as priests we serve royalty. We have not landed a maid-service position. We are part of God's "forever kingdom." **A holy nation** emphasizes that God has set apart the church for his use and that individual believers have a valuable contribution to make to his church.

"A chosen people," "a people belonging to God," and "the people of God" emphasize God's ownership in our lives. Throughout history God has claimed for himself his own people as his prized possession. Christians are a people for God to possess. A very ordinary thing acquires a new value if it has been possessed by some famous person.

Several years ago, an auction was held that focused on sports memorabilia. Dan Quayle's little league uniform was up for grabs, as were Michael Jordan's running shoes. Although in themselves these items were of little value, they were sold for incredible amounts of money simply because of who had owned them. Peter's repeated emphasis with the term *people* is that as a believer I may be a very ordinary person, but I acquire an immense new value because I belong to God and am possessed by him.

All of this has come to us not because we deserve it or have somehow earned it but because of God's mercy. The people who first read Peter's letter had lived without God and Christ for a long time. During that time they had tried through many ways to obtain mercy for themselves, but had failed. In coming by faith to Christ, they received the mercy that so long had eluded them. God's mercy came to them in tangible form, bringing the gifts of forgiveness and eternal life.

The New Testament is consistent in suggesting that these kinds of benefits—extended to us through the mercy of God—are not only to be received with gratitude but are to motivate each believer to testify verbally on behalf of God and Christ. Verse 9 contains a purpose statement that describes our response. We are to **declare the praises of him who called you out of darkness into his wonderful light.** *Declare* means "to advertise, to proclaim." A very literal rendering of the verb would be "to tell out or tell forth." This suggests we should give a high priority to verbal declarations.

The word is used in other contexts to describe the rehearsing in adoring language of God's righteousness and praises. The praises of God or Christ is a word picture for his character. One translator suggested that "praises" means his "excellent attributes." The Christian is to be an instrument that publicizes the attributes and character of God.

According to Grudem,

> The answer to our search for ultimate meaning lies in declaring the excellencies of God, for he alone is worthy of glory. Salvation is ultimately not man-centered, but God-centered. To declare God's excellencies is to speak of all he is and has done . . . This purpose is too often thwarted by our silence or pride, but even brief associations with a Christian whose speech fulfills this purpose invariably refreshes our spirits (Grudem, 112).

Ⓒ Living Out the Declaration of His Praises (2:11–25; 3:1–12)

SUPPORTING IDEA: *Becoming an advertisement for the excellent attributes of God includes not only a verbal testimony but also an active testimony of living day to day.*

2:11–12. A sense of urgency marks this section. It is important that we take very seriously our identity in Christ and begin to demonstrate spiritual growth through our daily lives. **Aliens and strangers in the world** repeats the opening address of this letter (see 1:1). It reminds us that as temporary residents in this world we should show a certain detachment from the world. A believer should **abstain** from certain behaviors. The word suggests a holding back, a walking away from, or an avoidance of what are described as **sinful desires, which war against your soul.** "Sinful desires" is best understood as "strong desires motivated by selfishness." Some desires are not wrong or sinful in themselves. These become wrong when the believer attempts to satisfy those desires in ways that are contrary to God's Word. Other desires are wrong "out of the gate" and are to be avoided. (For a more detailed description of what these desires are, see 1 Pet. 4:3 and Gal. 5:19–21.)

Why should Christians abstain from such things? Because these actions mount a full military campaign against our spiritual vitality and growth. Consistently satisfying our desires in a manner contrary to the Word of God or consistently giving in to sinful desires will ultimately tear down the believer. To entertain such desires may appear attractive and harmless, but they are enemies which inflict harm on the Christian's soul, making us spiritually weak and ineffective.

The opposite result is described in verse 12. This verse makes it apparent that the early church was under immense scrutiny and criticism. Rumors and false accusations abounded. Christians were accused of being disloyal to the state, or Caesar. They were accused of purposely hurting the business enterprises of the city and of being godless people because they did not own idols. Peter advised them not to try to defend themselves or to argue with words against their accusers. Instead, they should take a positive approach and demonstrate a different quality of life that non-believers will observe.

This verb refers to more than a casual observation of a person's behavior. It means "to watch over a long period of time." It suggests making mental notes and reviewing them. Our behavior over the long haul should be so positive that it will dismantle the negative accusations. That's why Peter wrote, **Live such good lives** *among* **the pagans** (italics added). That kind of lifestyle testimony may be the argument that wins the critic to Christ: **they may see your good deeds and glorify God on the day he visits us.**

Some interpreters suggest that this day of visitation refers to the judgment of God as the second coming of Christ. In light of the context, this seems unlikely. Peter's desire was for his readers to witness positively to nonbelievers through their lives, so it is more likely that the "day of visitation" refers to the time of their salvation, when God visits them with mercy and grace.

2:13–15. In 2:13–3:12 Peter illustrated several specifics of the "good" life. He first focused on the believer's response to leaders in their culture and government. **Submit** is the overriding action required of believers. The word means "to place yourself under someone, to rank under someone." Here it is essentially a synonym for obedience. Of course, submission to authority does not involve actions that are sinful or contrary to the Word of God. The believer is to obey except when commanded to sin. This is the Christian's responsibility toward all forms of human authority. The all-encompassing nature of this responsibility is underlined in Peter's emphasis on **every authority instituted among men.**

According to Grudem,

> The inclusiveness of the word *every* makes it appropriate to apply this statement to other legitimate human authorities (parents/children, church leaders/members, and authority structures in businesses, educational institutions, and voluntary organizations). God has established such patterns of authority for the orderly function of human life, and it both pleases and honors him when we subject ourselves to them (Grudem, 118).

The apostle Peter wanted believers to submit willingly, but his words are not presented as an option, but as a command. We are to submit because that is God's desire for his people. He wants us to trust him because all governments and authorities are ultimately appointed and controlled by him.

Doing good (v. 15) reconnects the reader with the living of **good lives** in verse 12. The emphasis is on doing what is right in God's eyes. This results in a positive behavior model of believers that provides a powerful testimony for the character of God and an argument against the false accusations of the non-Christian community.

2:16. Submission to authority does not eliminate freedom from the believer's life. Perhaps this concern prompted Peter to speak to the subject of freedom. The freedom of the New Testament is not political freedom but spiritual freedom. The great freedoms of the Christian life are: (1) freedom from the ruling power of sin in our lives; (2) freedom from guilt because our sins have been forgiven by God; and (3) freedom from the impossible obligation of attempting to earn favor with God through perfect obedience.

The Bible emphasizes that in those areas where the Word of God gives no command or primary principle, we are free and responsible to choose our own course of action. This is a freedom to choose what is right. Christian freedom does not allow us to do wrong. It does not permit us to disobey human laws unless these are in direct conflict with God's ways. Nor does our freedom permit us to disobey God, because we are **servants of God.**

This word (*doulos*) literally means "a slave." We are free, yet paradoxically we are slaves who serve God with our lives. Christian freedom is always conditioned by Christian responsibility. Christian freedom does not mean being free to do only as we *like*; it means being free to do as we *ought*.

2:17. Before returning to the subject of slaves in verse 18, Peter offered a summary word of counsel. **Respect** for everyone indicates that we should approach relationships with others with a positive point of reference. We should see others as having value or honor. In the culture of that day, this could easily have been missed. The Roman Empire included sixty million slaves. Roman law considered slaves not as persons but as commodities with no rights. In effect, Peter calls us to "remember the rights of human personality and the dignity of every person. Don't treat people as objects." With this as an operating principle, we have a special obligation to each other as believers: to love each other (cf. 1:22).

The next summary counsel is to **fear God.** This is the reverent fear that leads to obedience, introduced in 1:17. The last summary counsel concludes concisely the subject introduced in verse 13, adding that in our submission to authorities, we must do so with an honoring, valuing attitude. Otherwise, our submission is cheapened and it bears little positive testimony to the character of God.

2:18. An active testimony in day-to-day existence cannot ignore life's harshest realities. Nothing could be more real than the situation of slaves having to submit to their masters, even if those masters were abusive and unreasonable.

Slaves refers to those who worked in a family setting. Many of them were well-educated and held responsible positions in their households. These "slaves" of the first century included doctors, teachers, musicians, and secretaries. These "slaves" or "domestic servants" were to **submit,** or "place themselves voluntarily under the authority" of their employer or master **with all**

respect. *Respect* literally means "fear." The noun occurs in 1:17; 2:18; 3:2,14, while the verb is used in 2:17; 3:6,14. At the heart of Peter's meaning is the idea of reverence or reverential fear. The question is, Reverence or fear of whom? The best answer is, Fear of God. The slaves' attitude was to be one of fear or reverence for God as they worked. Their motivation for submission and service was not their respect for their master but their respect and reverence for God, who viewed their work as if it were done for him and whose character would be praised by their good behavior.

Some slaves or servants might respond to this injunction by asking about limits or exceptions. Peter addressed this subject at length. Many household servants were loved and trusted members of the families they worked for. Peter described the treatment they received from their masters with the words **good and considerate.** Submission to that kind of master would not be difficult.

But not all masters could fit under that label. Others are described as being **harsh** in their treatment of their slaves. The term describes a master who physically mistreated his servants or who was crooked and dishonest with pay, working conditions, and expectations about the job itself. The historical situation was accurately described this way: "Whatever a master does to a slave, undeservedly, in anger, willingly, unwillingly, in forgetfulness, after careful thought, knowingly, or unknowingly—it is judgment, justice and law" (Barclay, 211).

Even in that kind of environment, the command to submit still applies. The slave was to understand that greater issues were more important than the immediate injustice: the name of Jesus was at stake, as well as the possible salvation of his unreasonable master, who was the slave of sin.

2:19–20. Thus, Peter broadened his scope to include anyone who had experienced the pain of unjust suffering. The key in these verses is the emphasis on **unjust suffering** in verse 19 and **doing good** in verse 20. These expressions stand opposite **doing wrong** in verse 20. Peter was not commending suffering that enters our lives because we sin or do something wrong. His focus in this extended section was on living a good life on behalf of the Lord. He described a situation in which the believer does everything by the book but still suffers negative consequences and reactions.

Peter's praise was directed toward the believer, who in the vice of unjust suffering, **bears up under the pain,** or is able **to endure it.** These expressions suggest that the believer patiently endures or puts up with the mistreatment. How is that possible? Peter's answer is found in the NIV's translation of the last part of verse 19—**because he is conscious of God.** Paraphrasing Peter's words of verse 19 could suggest this wording: "For this wins God's approval when, because he is conscious of God's presence, a person who is suffering unfairly bears his troubles patiently."

Merely enduring unjust suffering and the accompanying pain is not what is pleasing to God. What pleases God is being mindful of God, cultivating a trusting awareness of God's presence and of his never-failing care while we endure pain. When we are conscious of the presence of God in our lives, God gives us the necessary strength to bear the pain, and he extends his grace and mercy to enable us to respond positively as we continue to trust in him.

2:21. Undoubtedly, even the strongest believer would raise the question, But why do we have to suffer? The believer has been called by God to the situation. God not only calls the believer **out of darkness into his wonderful light** (2:9); he also calls the believer to endure suffering that is unjust and painful. The believer's appropriate response to unjust suffering carries a powerful testimony to an unbelieving culture.

Peter referred to the life of Christ as motivation or illustration. Here it serves as both. Jesus' life was dominated by suffering (see 1:11). His life of suffering becomes an **example** for believers who follow him. We do not suffer the same agonies he endured, but we can follow Christ in the way in which he endured the suffering and responded to it.

2:22. Peter borrowed a stream of phrases from Isaiah 53:4–12. His description of Jesus Christ in verse 22 came from Isaiah 53:9. It illustrates pointedly the undeserved nature of Christ's suffering and how his response can become the believer's response. **He committed no sin** involves wrong actions in general. **No deceit was found in his mouth** refers to his not sinning with words and speech.

2:23. As he was suffering unjust pain during his arrest, trial, and crucifixion, Jesus refused to retaliate. Our natural inclination when we are being attacked is to protect ourselves verbally, at the very least. Sometimes a person will lie to prevent further pain. That is not the model of Christ. Furthermore, when we are being insulted, the instinctive response is to retaliate or to defend ourselves. At other times, uttering threats of revenge against the enemy, even if those threats cannot be carried out, seems to ease the pain. These responses do not follow the example of Jesus Christ in his moment of suffering. Christ's example was to endure or bear up under the pain. He did so when he **entrusted himself to him who judges justly**. Jesus Christ entrusted himself and the entire situation to God the Father.

In the words of Hillyer,

> Believers are not left to face suffering solely in their own strength, which might well prove inadequate. In the same confidence that Jesus had, they are to hand over their whole situation to God, for God, as all-knowing and all-seeing, judges justly. He alone can be relied upon to view all the evidence and to understand all the motives

which lie behind every human action—and in the final analysis to dispense perfect justice (Hillyer, 85–86).

2:24. The ultimate illustration of unjust suffering and pain is seen in the crucifixion of Jesus Christ. Christ's death was more than just an example of responding properly to unjust suffering. **He himself bore our sins in his body on the tree.** Christ took the consequences of our sins upon himself, and by his sacrificial death made atonement for them. **By his wounds you have been healed** cements this thought. Although there is some debate over the extent of the meaning of this phrase, it seems that Peter applied these words normally, in the sense that by Christ's wounds we have been "healed" from sin (Grudem, 132) through the free gift of forgiveness. Peter's emphasis was on spiritual healing or salvation, not physical healing.

Having said all of this, the idea of living a "good life" must not be lost. As we identify with Christ in salvation, the goal is to **live for righteousness.** The death of Jesus Christ enables believers, even in the midst of suffering, to live a life that is right with God, that models the characteristics mentioned in this chapter. "Righteousness," as it is used here, suggests the right kind of living, the ethical lifestyle that has been the focus of this major section. By living for righteousness, the believer continues to live out the declaration of God's praises not only through a verbal testimony but also as a lifestyle testimony.

2:25. This kind of lifestyle response is not easy. A believer in the midst of unjust suffering and pain has a tendency to walk away from the Lord and to become bitter and angry. Peter described such people as straying sheep who have recently returned to their shepherd, Jesus Christ.

Although the language here could be understood as a reference to their past way of life (**going astray**) and then their conversion to Christ at salvation (**returned to the Shepherd**), it seems more natural to see these pictures as a summary of the improper response to unjust suffering and the proper response to the same. Throughout these verses Peter exhorted his reader to be **conscious of God** (v. 19) and to follow the example of Christ who **entrusted himself to** [God] (v. 23). Such an extended section articulating this emphasis would not be necessary unless some of the believers were already going astray. It is not unusual for believers to respond to pain in this way. They cannot put together God's care and love for them with the intersection of suffering in their lives.

Peter reemphasized that Jesus Christ cares deeply for his people. He is their shepherd. Furthermore, he is the **Overseer** of their souls. He is the guardian, the bishop of their souls. Even throughout their pain and wandering away from the Lord, he remains their shepherd and overseer.

MAIN IDEA REVIEW: *Becoming a member of God's family initiates a lifelong building program. Just as buildings under construction improve in appearance as they near completion, so too should the behavior and attitudes of believers improve as we draw closer to our eternal reward.*

III. CONCLUSION

Spiritual Rigor Mortis

Peter insisted that we learn that living life involves spiritual growth verified by positive daily relationships and activities. General Douglas MacArthur focused on a similar perspective: "Life is a lively process of becoming. If you haven't added to your interest during the past year; if you are thinking the same thoughts, relating the same personal experiences, having the same predictable reactions, then rigor mortis of the personality has set in."

Relationships! We cannot go very far in life before we realize how important relationships are. In chapter 1 Peter put an exclamation point on the believer's relationship with God the Father. This relationship is never far from his mind or pen, but in this chapter, he carefully underlined the importance of positive relationships with one another. His premise is that those who have a secure relationship with the Father through Jesus Christ are now on a path of spiritual growth and development.

One of the crucial growth points on this path is how we can reflect positively the relationship we have with God. This reflection is not simply to be relegated to a verbal testimony or witness, but it takes form as we live day to day among our fellow Christians and before those who do not know Christ. Certain attitudes and actions need to be surrendered from the believer's pattern of living, lest our testimony be lost to others. We have a responsibility to live out a submissive relationship toward the government and to the employers we work under, even if those governments and employers are harsh and unfair.

PRINCIPLES

- Relationship sins are serious violations of God's grace.
- An individual either comes to Christ or rejects him—there is no middle ground.
- Jesus Christ is the centerpiece of the Christian church.
- Christians are a people whom God should possess.
- The Christian is to be an instrument that publicizes the attributes and character of God.

- God's grace gift of salvation must result in a positive change in the believer's behavior.
- God's desire for believers is that they submit to human governments.
- Christian freedom is not the freedom to do as we *like*; it is the freedom to do as we *ought*.
- Submission to those in authority should be done in a spirit of reverence toward God.
- The consciousness of the presence of God enables us to endure unjust suffering.
- Jesus Christ alone has provided atonement for our sins.

APPLICATIONS

- Spiritual growth should be a high priority for believers.
- Believers should make progress in dealing with anger, hatred, hypocrisy, envy, and slander.
- Do not say anything about other believers in their absence that you would not say to them personally.
- Unity should characterize the relationships and interactions of those who follow Jesus Christ.
- The believer is to proclaim the excellencies of Jesus Christ.
- Every Christian should be a good advertisement for Christianity.
- Moral purity is a mark of excellence in behavior.
- Christians must model a healthy respect and support for those in authority.
- Enjoy your liberty in Jesus Christ, realizing that this is not a license to do as you please.
- You may have to endure unjust suffering and should do so in the spirit and example of Jesus.
- Christians should resist the temptation to plot revenge toward others.

IV. LIFE APPLICATION

Did You Do Your Best?

For many years Admiral Hyman Rickover was the head of the United States Nuclear Navy. His admirers and his critics held strongly opposing views about the stern and demanding admiral. Rickover personally interviewed and approved every officer aboard a nuclear submarine. Those who went through the interviews usually came out shaking in fear, anger, or total intimidation. One Rickover interviewee was Jimmy Carter, who later became president of the United States. Carter described his interview with Rickover this way:

> We sat in a large room by ourselves for more than two hours, and he let me choose any subject I wished to discuss. Very carefully, I chose those about which I knew most at the time—current events, seamanship, music, literature, naval tactics, electronics, gunnery. Then he began to ask me a series of questions of increasing difficulty. In each instance, he soon proved that I knew relatively little about the subject I had chosen.
>
> He always looked right into my eyes, and he never smiled. I was saturated with cold sweat. Finally, he asked a question, and I thought I could redeem myself. "How did you stand in your class at the Naval Academy?" Since I had completed my sophomore year at Georgia Tech before entering Annapolis, I had done very well, and I swelled my chest with pride and answered, "Sir, I stood fifty-ninth in a class of 820!" I sat back to wait for the congratulations, which never came. Instead, he asked this question: "Did you do your best?" I started to say, "Yes sir," but I remembered who this was and recalled several of the many times at the Academy when I could have learned more about our allies, our enemies, weapons, strategy, and so forth. I was just human. I finally gulped and said, "No, sir. I didn't always do my best."
>
> He looked at me for a long time, and then turned his chair around to end the interview. He asked one final question, which I have never been able to forget, or to answer. He asked, "WHY NOT?" I sat there for a while, shaken, and then slowly left the room.

Throughout this chapter we see how Christians are to relate to one another and how we are to respond and relate to those who do not know Christ. This assignment is not easy. Relationships are hard work, and they require a great appreciation for the grace of God in our lives (2:2). The church has tolerated serious relationship sins within the body of Christ. Concentrating on the "big" sins, we have allowed relationship sins to go unchallenged.

We generally put all our energies into satisfying ourselves rather than living for Christ. As a result, our churches become places of pettiness and in-house fighting, and our lives reflect only hypocrisy to people outside the faith. The church has forgotten that our focus must not be on ourselves, but on God and those to whom we must minister. Without this other-directed approach, we erode the reputation of the church.

Christ has called us to model lives described with words like **light** and **good** (2:9,12) We are even to give up some of our rights, in an effort to respond well in relationships (2:13,18). This approach is vital to the

Christian because it may be the only way we have to witness for Jesus Christ at times. Unlike our culture—which demands justice, retribution, and pay-backs—the believer enjoys the privilege of honoring Jesus by modeling a life that does not require such self-serving rewards (2:21).

The key to such a positive approach appears in verse 12: **Live such good lives among the pagans that, though they accuse you of doing wrong, they may see your good deeds and glorify God on the day he visits us.**

One day at the judgment throne, Christ will ask you. "Did you do your best?"

"No, sir, I didn't always do my best," we will have to respond.

"Why not?" he will demand.

V. PRAYER

Lord, it is so hard at times to grow to be like you. Relationships that ought to be filled with grace seem poisoned by envy and slander. Forgive us, Lord. Help me to realize that you are my cornerstone and that in you I can trust. May this truth become more real to me each day even as I face people and circumstances that scream at me and cause pain in my life. Whatever painful realities I face, enable me to learn from them. Thank you for being my shepherd and my guardian. Amen.

VI. DEEPER DISCOVERIES

A. Zion (v. 4)

Zion first appears in the Bible in 2 Samuel 5:7. It was the name of the ancient Jebusite fortress that David captured. After he captured "the strong-hold of Zion," he called it "the City of David" (1 Kgs. 8:1; 1 Chr. 11:5). It was located on the southeast hill of Jerusalem.

Later, during the reign of Solomon, Zion came to include the temple and the temple area built on Mount Moriah, a separate and distinct hill from Mount Zion. Not long after this, Zion was used as a name for the entire city of Jerusalem, the land of Judah, and the people of Israel as a whole (Isa. 40:9; 60:14; Jer. 31:12). The spiritual meaning of Zion is extended into the New Testament, where it refers to God's spiritual kingdom and the heavenly Jeru-salem (Heb. 12:22; Rev. 14:1).

B. A Chosen People, a Royal Priesthood, a Holy Nation, a People Belonging to God (v. 9)

Scholars offer conflicting views as to the nature of the church. Some see the church as the direct continuation of Israel in the Old Testament, while others, although acknowledging similarities and parallels between the two, view Israel and the church as entirely distinct.

Those who see little, if any, distinction between the two point out that the church and Israel are portrayed in the Bible as being in a continuous relationship. The church, according to them, was present in some sense in Israel in the Old Testament. Acts 7:38 makes this connection when, alluding to Deuteronomy 9:10, it speaks of the church (*ekklesia*) in the wilderness. Additionally, if the church is seen in some New Testament verses as preexistent, then one finds in this the model for the creation of Israel (see Exod. 25:40; Acts 7:44; Gal. 4:26; Heb. 12:22).

Those who wish to make this connection further suggest that Israel, in some way, is present in the church in the New Testament. The many names for Israel that are also applied to the church seem to reinforce this point. Some of those names are: "Israel" (Gal. 6:15–16); "a chosen people" (1 Pet. 2:9); the true "circumcision" (Rom. 2:28–29); "the remnant" (Rom. 9:27); "priesthood" (1 Pet. 2:9; cf. Elwell, *Evangelical Dictionary of Biblical Theology*, 95).

Those who see a clear distinction between Israel and the church emphasize that a concordance study of the term *Israel* indicates that it is always used to indicate Jacob's physical descendants and is never used in a spiritualized way to refer to the church. They also teach that God has a distinct program for Israel and a distinct program for the church.

The commands given to one are not the commands to the other; the promises to one are not the promises to the other. God calls on Israel to keep the Sabbath (Exod. 20:8–11), but the church keeps the Lord's Day (1 Cor. 16:2). Israel is the wife of God (Hos. 3:1), but the church is the body of Christ (Col. 1:27). Those holding to this perspective maintain that a distinction between Israel and the church is continued after the birth of the church (Acts 3:12; 4:8; 5:21,31; Rom. 10:1; 11:1–29).

C. Submit Yourselves to Every Authority (vv. 13–14)

To submit to authorities and governments does not mean blind obedience. Peter, like Paul (see Rom. 13:1–2; Titus 3:1–2), teaches that government's authority is established by God to keep order on earth. Whether in the home or in society at large, Christians must recognize the authority over them, even if they don't always agree with it. If government parallels God's law, then Christians are to obey it. However, if a human law violates God's clear commands or laws, then it is wrong to obey that human law (Acts 4:19–20; 5:29).

The attitude of the Christian is important. A submissive Christian who constantly complains and criticizes the government does not provide a positive testimony for Jesus Christ. Christians must be careful in choosing not to obey civil laws that contradict the laws of God. They may break God's laws in their acts of resistance. Such an approach is arrogant, hypocritical, and contrary to the spirit of the Word of the Lord.

D. Slaves or Slavery (v. 18)

The New Testament consistently counsels Christians who were slaves to obey or submit to their earthly masters. The apostle Paul even asked Philemon to receive back Onesimus, a runaway slave who had become a Christian. In so doing, he also asked Onesimus to return to his position as a slave (Phlm. 16). The practice of slavery was a well-entrenched part of the culture of the first century, and the Bible contains no direct command or call to abolish slavery. The implications of the gospel, especially the ethic of love, stand clearly in opposition to slavery. As Abraham Lincoln once said, "As I would not be a slave, so I should not enslave."

In Christ, social and class distinctions are not to exist (Gal. 3:28; Col. 3:11). In Christ, all believers stand on equal ground as brothers and sisters in the faith (see Youngblood, 1186).

In the context of Peter's letter, his desire was to encourage believers to reflect Jesus Christ in their daily behavior. This applied to Christian slaves and masters. His emphasis was not on revolt, but on the reflection of Christ's character.

VII. TEACHING OUTLINE

A. INTRODUCTION

1. Lead Story: I Am Still Growing
2. Context: Pain and difficulties tend to make us believe that we are alone and isolated from God and others. In chapter 1 Peter reminded us that we are not isolated from God even in our most desperate circumstances. In chapter 2 he pointed out that we are also not to be isolated or alienated from one another in the body of Christ and that we have a great responsibility not to isolate ourselves from those who do not know Christ. We have the responsibility to introduce these people to Jesus through our words and actions.
3. Transition: This chapter leads us from the agony of suffering and the hope of Jesus Christ to the actions and attitudes of believers toward one another and the reflection of Christ in our lives.

B. COMMENTARY

1. Beginning to Grow Up (vv. 1–3)
   a. The Word of God helps to change our lives (v. 1a)

      b. Our relationships with others should demonstrate this change (v. 1b)

      c. The Word of God provides spiritual food for growth, while grace provides the motivation (vv. 2–3)

  2. Beginning to Grow Up Together (vv. 4–10)

      a. Spiritual growth begins with Christ (vv. 4–5)

      b. Christ is either rejected or believed (vv. 6–8)

      c. Growing believers take on a new identity and value (vv. 9–10)

  3. Living Out the Declaration of His Praises (vv. 11–25)

      a. The life of the believer is a testimony (vv. 11–12)

      b. The testimony of a believer with those in authority (vv. 13–17)

      c. The testimony of a believer as an employee-servant (v. 18)

      d. The testimony of a believer when suffering unjustly (vv. 19–20)

      e. The supreme example of a testimony (vv. 21–25)

C. CONCLUSION: DID YOU DO YOUR BEST?

VIII. ISSUES FOR DISCUSSION

1. What attitudes do you need to rid yourself of? Why? How will you begin?
2. What signs of spiritual growth does your daily behavior show?
3. What does it mean that you are a living stone like Jesus?
4. What identifying marks or characteristics in 1 Peter 2 describe you and your Christian life? What responses do you make to such an identity?
5. What evidence do your non-Christian associates have that you are a believer in Christ?

1 Peter 3

Declaring God's Praises at Home

Quote

"*Almost* all of our relationships begin and most of them continue as forms of mutual exploitation, a mental or physical barter, to be terminated when one or both parties run out of goods."

W . H . A u d e n

1 Peter

I N A N U T S H E L L

Chapter 3 teaches us that just as citizens should submit to government and slaves should submit to masters, so wives should submit to husbands. In return, husbands should be considerate and respectful of their wives. All Christians should live in harmony with one another. God will bless everyone who suffers for doing what is right, so always be ready to share this truth with others.

Declaring God's Praises at Home

I. INTRODUCTION

Let the Cheering Begin

*S*omewhere along the way I stumbled across a piece of prose entitled simply, "Marriage." As you read it, see if it makes your heart smile, even if it's just for a moment.

> When God made light, the angels drew near to let the refractions roll over their faces like a symphony. When God made earth, they poked their fingers into its moistness; they put a fleck to their nose and smiled. When God made a rose, they parted its petals and passed it among themselves, saying, "So fragile, yet how it grasps the soul." When God made a giraffe, they touched the strange hide and murmured to themselves that God was up to something magnificent. When God made man, each one retired to his chamber and peered into the writings, looking for some clue to the mystery. When God made woman, they came back out of their chambers and gazed, their jaws slack with awe. When God joined man to woman and said, "Let them become one flesh," everything suddenly made sense. And the cheering still shakes the galaxies.

God wants the cheering in the galaxies to continue. He wants the growing relationship between a husband and a wife to still provoke thunderous applause. Thus, the opening half of 1 Peter 3 concentrates our attention on husbands and wives. The latter half of the chapter is careful not to ignore other relationships that Christians have. The goal (as begun in chapter 2) is to assist believers in living a life that declares the praises of God positively and does so in the context of relationships with others inside and outside the church.

II. COMMENTARY

Declaring God's Praises at Home

> **MAIN IDEA:** *Wives must be submissive to their husbands, and husbands should be considerate and respectful of their wives. Everyone should live harmoniously with others. Even as we suffer under the hand of those who may be over us, we are to return good for evil and thus share our faith in Christ with others.*

Ⓐ Relationships in Marriage (vv. 1–7)

> **SUPPORTING IDEA:** *Marriage is a two-way relationship. Both husbands and wives must fulfill their respective roles.*

3:1. These words are addressed generally to all Christian wives, but with special attention to those women whose husbands are not believers in Jesus Christ. **In the same way** takes the reader back to something previously introduced. The manner of behavior is described with the words, **be submissive to your husbands.** Submission appeared first in 2:13 in reference to the believer's response to authority and again in verse 18 in discussing the slave's response to the master.

Opinions vary widely as to how these injunctions should be defined. One well-intentioned but misguided commentator says that "the meaning of the wife's submission to her husband concerns the sexual relationship and should not be taken in a more general and oppressive sense" (Hillyer, 92). Such an interpretation not only violates the meaning of the word but also violates the context of this verse. Submission is best understood as "to voluntarily yield your rights or will to someone else's wishes or advice, as an expression of love for that person." Another spin on the term would be to define it as simply considering the needs of your husband and fulfilling them (Marshall, 99).

In all discussions related to submission, if the wishes, desires, or needs of the husband involve a direct violation of the Word of God, then submission does not apply. In such cases, to practice submission would involve violating the higher principle of obedience to God and his Word previously held out as the believer's goal (see 1:14–15,22; 2:11).

Submitting oneself to another is the opposite of self-assertion, the opposite of an independent, autocratic spirit. It is the desire to get along with someone else. It involves being satisfied at times with less than what one may deserve or claim as a right. The goal of this type of behavior is to win over to Christ the non-believing husband. This occurs **without words.** This does not mean that a wife is never to speak, but rather that she is not to resort to constant arguments and nagging discussions. The husband will be more influenced by **the behavior** of his wife. This links this chapter to chapter 2, where verse 12 indicates that the non-Christian audience can be positively influenced for Christ as they observe the consistent and godly behavior of a believer.

As Christian wives live out the declaration of the praises of God, their husbands will be influenced. For the Christian wife living with a non-Christian husband, Peter's previous discussion of suffering even while doing what is right may have some application even within the context of her marriage and home. What a Christian wife says often will not change her husband; how she lives out her faith before him will make the difference.

3:2. Living a life of **purity and reverence** can make a difference. Purity signifies more than just moral or sexual purity, although this is included. The term suggests moral and ethical behavior that maintains a high standard. According to recent surveys, forty percent of the women polled by *USA Today* indicated that they have had extramarital affairs. Obviously, Peter's advice is still relevant today. Purity of life will generally not occur, however, unless "reverence" is also a part of it. The "reverence" is for the Lord and indicates a deep desire to keep his commandments. This desire to obey God should be the driving motive, resulting in a high moral standard.

3:3–4. These verses do not ban grooming or beauty aids, but they do put these adornments in proper perspective. If a woman relies only on these kinds of things to make her beautiful, she will miss the greater value of inner beauty. She must not go overboard patching up the externals while ignoring the internal character. Seneca, the Roman philosopher, referred to women in this time period who wore two or three fortunes in their ears. Peter encourages Christian women not to lose their sense of value. They are to recognize the beauty of character that is far more vital and important than external beauty. This beauty, available to all women, is much deeper and more valued by God. This beautiful character is described as having a **gentle and quiet spirit.**

The word *gentle* has a caress in it; yet behind gentleness stands the strength of steel. The supreme characteristic of the "gentle" woman is that she lives under perfect control. She is not given to panic, but exudes great strength. "Quiet," too, suggests being under control. It also means "to evidence a calming influence." Together, the two words speak of strength of character, strong self-control, describing a person of quiet elegance and dignity.

3:5–6. Support for this understanding of God's kind of woman comes from the example of **holy women** in the Old Testament (v. 5), specifically **Sarah**, Abraham's wife (v. 6). Submission characterized each woman's relationship with her husband. Sarah is singled out as the primary example of a woman who was submissive to her husband. Sarah **obeyed** Abraham. The verb used here can mean "to listen to someone." Translated this way, it fits well with the idea of submission, in that it indicates Sarah took an interest in her husband's conversation and articulated his needs and desires. Apparently, she responded to them in an appropriate manner throughout the course of their married life.

Sarah called Abraham **her master.** This statement is difficult to explain completely. Some suggest the reference is to Genesis 18:12, where Sarah verbalized to herself her disbelief that she was to become pregnant at her advanced age. There the term *master* was simply a respectful form of address, along the lines of our *sir* today. Others believe that the term *master* can be substituted for the word *husband*. Perhaps it would be better to conclude that Peter did not have one particular incident in mind, but rather was thinking about Sarah's overall approach to married life.

Sarah's characteristic attitude was one of loving submission. She willingly accepted a nomadic life, following her husband into unknown and uncharted territories. Scripture encourages Christian wives to follow Sarah's example. Thus, they **do what is right**. This summarizes the first six verses. The end of verse 6 adds a caveat: their behavior toward their husbands should **not give way to fear**. Submission to husbands should not arise from fear or intimidation. Christian women should not be bullied or forced into this kind of behavior by their husbands. This provides the bridge to verse 7 that speaks to the role and response of the husband. Obviously, Scripture is concerned about marriage as a mutual relationship, not a one-way relationship.

3:7. In order for the "cheering" in the galaxies to continue, both husbands and wives must work at modeling the characteristics of effective marriage relationships. Do not draw the conclusion, however, that because wives receive six verses of counsel to only one for husbands that the responsibility of a husband is any less exacting than that of a wife. The apparent imbalance exists only because the situation that a believing wife found herself in during that cultural time frame was more difficult and because Peter's counsel was so transforming that a more extended discussion was needed.

Husbands should be **considerate** as they relate to their wives. This word (*gnosin*) carries the meaning of "wisdom and understanding." Husbands should approach their marriage relationship intelligently. They are to live with their wives according to knowledge, not fantasy. Marriage is a real-life relationship, not a soap-opera drama. To live with your wife and demonstrate wisdom suggests a deep desire to understand your wife, to get to know her at more than just a surface level. It suggests a sensitivity to her needs and a desire to respond to these needs knowledgeably. In many ways, this sounds like submission, although the language is different. It hints at the concept of mutual submission (see Eph. 5:21).

Beyond this, husbands are to **treat** their wives **with respect**. "Treat" has a special significance. Classical Greek writers always used it in reference to what is due from one person to another. The giving of respect or honor to your wife is not simply a "nice guy" kind of thing to do. It is the husband's recognition of her because it is her due. This emphasis is reiterated in the word *respect*. This word is sometimes translated as "price" or "precious." It indicates value and esteem. It suggests the giving of respect because a wife is precious to her husband.

This kind of understanding, consideration, and respect is directed toward a wife for two reasons. First, she is **the weaker partner.** This weakness does not refer to intellectual, spiritual, or emotional weakness, but only to physical weakness. Such "weakness" does not make a woman any less important in God's eyes. Husbands should recognize and understand this physiological difference and adjust to wives in a positive manner. The second reason for an approach of consideration and respect is spiritual. In no way are wives inferior to their husbands spiritually. Each is an equal recipient of God's grace in salvation and should be treated in that light.

Finally, a husband's prayers will be hindered if this model is not adopted. **Hinder** means "to interrupt." Some interpreters suggest that this means that the husband's prayers are prevented from reaching their destination with God. A more likely understanding of "hinder" represents a more practical interpretation. A husband who treats his wife in the wrong manner will himself be unfit and unable to pray, not to mention that he will likely have little inclination to pray. To put it another way, a husband's spiritual health depends, in significant measure, on the way he treats his wife.

B Relationships in the Church (vv. 8–12)

> **SUPPORTING IDEA:** *Live in harmony with one another; return good for evil, and you will inherit a blessing from God.*

3:8,11. These verses present an ideal picture of the life of a church. The target audience (**all of you**) has expanded beyond husbands and wives to include everyone in the church. Harmonious living is displayed in the life of the church. **Live in harmony** translates a single word in the original text and means "to be like-minded." It describes an inner unity of attitude that makes division and mutiny within the body of Christ unthinkable.

This does not mean the church will never have any differences of opinion. The variety of gifts and talents God has given his people mean differences of opinion are bound to occur. The key is not the differences; the issue is how those differences are handled. Believers should live and minister together so that the differences do not divide the church but serve to enrich its life and work. To live in harmony means Christians should pursue the same primary purpose of serving God and extending love to one another, instead of being fueled by individual and selfish interests.

This emphasis on loving one another as brothers was introduced in 1 Peter 1:22. Its repetition here suggests that practical harmony within the body of Christ will not occur without a concerted effort by individual believers to approach their relationships within the body of Christ with a familial love.

Marshall observes, "The ideal Christian community is one which produces between people who have no blood ties the same bonds of affection as are expected between brothers (and sisters)" (Marshall, 106).

Verses 10–12 borrow from the pen of David in Psalm 34:12–16 to cement this emphasis. Verse 11 directs us to **seek peace and pursue it.** *Peace* means "agreement between people." That is what harmony is all about. Such harmony does not happen naturally. Believers must "pursue it." The verb is a hunting term, meaning "to pursue with intensity, determination and persistence." Believers have as their goal and calling the assignment to pursue peace.

Verse 8 adds a trio of virtues that reflect the active working elements of a harmonious group of people: sympathy, compassion, and humility. **Be compassionate** simply means "a tender heart." It underlines feelings that come from deep inside a person, especially when one observes the suffering and pain that another person is enduring. **Be sympathetic** goes beyond compassion in that it attaches action to a tender heart reaction. This word has a distinctly practical bent. Not only do believers understand the feelings of another; they act appropriately to assist that person.

Sometimes in the body of Christ people find it difficult to receive help from others. Something inside of us recoils from the need to be assisted. At other times, those who do the helping approach this action with a superior attitude. That's why **humility** is added. Humility is not a poor self-concept that shouts, "I'm no good! I am not worth anything to anyone. I don't deserve a thing!" Humility is an awareness of strengths and gifts as provided by God and a grateful attitude for them. It is also an awareness of areas of weakness and need and a desire to grow in these areas and the willingness to receive assistance with these needs. Furthermore, humility is the attitude that is content to minister in the background, away from the spotlight. Humility desires to put the interests of other people ahead of self-interest.

3:9–12. Verse 8 deals with teamwork (**live in harmony, love as brothers**) and team spirit (**be sympathetic, compassionate, humble**). Verses 9–12 emphasize team speech. **Evil** and **insult** in verse 9 refer to abusive speech. This is speech with a snarl attached. Verse 10 adds to this conversations that embrace evil or **deceitful speech.** This refers to things like slander, lying, gossip—any kind of speech that twists information and is designed to tear down. Obviously, evil and insulting words can achieve a temporary victory, but they inflict pain and destroy relationships and the believer's testimony for Jesus Christ.

Revenge is not part of the path a believer is to follow. This is quite an exhortation, since it comes from a man who chopped off a person's ear in an act of retaliation at one point in his life. That was a long time before these words were written. In his own spiritual growth, Peter came to realize there is a better way.

When believers receive insults and evil, they should not retaliate, but repay **with blessing**. This means several things: (1) You are to pray for those people who come after you verbally; (2) you are to treat them kindly, even with sympathy; and (3) you are to forgive them even when they have hurt you deeply.

Peter linked this response to the "calling" of a believer. His language was familiar (see 2:9,21) but intensely practical. God calls the believer to model right living within the church, with special emphasis on harmony in relationships with one another. When this happens, the believer **may inherit a blessing** (v. 9) and will **see good days** (v. 10). God directs his hand of blessing toward those who model this loving, humble behavior.

One motive for righteous living is the knowledge that such conduct will bring blessings from God. The blessings of the New Testament are not primarily material or physical; they are spiritual and relational. Verse 12 defines, in part, what some of these blessings look like. Living in harmony assures believers of God's listening ear when they pray (see 3:7). They are God's righteous people whom he regards with favor.

C Relationships with People Outside the Church (vv. 13–22)

> **SUPPORTING IDEA:** *When you suffer for doing what is right, God blesses you for it. So respond well to those who mistreat you so you can share your faith with others. Then no one can speak poorly of you as a Christian. This is what Jesus did.*

3:13. The last major section of 1 Peter begins with this verse. From here on Peter is primarily concerned with the believer's response to actual persecution and intimidation. His focus is the believer's response to specific attacks. He begins to zero in on this response by asking a question in verse 13: "Since we are doing good in our lives, will people harm us?" Peter has exhorted his readers previously to be good to others as a witness and defense against nonbelievers (see 2:12), so this question would naturally flow from such an exhortation. The question suggests an answer something like this, "Under normal circumstances when you do what is right and good, you should not expect pain or harm to be directed your way."

3:14. Circumstances are not always normal, however. Slaves face the prospect of suffering for doing what is good (see 2:20). All Christians need to hear about suffering and trials in general (see 1:6–7). Peter himself suffered under circumstances that were not "normal." Suffering in the believer's life requires discussion.

Right (*dikaiosunen*) is often translated as "righteousness." In this context, the emphasis is on right living, or living that parallels the standards of the Word of God. This kind of behavior sometimes produces a negative reaction from others. The believer is **blessed** in the sense of being a recipient of God's favor and grace and living out another dimension of his calling (see 2:21). Still, we have normal human responses to the harm directed toward us as believers. Peter hinted at one of the main responses: **Do not fear what they fear; do not be frightened.** A better translation of the first part of this sentence would be, "Do not fear their threats or intimidations."

Opponents often attempt to intimidate believers to change their "right" behavior or to deny their "right" beliefs. Inherent in "fear" is the suggestion of being put to flight, or running away. The word describes "terror that causes you to flee." In the midst of suffering for doing what is right, believers are sometimes intimidated into running from their belief system or running from their circumstances. Peter's counsel was that they should not allow this to happen.

3:15. Instead of running away, Christians need a renewed allegiance. **Set apart Christ as Lord** means "to treat as holy or to regard with reverence." Christians are to acknowledge Jesus Christ as the Holy One and also as Lord. "Lord" is the New Testament term for the Old Testament personal name for God (see Exod. 3:14–15; 6:2–3), often transcribed as "Jehovah" but more properly as "Yahweh." The New Testament applies the Old Testament title for God the Father to Jesus Christ, thus celebrating the deity of Christ.

The believer is to view Christ as holy, as worthy of reverence because of who he is. To reverence Christ as Lord means to believe that Jesus Christ is in control and that those who come against the believer are not. To have such reverence is to maintain a deep-seated confidence in Jesus Christ as the reigning Lord of the universe (see 3:22). When our lives are centered on Christ, who is in control of the universe, then we are able to respond properly to the uncertainties and inconsistencies of life.

When we have made this commitment, we can respond to harm by communicating a positive word regarding our hope in Christ rather than running away. Even while suffering unjustly, Christians are able to go on because of their hope in the future. Yancey observes, "When we awake in the new heaven and new earth, we will possess at last whatever we longed for. Somehow, from all the bad news, incredible good news emerges—a good without a catch in it somewhere. Heaven and earth will again work the way God intended. There is a happy ending after all" (Philip Yancy, *Disappointment with God* [Grand Rapids: Zondervan, 1988], p. 245.)

From the opening words of chapter 1, Peter has emphasized the **living hope** of the believer (see 1:3). The unbeliever does not enjoy this hope but is connected only to an **empty way of life**, and a life of spiritual darkness (see 1:18; 2:9). One of the distinguishing marks of believers in Christ is their possession of hope. Christian hope is to be so real and distinctive that non-Christians will be puzzled by it and ask for an explanation. We should seize the opportunities of witness presented in these kinds of situations. Our response should be characterized not by smugness or vindictiveness but by **gentleness and respect.**

These words suggest that the believer should approach others carefully and kindly. A Christian should not attempt to ram the truth down someone's throat or to speak patronizingly or critically to them. According to Grudem, "Such witness must be given with gentleness and (respect), not attempting to overpower the person with the force of human personality or aggressiveness, but trusting the Holy Spirit himself to quietly persuade the listener" (Grudem, 153).

3:16. If we maintain our testimony with gentleness and respect, we can be confident of operating with a **clear conscience.** This means that we should live in such a way that we won't have to keep looking over our shoulder, hoping that the wrong we have done isn't about to catch up to us.

By operating this way, our behavior and words will speak volumes to those who come against us. Peter promised that truth will prevail. What is not clear is whether the reference to the slanderers being ashamed refers to their present life or to the future day of God's judgment. Most likely the text looks to a change of heart by the persecutors in this life as they are confronted by the gracious responses of the people they are persecuting.

3:17. This verse is an effective summary of what Peter has already stated in 2:15,19–20: Suffering for doing good may be God's will for believers.

3:18–22. Suffering and persecution form the backdrop for everything in this section. These verses encourage believers to face their difficulties fearlessly and positively. We can do this by remembering the significance of Jesus Christ. This paragraph interrupts the pain of the persecuted readers just long enough to remind them of the pain that Jesus Christ experienced and of the spiritual significance that Christ's pain and death has for them.

3:18. This verse gives one of the Bible's shortest, simplest, and richest summaries of the meaning of the cross of Jesus Christ. This meaning begins with the fact that Christ died. The love God expressed through Christ has no value if Jesus Christ did not die physically on the cross. Beyond that, his death has no value spiritually except that Christ **died for sins.**

This expression finds its roots in the Septuagint, the earliest Greek translation of the Old Testament, where it speaks of the effects of sacrifices. The death of Christ is like a sacrifice in that it takes away sin and cancels sin's effects. Christ's death served as a perfect sin-offering for the sins of others because Christ himself was sinless (1:19; 2:22). In the Old Testament, sacrifices for sin were made repeatedly, but Christ died **once for all.**

Christ's death is all that is necessary to provide spiritual salvation. Christ's sacrificial death does not need revision or repetition. Christ died, **the righteous for the unrighteous.** This emphasizes again the innocence or sinlessness of Christ, because the term *righteous* means "without sin." In addition, this expression states clearly the substitutionary nature of Christ's death. In essence Peter said, "Jesus Christ, the sinless one, died once and for all for those who are not sinless, for all of humankind."

The ultimate purpose of Christ's death was **to bring you to God.** Jesus died to reach across the gulf between God and humanity. Taking our hand, he leads us across the territory of the enemy into the presence of God the Father. Jesus Christ opens the way and introduces us to God the Father. By removing sin as the cause of our separation from God, Jesus Christ provides access to God and makes us acceptable in his sight.

On the cross Jesus Christ paid in full the penalty for our sin. When Christ died, God's wrath against sin was expressed against his Son. God was then satisfied with Christ's sacrifice, which allowed all who would turn, in faith, to the son of God to be totally, once-for-all, and eternally forgiven. From the moment a person believes on Jesus, he or she stands forgiven, relieved of guilt before a satisfied and just God.

Peter added the exclamation point to this verse: **He was put to death in the body but made alive by the Spirit.** The saving action of Jesus Christ lies not simply in his death, but also in his resurrection. The resurrection secures and guarantees the results of his death. Christ's death on the cross initiated the path for salvation; his resurrection guaranteed this salvation.

3:19–21. Will our salvation last? Can Jesus Christ's work on the cross accomplish complete and final salvation forever? Or does our pain and suffering as believers indicate that something has gone wrong with the overall plan? Two vivid illustrations reassure us of Christ's victory and our security.

The first illustration concerns the imprisonment and judgment of disobedient spirits or angels. It finds a parallel in Jude 6. At least eighteen major theories have been suggested to explain these verses, and we cannot review all of them (see W. J. Dalton, *Christ's Proclamation to the Spirits: A Study of 1 Peter 3:18–4:6. Analecta Biblica* 23, Rome, 1965; Wayne A. Grudem, *The First Epistle of Peter,* Tyndale New Testament Commentaries, InterVarsity Press, 1988, 203–239).

After his resurrection and before his ascension into heaven, Jesus Christ went to the place where disobedient supernatural powers are imprisoned. There he proclaimed to them his victory over death and God's ultimate and final judgment on those evil spirits. Christ's proclamation to them is of his victory and of their doom, now sealed because of Christ's death and resurrection. In doing this, Christ reaffirmed that he is superior to all powers. These evil powers cannot separate the believer from Jesus Christ, so the eternal benefits of his salvation are assured.

Like Noah and his family, the Christians to whom Peter wrote were a small, persecuted minority who were surrounded by a majority that was disobedient to God. Christ's triumphant proclamation and the reference to the Flood remind them that they will be the delivered minority in eternity.

Verse 21 has also generated great debate. This writer believes that Peter used the historical account of Noah and his family as an analogy for the triumphant salvation provided through Christ. His reference to baptism, however, is not water baptism. The flood waters did not save Noah—quite the opposite. The waters of the flood destroyed everyone in judgment. Noah passed through those waters safely because he and his family were placed securely in the ark. Water baptism does not fit the picture and is not the point.

The point of the analogy becomes clear when we recall that when a person accepts Jesus Christ as personal Savior, he or she is placed into "the body of Christ." At that moment the Holy Spirit enters that person's life as a permanent resident. This action is described in the New Testament as "the baptism of the Holy Spirit" (see 1 Cor. 12:13). This is Peter's emphasis. When you accept Christ, you are placed spiritually in Christ. As this occurs, you stand before God with a "good conscience" (v. 21) because your sins have been forgiven. Water baptism does not provide a person with a clear conscience before God; baptism by the Holy Spirit does.

3:22. We find further assurance of the eternal nature of our salvation because Christ is **at God's right hand** in heaven. At this very moment Christ occupies an exalted position of royal dignity and authority alongside God the Father. The theme here is vindication. Christ, in his journey to heaven, has broken the power of evil; therefore, the future is assured in Jesus Christ. **Angels** includes good and evil spirits. Both angels and demons are subject to Christ. **Authorities and powers** indicate rulers and distribution of functions within the angelic world. All created spiritual authorities and powers are subject to Christ. He is the Lord indeed!

MAIN IDEA REVIEW: *Wives must be submissive to their husbands, and husbands should be considerate and respectful of their wives. Everyone should live harmoniously with others. Even as we suffer under the hand of those who may be over us, we are to return good for evil and thus share our faith in Christ with others.*

III. CONCLUSION

Do Not Short-Circuit Any Opportunities

The point cannot be missed: relationships inside and outside the church are vital to the witness of Christians. This chapter continues the emphasis begun in chapter 2. Peter now goes for the jugular. He brings the subject of relationships close to home by talking to husbands and wives about their relationship in the home. It's one thing to be a model of positive relationships at church. It's another to be a model of Christlike behavior to those outside the church. All of this means very little if we cannot bring it home. "Get it right at home" is Peter's point through the first part of this chapter.

From there, he rewinds the tape, and reemphasizes the importance of healthy relationships among the members of the body of Christ. Half-hearted efforts for harmony are not satisfactory. Life in the church family requires diligence from every member. Similar effort is needed to respond and act appropriately to those outside the body of Christ, particularly when they speak against you.

In each situation one thing should be uppermost in our minds: the continuing opportunity to present the gospel of Jesus Christ to those who stand in need. We must not short-circuit any opportunities to do so by our misguided and inappropriate responses and actions.

PRINCIPLES

- The biblical behavior of a Christian wife can present a powerful witness to her unbelieving husband.
- A husband's treatment of his wife impacts his prayer life positively or negatively.
- Harmonious relationships within the church are a priority for Christians.
- Revengeful behavior and speech are not consistent with Christian testimony.
- Doing good often leads to opposition from non-believers.
- Christians are to maintain a testimony for Jesus Christ even in the midst of serious opposition.
- The death of Jesus Christ is the only satisfactory and final sacrifice for sin.
- The resurrection of Jesus Christ guarantees the salvation work of Christ on the cross.

APPLICATION

- Submit to your husband, in the awareness that this does not reflect inferiority on your part or dominance on his part.
- Recognize that positive, biblical behavior and responses in marriage can have a profound effect on your spouse, whether he or she is a Christian or a non-Christian.
- Work diligently to promote harmony within your church.
- Look for ways to demonstrate love, sympathy, and compassion to members of the body of Christ.
- Be aware of the power of the tongue for good and evil.
- Take advantage of every opportunity to speak to others about Jesus Christ.
- Remind yourself that suffering for doing what is good is a part of your Christian experience and testimony.
- Never stop thanking God for your salvation gift in Jesus Christ.

IV. LIFE APPLICATION

Cells Growing Out of Control

In a book about the human body and the body of Christ entitled *Fearfully and Wonderfully Made,* Dr. Paul Brand and Philip Yancey make this sobering statement:

A tumor is called benign if its effect is fairly localized and it stays within membrane boundaries. But the most traumatizing condition in the body occurs when disloyal cells defy (restrictions). They multiply without any checks on growth, spreading rapidly throughout the body, choking out normal cells. White cells, armed against foreign invaders, will not attack the body's own mutinous cells. Physicians fear no other malfunction more deeply: it is called cancer. For still mysterious reasons, these cells grow wild, out of control. Each is a healthy, functioning cell, but disloyal, no longer acting in regard for the rest of the body.

Because I am a surgeon and not a prophet, I tremble to make the analogy between cancer in the physical body and mutiny in the spiritual body of Christ. But I must. In his warnings to the church, Jesus Christ showed no concern about the shocks and bruises his body would meet from external forces. "The gates of hell shall not prevail against my church," he said flatly (Matt. 16:18). (Christ) moved easily, unthreatened, among sinner and criminals. But he cried out against the kind of disloyalty that comes from within.

From within it does come, whether it is the way that husbands diminish their wives, or a church brutalizes a pastor, or individuals attack one another with cancerous ferocity. Like a darkened, shroud-like fog, mutiny, disloyalty and disharmony march up to the door of the church and seep through the cracks and then slide down the aisle and join us in our seats. If we are not careful, they will ultimately walk out with us on their arms.

The third chapter of 1 Peter focuses on the relationship between husbands and wives. How easy it is to concentrate our efforts on every other kind of relationship and neglect to apply ourselves at home. For a marriage to be successful, both partners must make every effort to complete their biblical assignments. For too long, the church has hammered on the role of Christian wives with constant reminders about "submission." Many of those reminders have gone well beyond the biblical understanding of the word and have degenerated into a biblical club for a sexist and patronizing view of women. Such is not the view of Peter or the rest of Scripture. Furthermore, not enough emphasis has been placed on the responsibility of the Christian husband. To model effective marriage relationships, both partners must be accountable.

As our marriage relationships move toward wholeness, our healthy relational living will attach itself to our connections within the body of Christ. The same spirit that is to dominate our marriages needs to enter our relationships in the church. *Consider the other person first* is the simplest way to summarize Peter's emphasis. The church will succeed only when its members follow Jesus Christ's model of serving others.

No longer should we be allowed to excuse the sins of our tongue by saying, "Well, that's just the way he is," or "Look, she didn't mean anything by it," or "He was just joking; can't you take a joke?" The serious sins of our tongues must be confronted with the gravity that Scripture attaches to them. The cancer of division and disharmony must not be allowed to gain a foothold. Sin is sin, and God is not in the business of categorizing them into big or little transgressions.

After concentrating our spiritual energies at home, we have a greater opportunity to succeed in our witness outside the church. Our positive behavior will make a statement for Christ, but more is necessary. We must be willing to speak up for Christ, graciously and respectfully, even when we are speaking to those who make it their business to bully or assault us verbally. Perhaps this combination of action and word will nudge them toward the good news of the death and resurrection of Jesus Christ.

V. PRAYER

Lord, I confess to you that my reflection of you to others is often distorted and clouded because of my inappropriate attitudes and actions. I find this to be so true at home and at church. Forgive me, Lord. Continue to extend grace to your servant so I may declare your praises through my life. Lord, that is even more true when people come against me. My inner nature wants to strike back, to get even. Again, I need your grace to respond with gentleness and respect, reflecting you, not defending me. May I continue to find strength and courage in you, my resurrected and sovereign Lord. Amen.

VI. DEEPER DISCOVERIES

A. Wives, Be Submissive to Your Husbands (v. 1)

In today's culture any discussion regarding the role of women that includes the word *submission* always produces intense reactions. Unfortunately, a great deal of damage has been done to women under the over-zealous banner of evangelical men, who have assumed that submission gives them the right to mistreat and dominate their wives. Such a misunderstanding and misrepresentation of submission must not go unchallenged. This prejudicial approach to the subject has also led to incorrect teaching regarding the role of women within the church. Much of the rhetoric from this group seems to stem from a desire to rule over rather than to serve one another in love.

The *Handbook of Biblical Application* offers an excellent word on the subject:

> Biblical submission is a mark of equality rather than inequality. Submitting to another person is an often misunderstood concept. It does not mean becoming a doormat. Christ—at whose name "every knee shall bow in heaven and on earth and under the earth" (Philippians 2:10)—submitted his will to the Father, and we honor Christ by following his example. When we submit to God, we become more willing to obey his command to submit to others, that is, to subordinate our rights to theirs. In a marriage relationship, both husband and wife are called to submit to one another. For the wife, this means willingly following her husband's leadership in Christ. For the husband, it means putting aside his own interests in order to care for his wife. Submission is rarely a problem in homes where both partners have a strong relationship with Christ and where each is concerned for the (well-being) of the other.
>
> Although some people have distorted (Peter's) teaching on submission by giving unlimited authority to husbands, we cannot get around it—(Peter and) Paul told wives to submit to their husbands. The fact that a teaching is not popular is no reason to discard it. According to the Bible, the man is the spiritual head of the family,

and his wife should acknowledge his leadership. But real spiritual leadership involves service. Just as Christ served the disciples, even to the point of washing their feet, so the husband is to serve his wife. A wise and Christ-honoring husband will not take advantage of his leadership role, and a wise and Christ-honoring wife will not try to undermine her husband's leadership. Either approach causes disunity and friction in marriage (Wilson, 605–606).

B. The Spirits in Prison (v. 19)

The identity and location of the spirits in prison is the center of great debate and confusion. The following are the major interpretive views:

1. These are disembodied spirits of men after death, awaiting the day of judgment. The victory of Christ's death is proclaimed following the crucifixion. In favor of this view is the fact that the word *spirits* is used sometimes to refer to departed men in the New Testament (for example, Heb. 12:23) and this fits the sequence of thought in verses 18–22: death, preaching, resurrection, ascension. However, the mention of Noah forces this view to be questioned, for this view has no need for Noah. If the men are those of Noah's generation, there is no explanation as to why Christ confined his preaching to this one group of dead.

2. These are men who did not listen to Noah's preaching before the Flood. They are here being offered another chance to repent after death. This is similar to the first view, except that it specifies the dead generation as belonging to the generation of Noah. The same objection mentioned under the first view applies here.

3. These are men of apostolic times who heard and refused the gospel as preached by Christ through the apostles. They are prisoners of sin because of their rejection of the gospel. This view finds approval because this was the preaching that transpired after the resurrection of Christ. The preaching that opens verse 19 follows the event that closes verse 18—the resurrection. One difficulty with this view however, is that it cannot explain the reference to Noah in verse 20. The "spirits" cannot be placed in the apostolic era.

4. These are the men of Noah's day to whom the preincarnate Christ through Noah preached. These rejected the preaching and now are in prison. In favor of this view is that the preincarnate Christ was certainly active in Old Testament times and that this may have been alluded to by Peter in 1:11, where he spoke of the Spirit of Christ working in the prophets of the Old Testament. The difficulty of this view is that the text says that Christ, not Noah, was the preacher. Furthermore, this view separates the preaching (Noah's time) from the imprisonment (Christ's time).

5. These are angelic beings, specifically fallen angels, who have been imprisoned until judgment. Christ's preaching to them following his death

was a victory proclamation. This view seems to find a parallel in Jude 6 and 7, where Jude spoke of angels being kept in prison, awaiting their judgment (cf. 2 Pet. 2:4–6). The usage of the word *spirit* without a qualifying genitive indicates that the term describes angels. Also, angels are spoken of in the context as having been brought into submission following this event (v. 22). A variation of this view suggests that this refers to Christ's announcement to departed spirits of the triumph of his resurrection, declaring to them the victory he had achieved by his death and resurrection. Some interpreters suggest that Jesus offered no hope of salvation to these spirits. He did not evangelize them but simply proclaimed the victory of his resurrection to them. Either variation of this view would seem to be the best alternative (see Geisler and Howe, 534).

C. Baptism That Now Saves You (v. 21)

Larry Richards offers a clear and concise explanation for this verse:

This is another one of the Bible's more difficult passages. The thought is not hard to understand, but people tend to snatch the verse out of context and try to understand it without seeing it in context. We must remember that Peter draws a comparison between the days of Noah and the age of Christ. His analogy is intended to show the far-reaching effect of Jesus' work. To do this he goes back to the Genesis flood and compares the Christian experience to the experience of the eight people who were carried in the ark through the waters of raging judgment. Baptism is used here to indicate our union with Christ (see Matthew 3:11; Romans 6:1–4). Like Noah and his family, we Christians have been lifted beyond danger of judgment and deposited in a new world in which we are to live new lives. Freed by Jesus, we are to live these new lives not "for evil human desires, but rather for the will of God" (4:2).

Note the appropriateness of the analogy. Noah and his family were snatched from an old world that was destined for destruction and carried safely through the waters of judgment in the ark. When the waters receded, Noah made landfall on a changed earth, empty of human habitations, rich with new, budding vegetable life. In the same way, we have been lifted out of the spiritual kingdom ruled by Satan, which is destined to be judged by God, carried through the judgment in Christ, and brought into the kingdom of God's son. Now we live in that kingdom and everything about our lives is fresh and new (Richards, 377–378).

VII. TEACHING OUTLINE

A. INTRODUCTION

1. Lead Story: Let the Cheering Begin
2. Context: Relationships and our reactions to those relationships, whether positive or negative, continue to be the emphasis of Peter. Having introduced these subjects in chapter 2, he filled in more of the details in chapter 3, particularly as it relates to relationships at home.
3. Transition: This chapter continues the primary concerns of Peter for his friends—their reactions and responses to one another and to their neighbors and friends who do not know Christ. He was concerned about our ability to maintain a positive testimony on behalf of Jesus Christ in the day-to-day interactions of our lives.

B. COMMENTARY

1. Relationships in Marriage (vv. 1–7)
   a. The attitude and actions of wives (vv. 1–6)
   b. The attitude and actions of husbands (v. 7)
2. Relationships in the Church (vv. 8–12)
   a. Team work (v. 8)
   b. Team spirit (v. 8)
   c. Team speech (vv. 9–12)
3. Relationships with Those Outside the Church (vv. 13–22)
   a. Life in normal circumstances (v. 13)
   b. Life in abnormal circumstances (vv. 14–17)
      (1) Suffering for right (v. 14)
      (2) Responses that are right (vv. 14b–16)
      (3) A principle to remember (v. 17)
   c. Illustrating the Principle (vv. 18–22)
      (1) The suffering and victory of Christ (vv. 18–20a)
      (2) The security of Noah (vv. 20b–21)
      (3) The supremacy of Christ (v. 22)

C. CONCLUSION: CHRISTIAN TUMORS

VIII. ISSUES FOR DISCUSSION

1. Describe the proper roles of husbands and wives in the relationship which the Bible describes for them. How do these roles work out in

everyday decision making, work assignments, parenting, schooling, and discipline?

2. How should a woman adorn herself?

3. What threatens to disturb the harmony of your church? What can be done to restore or maintain harmony?

4. How is your suffering or pain related to your salvation?

5. Describe what Christ has done to bring you salvation? What assurance do you have that this salvation will last forever?

1 Peter 4

He Is Faithful in Our Suffering

I. **INTRODUCTION**
Regardless of the Cost

II. **COMMENTARY**
A verse-by-verse explanation of the chapter.

III. **CONCLUSION**
News About Our Suffering

An overview of the principles and applications from the chapter.

IV. **LIFE APPLICATION**
Day by Day

Melding the chapter to life.

V. **PRAYER**
Tying the chapter to life with God.

VI. **DEEPER DISCOVERIES**
Historical, geographical, and grammatical enrichment of the commentary.

VII. **TEACHING OUTLINE**
Suggested step-by-step group study of the chapter.

VIII. **ISSUES FOR DISCUSSION**
Zeroing the chapter in on daily life.

Q u o t e

"*G*od, You are relentless. I have yielded everything to You—everything but one small exception—an exception so small I'm truly amazed You would even take notice. Yet it is invariably to that one small exception that You keep bringing me back, and back, and back. Why does it matter so much to You? (My child, Why does it matter so much to you?)"

R u t h   H a r m s   C a l k i n

I N   A   N U T S H E L L

*C*hapter 4 teaches us that since Jesus suffered, we must be prepared to suffer. We've had plenty of time to sin. It's time to stop and live for God. The end is near, so do what is right toward others, so that God will be praised. We will suffer for doing what is right. When we do, we should commit our lives to God and keep on doing what is right.

He Is Faithful
in Our Suffering

I. INTRODUCTION

Regardless of the Cost

*Y*ou probably have never heard of Miss Aida Scripnikova. She was born in 1941 in St. Petersburg, when the Russian people were fighting to free themselves from their invaders, the German armies. The enemy was eventually driven out, but for many decades there was no true freedom in her homeland. In the fall of 1961, Aida came to know Jesus Christ as her personal Savior. She was nineteen years old. With her new faith came the impulse to share it with others. So she purchased some postcards with a beautiful picture on one side and then she wrote a poem on the reverse side. The poem expressed her perception of life and the need for people to find God.

Aida then took her postcards, stood on the Nevski Prospect (which is the equivalent in St. Petersburg of Fifth Avenue in New York City), and handed out the cards to people who passed by. She was, of course, arrested.

In April of 1962 Aida was tried by a Communist court. She was exiled from St. Petersburg and lost her job as a laboratory assistant. She was arrested again in 1965 and sent to a labor camp for a year. In 1968 she was arrested again and sent to a labor camp for an additional three years.

I do not know if Aida Scripnikova had ever come across 1 Peter 4, but she obeyed the instinct of her heart. In the midst of unrelenting persecution she shared the message of Jesus Christ, regardless of the cost. In so doing, she lived out the implications of 1 Peter 4.

This chapter continues the dominant theme of the letter: the reality of a fleshed-out faith in the midst of oppressive circumstances. Believers in Jesus Christ should direct their hearts and minds toward living out the will of God, regardless of the cost. True believers must pay a price, but, in light of eternity, it is worth the cost.

II. COMMENTARY

He Is Faithful in Our Suffering

MAIN IDEA: *Do not continue to live in sin. Instead, since the end is near, live in love toward others. When suffering comes, commit yourself to God and continue to do good.*

A Living for the Will of God (vv. 1-6)

SUPPORTING IDEA: *Have the same perspective on suffering that Jesus did. In the past you've spent enough time sinning. God will judge sin, so live for God.*

4:1-2. Therefore connects this chapter to the discussion of the sufferings of Jesus Christ at the end of chapter 3. The suffering that Christ endured was, in part, because of the righteous life that he lived. Believers in similar fashion should **arm yourselves also with the same attitude.** As believers in Jesus Christ, we are to adopt the same attitude Christ had toward his suffering. We are to be willing to suffer because we have chosen to live righteous lives. We are to think as Christ did about obedience and suffering: to be convinced that it is better to do right and suffer than to do wrong.

Because he who has suffered in his body is done with sin does not suggest that the believer, because he suffers for doing what is right, will never stumble or sin again. A Christian does not, through suffering, magically vault to the level of moral perfection. Verses 1-2 indicate that believers take seriously their struggle against sin and their commitment to obedience. By following this counsel, you demonstrate to others that obeying God is the most important motivation for your life, more important by far than avoiding hardship and pain. The Amplified Bible's rendering of this section clearly conveys the meaning Peter wished to communicate: "So, since Christ suffered in the flesh, arm yourselves with the same thought and purpose (patiently to suffer rather than fail to please God). For whoever has suffered in the flesh has done with (intentional) sin—has stopped pleasing himself and the world, and pleases God" (1 Pet. 4:1-2, AMP).

4:3. This verse says quite bluntly that our past experience of sin is sufficient. The Greek perfect tense emphsizes that the kinds of activities listed in verse 3 are over; this part of our lives is a closed chapter.

The staccato-like descriptions come quickly and clearly—without detailed explanations. The original readers knew precisely what was meant. **Debauchery** and **lusts** refer to unbridled and unrestrained living. They describe a person who knows no restraints, has no checks and balances for life. Specifically, such a person has no restraint when it comes to sexual morality or violent behavior.

Drunkenness, orgies, carousing also stand together. "Drunkenness" emphasizes the habitual nature of a person's sin. The other two terms could be translated as "drinking parties." These two words originally described a group of friends coming home from a big athletic contest. Along the way, they imbibed their favorite beverage and then stopped off at the local gathering place and drank one too many. They were out having a good time, grabbing for all the gusto, and disturbing people in the process. For believers, that is not part of our present experience; it is in the past.

Detestable idolatry simply reinforces this point. In the first century, sexual and alcoholic excesses had become idols in many people's lives. Believers may continue to struggle with the temptations of these kinds of activities, but they must remain a part of our past history.

4:4. Continuing in these activities, unbelievers will **think it strange that you do not plunge with them.** "Think it strange" suggests that the nonbeliever will be astonished or surprised that you don't run with them. Unfortunately, their response does not remain neutral. To "think it strange" also suggests that they become offended. That offense is not silent. They **heap abuse** on the believer. In other words, they defame and injure the reputation of the believer, primarily with verbal abuse and slander. Nonbelievers of every era tend to resent the convicting purity of the believer's life, and as a result, the Christian becomes the victim of their slander. Through such slander they seek somehow to justify their own behavior by painting the nonparticipant in a negative way.

The letter never moves far from the dominant theme of suffering. Believers serious about righteous living will invariably suffer. One way they suffer is from verbal abuse.

4:5–6. Why should I stand against an ungodly life? What support do I have? The answer comes loud and clear: the coming judgment. This judgment is **near** (v. 7). It will be universal, for it will embrace all the living and the dead. Unbelievers will have to give an account of their lives but will not be able to withstand the divine scrutiny. God is **ready to judge,** so this judgment could come suddenly, without warning.

Those people who practice these things and who abuse Christians for failing to live the same way may seem to have the upper hand for the time being, but the last word will be with God. He is already prepared. A time is coming when the world as we know it will come to an end and God will judge the world. Those who are still alive will face God, and those who have died will be raised up to answer for themselves before God.

🅑 Living for the Will of God in the Church (vv. 7–11).

SUPPORTING IDEA: *Since the end is near, live in love toward others. Minister to them with your spiritual gifts. As you serve others, God will be praised.*

4:7–11. Marshall summarizes well the big picture of this paragraph:

> In the church where there is a lack of love and common purpose and where the spiritual lifeline of communication to God is broken, the forces of opposition will weaken and eventually destroy the church. In these verses Peter emphasizes how crucial it is that local churches be strong in fellowship with firm links of life and loyalty between the members and also between the members and God (Marshall, 140).

4:7. All the major events in God's plan for redemption have occurred, and all things are now ready for Jesus Christ to return and rule. **Therefore** connects this doctrinal word to the behavioral and ethical consequences that ought to be demonstrated in the believer's life and in the life of the church. One of the proofs of being a Christian is not simply having a hope for the future; the proof is having a hope that makes a difference in our lives today, in the present. As we live in the expectation of the second coming of Christ, some things need to take priority in our lives.

First on this list of priorities is purposeful prayer. Such prayer must be **clear minded and self-controlled.** To "be clear minded" suggests that believers pray intelligently or that they think about and evaluate their situations in life maturely and correctly as they begin to pray about them. In light of the context, perhaps Peter was cautioning them against giving way to eschatological frenzy and panic. To be "self-controlled" as one comes to prayer suggests that believers are to pray with a mind that is focused and alert. In other words, prayer should not be practiced nonchalantly or flippantly. Believers are to take prayer seriously.

4:8. The second priority is forgiving love. **Above all, love each other deeply** burns into our minds the supreme importance of love as the controlling factor in all relationships in the church (see 1:22; 2:17; 3:8). This kind of love (*agape*) can be commanded because it is primarily a decision of the mind, not a feeling into which a person falls. The goal of *agape* love is always to seek the good of the other person. The evidence of *agape* love is action, not words. The extent of *agape* love is sacrifice. Thus, believers are to love each other "deeply." This word means "to be stretched." True *agape* love is constantly being stretched to the limit by the demands made on it. This is precisely where *agape* love shines, because it is not exhausted when it becomes difficult or inconvenient.

One of the most difficult and inconvenient times to extend love is when someone in the church has hurt or wronged us. We must demonstrate a love that is willing to be stretched **because love covers over a multitude of sins.** "Covers" means "willing to forgive." The present tense indicates that which is to be constantly true in the life of the believer.

Love does not ignore the reality of personal sin any more than it justifies or condones sin. Confrontation of sin is appropriate and necessary, especially when we demonstrate love. However, it is just as important to demonstrate a willingness to forgive and then to move on. Forgiveness, like love, is an act of the will, a personal choice. A person chooses either to forgive or not to forgive. According to Grudem, "Where love abounds in a fellowship of Christians, many small offenses, and even some large ones, are overlooked and forgotten. But where love is lacking, every word is viewed with suspicion, every action is liable to misunderstanding, and conflicts abound" (Grudem, 174).

4:9. Believers should put action into the love command. Hospitality among Christians is an important and tangible expression of love. In the first century, hospitality was a common courtesy that even nonbelievers extended to others. Scripture lifts Christian hospitality to a higher level. A believer's attitude toward the necessity and courtesy of hospitality should be **without grumbling.** This expression speaks of murmuring and of repeated words of complaint. Such words were often spoken, not quietly to themselves, but to others. Obviously, the arrival of guests in any century can be inconvenient for a variety of reasons. Even the best-behaved guests can overstay their welcome. Therefore, Christians are to provide hospitality without complaining or whining about the time and expense involved. This is an expression of agape love.

4:10–11. One final priority remains for believers who live in the light of Christ's second coming and who wish to demonstrate *agape* love toward one another. This priority can best be summarized as *intense serving.* Every believer is to heed this injunction. **Each one should use whatever gift he has received to serve others.**

Every believer in every church has received a spiritual gift from God for use in the life of the church. Within the body of Christ, love for each other finds expression in the use of spiritual gifts, not for self-advancement or as an attention-getter, but for the benefit of others. Every Christian, then, is capable of ministering to others within the body of Christ.

"Gift" (*charisma*) literally means "a gift of grace." When Christians receive God's grace in this way, we have the responsibility to share this gift with other Christians. Through such sharing we are **faithfully administering God's grace in its various forms.** What has been given to the individual as a gift of grace has also been given for the benefit of the body as a whole. Believers are agents of God in passing on the benefits of his grace in our life. God does not grant us gifts of grace for our personal use; he gives them for the benefit of the body of Christ.

Verse 11 illustrates this point by dividing the many gifts of grace into two broad categories: speaking and serving. *Speaking* includes not simply preaching or teaching, but many kinds of gifts involving speech, such as evangelism, speaking in tongues, prophecy, encouragement, and leadership. *Serving* includes any type of assisting or encouraging ministry that directly targets the benefit of others within the body of Christ, such as contributing to the needs of others, healing, miraculous powers, showing mercy, and encouragement.

Believers are to take these gifts seriously and to exercise them with an attitude of dependence on God (speak the very words of God, do it with the strength of God). When the gifts of grace are applied in this way, the attention and praise shift from the individual believer to God, the one who has gifted the believer in the first place.

C Living for the Will of God During Suffering (vv. 12–19)

> **SUPPORTING IDEA:** *Rejoice in suffering for Christ so that you will be overjoyed when you get to heaven. Return good for evil. When you suffer for doing the will of God, commit your suffering to God, and keep doing good.*

4:12. Four times this section uses the words **suffering** or **suffer**, and this verse talks about **the painful trial.** This phrase could be read as "the painful trial that burns among you." The original readers would hear this as martyrdom by being burned at the stake. It could describe the fact that followers of Jesus in the city of Rome (where Peter wrote this letter) were being dragged from their families, dipped in tar, and used as living torches to light the gardens of Nero. At the very least, Peter described experiences of pain comparable to the pain of being burned with fire, though his definition of these trials remains deliberately vague.

Verse 14 does hint at one specific type of persecution: being **insulted because of the name of Christ.** "Insulted" refers to being slandered by someone. It describes the dismantling of a person's character with false information. This reminds us of James's words: "The tongue also is a fire, a world of evil among the parts of the body. It corrupts the whole person, sets the whole course of his life on fire, and is itself set on fire by hell" (Jas. 3:6)

Believers must not **be surprised** when things like this assault their lives. *Surprised* means to be "astonished, upset, and bewildered." It does not refer, however, to the very normal and short-term surprise or shock that an individual experiences in the face of this kind of pain. The present tense of the verb suggests a continuing attitude of bewilderment and astonishment at what is happening in the believer's life.

Hidden in the word *surprised* is not only the thought of being bewildered over time, but also the idea of becoming resentful and bitter about the circumstances. Long-term bewilderment often leads to long-term bitterness, but believers should not view suffering as something **strange** or foreign. Our sufferings are not accidental, nor are they interfering with God's purposes for our lives. In fact, these sufferings are part of his purpose.

This insight is suggested by the phrase **painful trial.** This expression contains the picture of a refining fire or a testing process that produces a positive result. The fires of suffering are designed by God to purify and strengthen the lives of his followers.

4:13. Again, the believer should not be surprised at this. Our suffering is the same kind of thing that Christ received, and therefore, in some sense, suffering is an indication of the believers' identification with Christ. Believers **participate in the suffering of Christ.** *Participate* is taken from the familiar word *koinoneo*, "to share or fellowship with someone." How does this work? Think of it this way: Your closest friends are those with whom you have suffered and hurt. As you stumble and crawl through pain together, you grow together as friends.

The same thing happens in our spiritual lives. As we view our persecutions as suffering for Christ and with Christ, we love him more deeply and trust him more completely. As this occurs, we are able to rejoice in the midst of our pain. Our present-tense joy will be turned into super joy when the pain is gone at the return of Jesus Christ (**when his glory is revealed**). This kind of joy should not be surprising, but in fact it should be expected. However, it is the present tense rejoicing that comes as a surprise.

Joy in suffering is not a trick of the mind. Rejoicing in pain has nothing to do with deriving pleasure from being mistreated in some way. Suffering has meaning as it puts us into deeper fellowship with Jesus Christ. As this occurs, our level of trust in his wisdom and care in our lives increases so that we are able to rejoice. Joy, in its most sublime meaning, is a deep confidence that God is in control of every area of our lives, even the painful places. The fullness of joy comes from a deep sense of the presence of God in a person's life. Joy occurs when our pain drives us to depend upon God.

4:14. This verse mentions a specific kind of suffering: **if you are insulted because of the name of Christ.** *Insulted* means "to be abused or slandered." It pictures unjustified denunciations being hurled against the believer. For sensitive people, "there is often more bitterness (in such attacks) than in the loss of goods, or in the torments or agonies of the body" (Hiebert, quoting John Calvin, 268).

The Christian who suffers these kinds of abuses is uniquely blessed of God because **the Spirit of glory and of God rests on you**. This refers to the indwelling presence of the Holy Spirit within those who are believers in Jesus Christ. "Rests" indicates that the Holy Spirit is within the believer continually to refresh and to strengthen. At any moment we can draw on the Spirit of God. Especially in moments of crisis and suffering, God's Spirit is available to strengthen and refresh the believer.

4:15. This verse offers a disclaimer or clarification regarding the suffering Christian's experience. Believers should not rejoice in certain kinds of pain and suffering and should not consider themselves blessed to be a part of such suffering. In these cases even the staunchest believer should not look for the refreshment and strength of the Holy Spirit. Those sufferings are detailed with four descriptive phrases. **Murderer or thief or any other kind of criminal** form one group and should be taken literally. They refer to breaking the laws of society and suffering the consequences of those actions. When that happens, the believer is not to say, "I am suffering for Jesus' sake or for the sake of righteousness." You are not. You are suffering because you broke the law.

The fourth term may be the real concern: **meddler**. This refers to Christians who stick their noses into situations where they have no business. Words like "agitator," "disrupter," or "troublemaker" give the proper sense of the term *meddler*. By interfering in the lives of others, a meddler disrupts the peace and harmony of the local church and community.

Everyone has had experience with such meddlesome people. They stick their nose in, get caught, and get called on the carpet. Invariably they respond, "They are just picking on me because I am a Christian," or, "I am just suffering for the Lord." Scripture says, "Call it whatever you want, but you are not suffering on behalf of Jesus Christ; you are suffering because of your own meddling behavior." If you are behaving this way, stop your negative behavior.

4:16. Legitimate suffering for the name of Christ is again mentioned in this verse in direct contrast to the behavior pattern described in the previous verse. **Christian** appears only three times in the New Testament, but in each case it identifies the true followers of Jesus. Peter connected this name with true and valuable suffering. Some readers were suffering because of their faithful identification with Jesus Christ through their lifestyle choices or their verbal testimony. Faithfulness to Christ will produce suffering and persecution. The reverse also seems to be true: a lack of persecution in a believer's life may suggest a less-than-faithful lifestyle and testimony.

4:17–18. These two verses, although somewhat connected to verse 16, are better understood in their connection to the entire paragraph, beginning with verse 12. For the believer in Jesus Christ, trials and sufferings can have a positive impact. They have a refining and purifying purpose. Verse 17 develops this idea by suggesting that trials, in the form of persecution, have redemptive value for the believer, even when seen as the judgment of God in the life of the believer. One commentator puts it in these words: "The effect of persecution is to show up in the church those who really believe and are prepared to stand firm and those who do not really believe and so fall away when under trial. This judgment also purifies the true believers, encouraging them not to commit shameful acts" (Marshall, 156).

A quotation from Proverbs 11:31 reinforces this point from the perspective of the unbeliever. Unbelievers, unlike the followers of Christ, are not a part of the refining judgment of God. The judgment they face is judicial; it takes the form of punishment. When Jesus Christ returns, they will face the fire of his anger in judgment.

4:19. This is not the destination of the believer who receives quick reassurance of his or her connection to God in this verse. In this one verse the teaching of the entire letter of 1 Peter could be summarized. Believers do not suffer accidentally or because of irresistible forces of blind fate. Rather, they suffer according to God's will. This should be enough for his followers to **commit themselves** to God. *Commit* means "to entrust yourself for safe keeping." Believers are in good hands, not with a human insurance agency, but with an all-loving and faithful God who has cared for us from the beginning. He asks us to commit ourselves **to [our] faithful Creator.**

The combination of "faithful" and "Creator" reminds us of God's love and power, even in the midst of suffering and pain. God created the world, and he has faithfully ordered it and sustained it since the creation. Because we know that he is faithful, we can count on him to fulfill his promises to us. If he can oversee the forces of nature, certainly he can see us through the trials we face.

The committed believer can obey the final injunction of this paragraph: **and continue to do good.** This means doing those things God views as good. The believers to whom Peter addressed these words had not rejected their Christian faith. They had not stopped living out their faith. Perhaps they were beginning to feel weary and to weaken in their resolve. They needed encouragement to depend on God's care and the will to keep on keeping on.

Grudem summarizes this paragraph well:

> Upon reflection, no better comfort in suffering can be found than this: it is God's good and perfect will. For therein lies the knowledge that there is a limit to the suffering, both in its intensity and in its duration, a limit set and maintained by the God Who is our creator, our savior, our sustainer, our Father. And therein also lies the knowledge that this suffering is only for our good: it is purifying us, drawing us closer to our Lord, and making us more like him in our lives. In all of it we are not alone, but we can depend on the care of a faithful

Creator, we can rejoice in the fellowship of a Savior Who also suffered; we can (delight) in the constant presence of a Spirit of glory who delights to rest upon us (Grudem, 184–185).

MAIN IDEA REVIEW: *Do not continue to live in sin. Instead, since the end is near, live in love toward others. When suffering comes, commit yourself to God and continue to do good.*

III. CONCLUSION

News About Our Suffering

This section of 1 Peter might be described as "a chapter of reality." Peter has lived a real life, experienced real pain. Most of this pain was inflicted by others. Often those who crack the whip in our direction are angry or jealous toward us. Sometimes that is because we model a lifestyle that troubles them because it illumines the darkness of their life. In response, they either become enraged and lash out at us with ridicule and slander, or they respond with jealousy, never admitting that they want what we have. Either way, we end up on the receiving end of pain simply because we have chosen to follow Christ. That is what makes this letter so practical and relevant for our lives. This chapter challenges us to continue to trust our faithful God in the midst of all circumstances.

PRINCIPLES

- Followers of Jesus Christ are to adopt his attitude toward suffering.
- A Christian's lifestyle is to be distinctly different and morally superior.
- God's final judgment could come at any time.
- Jesus Christ's second coming is always near.
- Relationships of love and forgiveness are priorities within the church.
- Every Christian has received at least one spiritual gift to be used in serving the church on behalf of Christ.
- God, in his sovereignty, sometimes deems necessary the suffering of his children.
- The Holy Spirit continually strengthens the believer.
- Faithfulness to Jesus Christ will produce suffering and persecution in a believer's life.
- Followers of Jesus Christ are not out of God's will when they suffer for Christ.

APPLICATION

- Take seriously your struggle against sin and your commitment to obedience.
- Establish clear moral boundaries and restraints for your life, based on the clear teaching of the Word of God.
- Be committed to prayer, forgiveness, hospitality, and ministry within your church.
- Don't be surprised when you experience suffering and persecution because of your commitment to Jesus Christ.
- Avoid the tendency to become a meddler or busybody.
- Search for the positive meaning and purpose that God has for suffering in your life.

IV. LIFE APPLICATION

Day by Day

Her name was Lina Sandell. Swedish. Born in 1832. She loved her dad, idolized him, in fact. As she grew older, she often ministered alongside him. When she was only twenty-six, her father died. They were traveling together by ship and were standing together on the deck, reveling in the beauty of creation. For some reason, the ship lurched unsteadily, and Lina Sandell's father fell overboard. No rescue was possible. He drowned before her eyes. The one she loved, cherished, and idolized was gone. That is when Lina Sandell dug deep within for help and found it. That is when she wrote these words:

> Day by day and with each passing moment,
> Strength I find to meet my trials here.
> Trusting in my Father's wise bestowment,
> I've no cause for worry or for fear.
> He whose heart is kind beyond all measure
> Gives unto each day what He deems best.
> Lovingly, it's part of pain and pleasure,
> Mingling toil with peace and rest (*Baptist Hymnal* 1991, 66).

Day by day Christians face the same routine: relationships with people outside the church, relationships with people inside the church, and our reactions to both groups. Whenever we grow spiritually, emotionally, or intellectually, those who were with us before our growth often have serious difficulties with the changes in our lives, unless the same growth has happened to them. That is certainly the case when a person becomes a Christian and begins the life-changing journey of spiritual growth. It usually results in some significant lifestyle changes. Those changes usually prompt some significant reactions, many of which are negative (vv. 2–4).

The church has often resisted this kind of opposition, choosing instead to surrender clear biblical guidelines for living, in order to avoid any pain or persecution. The United States remains perhaps the least-persecuted Christian country in the world. What does this suggest about the reality of our faith? Gratefully, however, there have been exceptions to this. Responding to abuse, slander, and persecution can be difficult and take the Christian off guard. That's why Peter made this a focus of his letter (v. 12)

When we are feeling the heat, it is easy to curl up into a ball and forget about everything and everyone. Peter's advice is to go out of our way, through the enablement of the Holy Spirit, and to continue to love and serve one another in the body of Christ. We need one another. We need to draw strength from the Lord and from our relationships (vv. 7–11)

The community and fellowship of our local churches has not been heralded as the biblical priority that it is. Our culture of narcissism has so invaded our lives as Christians that at the first sight of conflict or difficulty, we are prone to run to another congregation and bad-mouth the one we have just left. Quite the opposite pattern is seen in the New Testament. These Christians needed one another and were encouraged to pray together, work together, and extend grace, love, mercy, and forgiveness to one another. This is necessary for the health of the body and the cause of Jesus Christ.

In the midst of our pain, we are able to go on because we have one another and because we have the Lord as our example. He is the one we hang on to and trust with our lives. His faithfulness is our anchor (vv. 13–19)

V. PRAYER

It is so hard, Lord, to weave all the dark threads of suffering through my life and to see any kind of pattern or reason for them. They seem so out of place, so dark, so foreign to my dreams. I wonder if your Son felt this way when he suffered. Help me, Lord, to see your hand, your will directing the circumstances of pain. Help me, Lord, not to abandon right living just because living is hard. May my obedience to you direct praise and glory your way even if it means that insults and suffering are directed my way. Thank you, Lord, for helping me see that the colors of suffering are necessary. Without them, the canvas of my life could not reflect the image of your Son. Amen.

VI. DEEPER DISCOVERIES

A. The Gospel Was Preached Even to Those Who Are Now Dead (v. 6)

Scholars disagree about the meaning of this expression. It would be, as one commentator suggests, "perverse—and it would not fit the context—to interpret verse 6 as teaching that a further chance of embracing new life is given after death. The Bible is quite clear that the books are opened and all men's accounts are settled when the tale of our earthly existence has been told (e.g., Heb. 9:27), and Peter himself says as much in 4:17–18" (Elwell, 1168–1169).

In spite of such statements, the following views have emerged regarding this verse:

1. These are people who are spiritually dead. The difficulty with such a view is that the word for the "dead" is the same word used in verse 5. In that verse, the literal meaning of physical death is clearly the emphasis, and it is extremely difficult to justify the shift of meaning in the very next verse.

2. These are people, including the spirits in prison, who are given an opportunity to hear the gospel after death. Proponents of this view suggest that since the object of the preaching was salvation and since Peter does not say that this has been accomplished, the idea must be that God will not judge any person finally until the whole truth has been revealed to him or her. This view is heretical in that it is contrary to the teachings of Christ and the apostles. It finds absolutely no support in Scripture. There is no hope held out anywhere in Scripture for salvation after death. Death is final, followed by one of only two destinies—heaven or hell.

3. These are people who had the gospel preached to them while they were alive but are now dead. As Geisler notes, "In favor of this is cited the fact the Gospel 'was preached' (in the past) to those who 'are dead' (now, in the present)" (p. 535).

B. Spirit of Glory (v. 14)

The Bible identifies the Holy Spirit with a variety of titles that emphasize the variety of ministries that the Holy Spirit undertakes. Some of the biblical titles for the Holy Spirit include:

1. Seven Spirits (Rev. 1:4; 3:1). This emphasizes his perfection and completeness and perhaps his omnipresence.

2. The eternal Spirit (Heb. 9:14). This emphasizes his existence prior to creation, extending beyond the destruction of this universe. This

eternal nature he shares with God the Father and God the Son as the only beings who always have been and always will be.

3. The Spirit of glory (1 Pet. 4:14). This emphasizes the perfect character and majesty of the Holy Spirit and confesses an equality of deity to the Holy Spirit.

4. The Spirit of life (Rom. 8:2). This could be understood as "the Spirit who provides life," thus emphasizing one of the gifts that the Holy Spirit provides the believer. The life that he gives could be eternal life and/or a quality of life, much like the abundant life Jesus spoke of in John 10:10. On the other hand, this description could refer to the vitality and aliveness of the Holy Spirit and thus be a self-description.

5. The Spirit of holiness (Rom. 1:4). This title focuses on the character of the Spirit of God. He is completely separate, transcendent, and perfect by his very nature. There is nothing common about the Holy Spirit or his ministry in our lives.

6. The Spirit of wisdom, understanding, counsel (Isa. 11:2). This emphasizes the omniscience of the Holy Spirit. The Spirit of God is not on a learning curve; he is the personification of wisdom and truth. Part of his ministry in our lives is to lead us into truth and to guide us into wisdom (cf. 1 Cor. 2:10–13; see House, 68).

C. If You Suffer as a Christian (v. 16)

Youngblood makes the following observations about suffering:

Suffering has been part of the human experience since people fell into sin (Gen. 3). The Psalms, one-third of which are laments, include graphic descriptions of suffering (Ps. 22). A theme of the book of Job is the problem of suffering and why God permits the righteous to suffer.

The Bible makes it clear that some suffering is the result of evil action or sin in the world. This type of suffering came upon people after the fall in the Garden of Eden (Gen. 3:16–19). But some suffering is not related to the past. It is forward-looking in that it serves to shape and refine God's children (1 Pet. 1:6–7; 5:10). The book of Hebrews declares that Jesus learned obedience by the things he suffered (Heb. 5:8), and that he was perfected through suffering (Heb. 2:10). Suffering has the potential of demonstrating God's power (2 Cor. 12:7). Those who suffer are in a position to comfort others (2 Cor. 1:3–6).

Suffering also helps believers identify with Christ, which is more than suffering for Christ. Through persecution and tortures, people have suffered for the sake of Christ and his kingdom (Phil. 1:29; 2 Thess. 1:5; 2 Tim. 3:12). To suffer with Christ, however, is another matter. Paul speaks of the "fellowship of His [Christ's] sufferings" (Phil. 3:10). Believers share in the suffering of Christ in the sense that through suffering they identify with Christ. To be a disciple involves suffering like the Master. Christ as Lord and His believers as disciples are bonded even further through the experience of suffering (Youngblood, 1207).

VII. TEACHING OUTLINE

A. INTRODUCTION

1. Lead Story: Regardless of the Cost
2. Context: The early Christians, unlike many of their twentieth-century relatives in the faith, underwent severe persecution and opposition because of their commitment to Jesus Christ. This chapter addresses why that is the case and how to respond to persecution in a manner that would honor Jesus.
3. Transition: Pain and suffering are never easy to deal with. They become almost unbearable when they are inflicted upon us from other people. The model of Jesus becomes our inspiration and our guide as we, along with these early believers, face opposition to our faith.

B. COMMENTARY

1. Living for the Will of God (vv. 1–6)
   a. The attitude of Christ (vv. 1–2)
   b. The past actions of believers (v. 3)
   c. The antagonism of nonbelievers (v. 4)
   d. The anticipation of judgment (vv. 5–6)
2. Living for the Will of God in the Church (vv. 7–11)
   a. The motivation (v. 7a)
   b. The ministering lifestyle (vv. 7b–11)
3. Living for the Will of God During Suffering (vv. 12–19)
   a. Responding to suffering (vv. 12–13)
   b. Right reasons for suffering (vv. 14–16)
   c. Recognizing God's hand in suffering (vv. 17–19)

C. CONCLUSION: DAY BY DAY

VIII. ISSUES FOR DISCUSSION

1. How does the example of Christ help you when you endure suffering?
2. Describe the difference between your life before you became a Christian and your life now. What practices have disappeared? What practices still need to disappear?
3. In what ways are you suffering? What are the causes of this suffering? Can you truly say you are suffering for the sake of Christ? or have you brought suffering on yourself with conduct that is not Christlike?
4. In what sense is the end of time and the return of Christ near?
5. What spiritual gifts has God given you? How are you using your gifts to bring harmony and blessing to your church?

1 Peter 5

Resisting Satan

"*Do you wish to rise? Begin by descending.*

You plan a tower that will pierce the clouds?

Lay first the foundation of humility."

A u g u s t i n e

I N   A   N U T S H E L L

Chapter 5 concludes 1 Peter with instructions for suffering pastors: Elders, shepherd those under your care with a willing heart, living an exemplary life before them. If you do, Jesus will reward you. Young men should be submissive to elders, and everyone should live humbly with others. If you don't, Satan might gain an advantage over you. Resist him; even in your suffering. God will help you.

Resisting Satan

I. INTRODUCTION

Satan on the Prowl

*I*n November of 1988 Thomas Sullivan Jr.'s Catholic schoolteacher assigned students to research other religions. The studious fourteen-year-old did his paper on Hinduism, but police say he became more interested in the subject that earned his friends an A: Satanism.

Within weeks, the all-American neighborhood paperboy became a defiant, hostile teen buried in library books on the occult and listening to heavy-metal rock music. His teachers noticed the transformation and warned his mother on January 7. Two days later, both mother and son were dead. Police say Sullivan, entranced by the occult, stabbed his mother at least twelve times and tried to kill his father and ten-year-old brother by setting fire to the house. He then slit his throat and wrists with a Boy Scout knife.

The boy's father told the *New York Daily News* that his son had told a friend about a vision in which Satan came to him, wearing his face, and urged him to kill his family and preach Satanism. Detective Sandi Gallant of the San Francisco police receives four calls a day from around the country on crimes with satanic or occult overtones. Commenting on this subject, she said: "Three years ago, nobody wanted to hear it, nobody believed it was real. Now I'm seeing them tuning into it, looking to see it as a reality and facing it head-on."

At the Chicago-based Cult Awareness Network, every month brings news of a teenager involved in crime believed linked to devil worship. At least ten percent of the two hundred and fifty calls they receive each month are about satanic cults. Some estimates indicate that there are as many as sixty thousand deaths a year due to satanic ritual murders.

All of this brings a stark reality to Peter's words in 1 Peter 5, because Peter certainly understood the reality and danger of Satan (see Matt. 16:23; Luke 22:31). This chapter revolves around his understanding of the tactics and attacks of Satan, summarized in verses 8–9. At the very least, Satan can be seen as the one who stirs up suffering and persecution to test the faith of the followers of Christ. This chapter provides courage and encouragement for all who are in the church, from the leadership down, so they might effectively resist the assaults of Satan.

II. COMMENTARY

Resisting Satan

> **MAIN IDEA:** *Elders, shepherd those under your care. Jesus will reward you. Everyone should live humbly with others. Trust God. Otherwise, Satan may gain an advantage over you. God will strengthen you in your suffering.*

A Leadership in the Church When the Heat Is On (vv. 1–4)

> **SUPPORTING IDEA:** *Elders, you should willingly shepherd the people under your care, not for personal gain, but as an example of Christlikeness. If you do, when the Chief Shepherd appears, he will reward you.*

5:1. Peter addressed this section pointedly to the **elders** who served among the congregation. "Elder" (*presbuteros*) refers to the officials who acted as pastoral leaders of the congregations. Because of the intense suffering and persecution that these believers faced, the need for pastoral leadership was crucial. Wisely, Peter did not simply challenge the pastoral leaders. He included himself as one of them and as one included in his challenge when he chose the identifying term **fellow elder** to describe himself and part of his ministry.

Peter paused to make two significant statements of introduction for himself. First and remarkably, he described himself as **a witness of Christ's sufferings**. Had he said "a witness of the resurrection," we would be impressed. Had he said "a witness to the transfiguration," we would have thought highly of him.

"A witness of the sufferings of Christ" bluntly recalled, for Peter and anyone else who remembers him, the most painful event of his life. Most everyone does remember Peter. They remember what kind of witness Peter was. Drop his name into a conversation, and someone recalls the rooster story, the swearing, and the denial. That very night, immediately after his denial of Christ, Peter came eyeball-to-eyeball with Christ's initial suffering. "Peter replied, 'Man, I don't know what you're talking about!' Just as he was speaking, the rooster crowed. The Lord turned and looked straight at Peter" (Luke 22:60–61).

Peter was a witness . . . a witness who stood forgiven, who stood restored, who basked in the warmth of God's grace. This is why he described himself **as one who also will share in the glory to be revealed**, the future glory that will come to believers when Christ returns. Peter was a spiritual leader, a pastor, who had sinned, repented, and been restored. He was a sinner who would share with Christ in glory (Wayne Grudem, *1 Peter,* Tyndale New Testament Commentary [Grand Rapids: Eerdmans, 1989], p. 187.)

5:2. Out of his personal history and his identification with his fellow elders, Peter encouraged and challenged them. The primary role for pastors is to **be shepherds of God's flock that is under your care.** This is not an optional assignment but a command. It echoes Christ's command to Peter to "take care of my sheep" (see John 21:16). To "shepherd" means "to lead, to guide, and to rule."

Since the pastor is the leader of a church, one commentator suggests the following functions of the pastor: "(They) had charge of the financial administration of the church . . . they were the counselors and administrators of the church. They oversee all the activities of the church and are defenders of the faith. They are also called rulers and teachers and were the paid leaders of the church" (William Barclay, *The Letters of James & Peter,* Daily Study Bible [Toronto: G. R. Welch Co., 1976], p. 264.)

Although Peter did not allude to the shepherd image in Psalm 23, the model presented there can be applied here. According to that psalm, the tasks of a shepherd are to lead (v. 2), to provide spiritual guidance and feeding (v. 3), to offer comfort (v. 4), strengthening (v. 5), and correction (v. 2).

To accomplish this kind of ministry, a pastor's motivation must be positive. He must view his role as an overseer of the church not because **you must, but because you are willing.** "Not because you must" suggests a false sense of unworthiness, a reluctance for responsibility, or a desire to do no more than is absolutely necessary. Ministry should not be an unwanted burden; pastors are not to serve out of a sense of false guilt or fear, or in an attempt to please people. Any of these attitudes or motives can lead to an unwillingness to shepherd or to shepherd in an inappropriate manner.

One of the most inappropriate shepherding motivations is highlighted next: serving because one is **greedy for money.** Peter did not suggest that pastors should not be paid a salary for their shepherding ministries. The New Testament is very clear that generous remuneration for pastors is incumbent upon the churches (see 1 Tim. 5:17–18). Scripture opposes a motivation for ministry driven by greed, so much so that the pastor either appropriates money dishonestly or is concerned only about personal financial needs. When this occurs, the pastor is not helping the church resist the attacks of Satan, because this is something that Satan often uses to distract us.

How much better to be **eager to serve.** *Eager* is a strong term meaning "with enthusiasm, with energy and excitement." This is certainly difficult when facing the attacks of Satan and when one is attempting to lead a church through a maze of suffering and persecution. At the same time, it is an indispensable characteristic for pastor-leaders to model. It doesn't suggest that a pastor is never discouraged or that he does not have days when he is not enthusiastic about ministry. This is a big-picture word, a long-haul term that describes the overall tone of his shepherding. Without this, pastors have a tendency to drift toward a harmful approach to ministry.

5:3. Lording it over the people in a congregation is not the same as leading people in the congregation. The words *leading* and *lording* should not be confused because they are distinctly separate in meaning and tone. "Lording it over" people means to rule forcefully. It is a word of harshness that implies excessive use of authority. It is a high-handed, autocratic style that should not be practiced by pastors.

A pastor should not delight in the use of authority (although at times he must exercise it), nor should he seek to increase, preserve, or flaunt his authority. This characterizes leadership that has degenerated into dictatorship. Godly leadership in the church that can serve as **examples to the flock** involves sensitivity to peoples' needs, affection for people, authenticity of life, and enthusiastic affirmation, without deception, greed, flattery, or authoritarianism.

5:4. This section concludes with the highest motivation for positive shepherding: the second coming of Jesus Christ. Jesus Christ is the **Chief Shepherd.** To him all pastor-shepherds are responsible (cf. Heb. 13:17). The Chief Shepherd will honor those who have been faithful, godly pastors. **Crown of glory** is borrowed from the world of athletics. The crown is not a physical crown; rather, the crown is the glory of being accepted by God, or perhaps it serves as a picture of the glory that the church leaders will share with Christ at his second coming.

A crown **that will never fade away** adds a wonderful touch. This expression emerges from one word (*amarantinon*), meaning "of amaranth," a flower which took its name from the word *amaranton* because it was thought to be a flower that did not fade or wither. This contrasts with the fading crowns of laurel leaves awarded to the winners in the Greek and Roman athletic games.

If pastors model this kind of responsible shepherding in the church, they offer their own resistance to the assaults of Satan and motivate the congregation to do the same.

B Responsibilities of Those Being Led (vv. 5–7)

SUPPORTING IDEA: *Be humble in all your relationships, for God opposes the proud but helps the humble. Cast your anxieties on God, for he cares for you.*

5:5. Young men should not be restricted to men, but can refer to a mixed group of men and women. Specifically, it identifies all those in the church who are not pastors and who are likely younger in the faith, in Christian maturity, and in experience. Just as pastors have a primary responsibility to shepherd the members of the flock, the members of the flock have a primary responsibility: "submission" to their pastors who have been given the responsibility of leadership. **Be submissive** is a command, an imperative, a directive which should be obeyed. Such a command is not to be debated. The verb means "to defer to the authority of." It indicates a spirit of cooperation as opposed to dissatisfaction with the leadership. It describes a willingness to support the pastors' directions.

Some church members believe they have a right to sabotage pastoral leadership, to speak critically of pastors, to slander them, to castigate them simply because they don't like them or their leadership. God has not given the members of the flock this responsibility. When they take this upon themselves, they allow Satan to use them as his tool for division and destruction in the church. The message here is clear: when pastor-shepherds lead their congregation with responsible and godly leadership and members of the flock resist this leadership, those members are in disobedience to the Lord and have opened the door for Satan.

The combination of godly leadership and submissive followership should flow into an attitude of humble respect for one another throughout the church body. **Clothe yourselves with humility** suggests that humility should be a part of the believer's wardrobe. "To clothe" refers to a slave or servant putting on an apron or towel to serve someone else. This image was forever ingrained in Peter's mind. He had firsthand knowledge of this kind of humility. The same night on which Peter denied Christ, Jesus took a towel and washed the feet of the disciples (see John 13).

True humility does not involve an attitude of self-depreciation. As Charles Spurgeon once wrote, "Humility is to make a right estimate of one's self." Humility is to be aware of personal strengths and to be thankful to God for them. Humility is to be aware of personal weaknesses and to be dependent upon God to help you improve in those areas. Beyond this, humility describes an attitude which puts others first, which thinks of the desires, needs, and ideas of others as more worthy of attention than your own.

To emphasize this point, Peter completes verse 5 with a quotation from Proverbs 3:34. Instead of quoting the Hebrew text, Peter followed the common practice of the early church and quoted the Septuagint, the earliest Greek translation of the New Testament. God stands against pride, while extending grace to the humble. Why does God act this way? Because proud people invariably trust only in themselves, not God. Furthermore, the proud see themselves only with strengths, not weaknesses. They consider themselves the standard for others to follow. They display an attitude of arrogant superiority and generally exude a self-centered and self-sufficient odor.

Peter knew from experience what he was talking about. For a part of his earlier life, Peter operated from a base of pride. He said something along these lines: "Lord, everybody else may bail out on you, but when the fur flies, you can count on me. I'll be right at your shoulder. These other wimps will walk, but not me. You can count on it!" (see Matt. 26:33; Mark 14:27–31; Luke 22:31–34).

People who dance with pride trust only in themselves, in their own opinions, in their own ideas. Inevitably, they seek attention and glory for themselves. God stands opposed to this attitude. God applauds the model that resists or fights off the arrogance of Satan through the attitude of humility. Is it possible that Peter remembered his own self-glorifying behavior and Jesus' words of rebuke to him? (See Matt. 16:23.)

5:6. In humbly following the Lord and submitting to him, we are bowing to his **mighty hand** or power. This is a far greater power than that of Satan (see Eph. 1:19–21 for a description of this power). The Old Testament speaks of God's power to intervene in history for the sake of his people (Exod. 13:9; Deut. 26:8) and to exercise discipline by imposing suffering on his people (Job 30:21). The followers of Christ are to humble themselves under God's mighty hand. Although it may allow us to experience deep pain and suffering, it will still protect us and bring us safely through.

Those who obey God in this manner find the promise that God **may lift you up in due time.** Trusting God in this way is another way to resist Satan, who would invite us in the midst of our pain to curse God and die. Trusting God ultimately leads to exaltation by him in "due time." This description means either the time of Christ's second coming or a time near at hand. God will bring persecution to an end. This truth is expressed by Grudem:

> In the time that God deems best—whether in this life or in the life to come, He may lift you up from your humble conditions and exalt you in the way that seems best to Him—perhaps only in terms of increased spiritual blessings and deeper fellowship with Himself, perhaps in terms of responsibility, reward or honor which will be seen by others as well (Grudem, 195).

5:7. Satan and his attacks have not been mentioned overtly, but another resistance method for believers appears here. As we trust God and his mighty power, we follow a God who cares deeply for us. Peter may have had in mind the words of Jesus (Matt. 6:25–34). If so, he borrowed them and placed them in the context and crucible of suffering and persecution.

Cast means "to throw something upon someone or something else." This word suggests a deliberate decision of trust. We are to trust God with our **anxiety,** the things we worry about. The term (*merimnan*) means "to be drawn in different directions, to be divided or distracted." Whatever we are anxious about tends to distract us from trusting God. It tends to pull us in different directions so that we do not depend on him. When we limp in this direction, we do not resist Satan, but play into his hand. He wants us to put more trust in ourselves and others as opposed to God.

Peter's first-century readers, like their twentieth-century cousins, failed to remember this truth even in the midst of anguish and pain: God **cares for you.** The form in which the verb appears (present active indicative with the dative) indicates that God's care and concern for believers is constant, ongoing, and unending. God is not indifferent to the suffering of his followers, but desires our active, humble trust in him, especially during difficult days.

ⓒ Rallying Together in Resisting Satan (vv. 8–11)

SUPPORTING IDEA: *If you do not cast yourself on God, Satan may gain an advantage over you. Be alert, and resist him, firm in your faith. After you have suffered for a little while, God will restore you.*

5:8. C. S. Lewis once suggested that the two mistakes Christians make in talking about Satan are that we either joke about him or we ignore him. According to this verse, neither of these is an option. In essence, this verse says, "Wake up! Pay attention! We are involved in a spiritual battle. You need to know the enemy and his characteristics. You need to understand that we are in a life-and-death battle."

Biblically, Satan or **the devil** (*diabolos,* the slanderer) is described as the prince of this world. His residence is on this earth, and he moves from place to place. Because this earth is the devil's territory, believers are constantly under attack. Additionally, the Bible speaks of the devil as a personal spiritual being in active rebellion against God. He leads many demons like himself. Peter envisions the devil as a cunning and evil personal being who has the ability to attack Christians and to disrupt the life and unity of the church.

The biblical writers take the existence of Satan and evil spirits for granted and portray them as opposing God's purposes and the welfare of his people. Satan and his henchmen are bent on destroying life and introducing every sort of evil. They use deceit to attack believers and to blind unbelievers to the gospel. The commander-in-chief of these opposing forces is Satan himself. He is the master of ingenious strategies, and his tactics must not be allowed to catch us unaware. One scholar adds to our understanding:

> A survey of the results of demonic influence in the New Testament will indicate certain characteristics which a (self-controlled) and (alert) Christian may suspect to be caused, at least in part, by the devil or demons: bizarre or violently irrational evil behavior, especially in opposition to the gospel or Christians; malicious slander and falsehood in speech; increasing bondage to self-destructive behavior; stubborn advocacy of false doctrine; the sudden and unexplained onslaughts of emotions (such as fear, hatred, depression, violent anger).

(Still) caution is appropriate here, for there is much evil in the world which is not directly from Satan or demons but simply from sin remaining in our own hearts or in the lives of unbelievers around us (Grudem, 197).

5:9. The Christian response to satanic opposition is not panic or fear but firm resistance. **Resist** means "to withstand," or "to stand up against." It is a term of defense and victory. Theologically, Jesus Christ's death and resurrection won the decisive victory in the war against the powers of darkness. This, however, does not mean that the battle is over. Because of the cross, believers have the assurance that these evil powers have been disarmed. Believers share in Christ's authority over them. This does not mean that Christians have an automatic immunity to the influence of Satan and his demonic powers; otherwise, Peter's counsel regarding resisting him would make no sense.

To **resist** the devil effectively, we must draw on the power of Christ and not yield to Satan in our lives. Furthermore, to resist the devil, the believer must be **standing firm in the faith.** We should draw strength from what we believe.

First Peter overflows with reminders of the firmness of the faith of believers. We have been **chosen** by God the Father (1:2), given a **new birth** into a living hope (1:3), and provided with an **inheritance** that can never perish (1:4) because we are **shielded** by God's power (1:5). Furthermore, we have been called **out of darkness** into God's wonderful light (2:9). God himself is building up individual believers into a **spiritual house** (2:5). He views his followers as a holy and **royal priesthood**, a holy nation and **a people belonging to** [him] (2:5,9).

This is the kind of faith in which the believer must stand firm. Regardless of personal suffering, we must join many other Christians suffering in other parts of the world in standing firm together in a united and active resistance to the assaults of the devil. Followers of Jesus Christ need to trust the God who provides them with this faith.

5:10–11. The body of the letter concludes with a powerful statement of the gracious and restoring power of God. This repeats a promise introduced in 1:6, and it offers in a capsule statement a picture of Peter's life by borrowing similar language from his past experience. Peter's own restoration from pain and failure puts credibility behind the promise in verse 10.

This is more than a hope; it is an assertion of what God will do. God will **restore** or repair whatever is damaged, so the believer will be able to face up to whatever lies ahead. Failure in the past does not doom a person to failure in the future. "Restore" could be used in a medical sense of "setting a broken bone" or of repairing and refitting a damaged boat. Peter the denier who became Peter of Pentecost spoke from deep experience.

Additionally, God will make followers of Christ **strong** or stable, providing us with courage to go on. He will make us **firm and steadfast**, so that our foundation in him is secure. "Made strong" (*steridzo*) is a word Jesus used in talking to Peter years before. Verse 10 may be a partial fulfillment of Christ's earlier word to him in Luke 22:31: "Simon, Simon, Satan has asked to sift you as wheat. But I have prayed for you, Simon, that your faith may not fail. And when you have turned back, strengthen (*steridzo*) your brothers."

5:11. The only appropriate response to the restorative and strengthening power of God is to celebrate this grace in a doxology of praise.

D Final Greetings (vv. 12–14)

SUPPORTING IDEA: *Trust Silas as I do, and stand fast in God's grace. Your friends greet you. Good-bye.*

5:12. Silas was Peter's faithful and trustworthy associate. This is the same Silas, no doubt, who traveled with the apostle Paul during some of his missionary work (see Acts 15:40). Peter trusted Silas enough to have him deliver this letter to his readers.

The basic thrust of the letter is summarized: a testimony or witness designed to encourage and exhort the readers to grasp the true grace of God and to recognize that God's grace includes room for suffering and persecution, while at the same time offering strength to endure.

5:13. Modern letter writers generally extend greetings at the beginning of a letter. Peter followed first-century custom by offering words of greeting at the conclusion of his letter. He extended greetings from **she who is in Babylon**. Babylon is a reference to the city of Rome, which was increasingly called by this name by both Jews and Christians. The nickname expressed the fact that the Christians in the city felt themselves to be in exile in a foreign land, a city of luxury and sin and the oppressor of God's people. This identification also corresponds to Peter's earlier description of the Christians in the city as **aliens and strangers in the world** (2:11).

Mark is likely to be understood as John Mark, a former traveling companion of the apostle Paul and writer of the second Gospel. His link with Peter is not clear from the biblical record, since virtually nothing is known of John Mark's ministry after his separation from the apostle Paul (Acts 15:39). Apparently, Mark increasingly became linked to Peter so that Peter could now identify him as his closest colleague.

5:14. The **kiss of love** is similar in intention to our Western handshake. It was a common gesture of fellowship among Christians and was part of the ritual of public worship in the early churches. It is still common in many parts of the world today. Peter's final blessing or wish for his readers is for peace, just as it was his desire at the beginning of his letter (1:2).

MAIN IDEA REVIEW: *Elders, willingly shepherd those under your care. Jesus will reward you. Everyone should live humbly with others. Trust God. Otherwise, Satan may gain an advantage over you. God will strengthen you in your suffering.*

III. CONCLUSION

Your Incredible Calling

What an incredible way to end this letter. The challenge goes out to pastors to lead the congregations in which God has placed them with assurance and care because Satan is on the prowl. He is looking to divide and destroy Christians and the churches that they belong to. It is a monumental assignment to lead a congregation as a pastor, especially during times of difficulty and suffering. However, this is the calling of these pastors.

As the chapter concludes, Peter once more drew the hearts of his readers back to the grace of God on which they must depend and to the eternal glory that they shall enjoy with him. They must remain confident even as they face the varied trials of their growing faith.

PRINCIPLES

- Failure in ministry is not necessarily fatal to future ministry.
- The pastor of a local congregation is the primary leader of that congregation.
- Pastoral ministry must not be motivated by greed.
- Pastoral ministry uses authority appropriately without becoming authoritarian.
- Members of a local congregation have the responsibility to follow godly pastoral leadership.
- An attitude of humble respect for one another should characterize the members of a church.
- God can be trusted during our most severe times of anxiety.
- Satan is a personal spiritual being who is in active rebellion against God.
- The life of the Christian is an intense spiritual battle.
- The God of grace whom we follow is the God of restoration.

APPLICATION

- Be supportive of and willing to follow godly pastoral leadership in the church.

- Avoid any pastor or Christian leader who abuses his authority and is preoccupied with money and material gain.
- Evaluate your life and attitudes at all times to make sure you are not motivated by pride.
- Attempt to model in your church the attitude that says, "What can I give to this ministry with thanks from God?" as opposed to the attitude that says, "What can I get out of this church?"
- Cultivate an active trust in God, especially during times of stress.
- Ask the Lord to increase your willingness and ability to trust him.
- Remind yourself where you might be if it were not for the grace of God in your life.
- Write down the names of some people who have been an encouragement or help to you during the last year.

IV. LIFE APPLICATION

Forgiven Souls

The late bishop J. C. Ryle summarized what Peter wants to teach us:

> Forgiven souls are humble. They cannot forget that they owe all they have and hope for to free grace, and this keeps them lowly. They are brands plucked from the fire—debtors who could not pay for themselves—captives who must have remained in prison for ever, but for undeserved mercy—wandering sheep who were ready to perish when the Shepherd found them; and what right then have they to be proud? I do not deny that they are proud saints. But this I do say—they are of all God's creatures the most inconsistent, and of all God's children the most likely to stumble and pierce themselves with many sorrows.

As you read this chapter, you sense Peter is writing to you personally. His gaze is locked in, and we are the target. Sometimes pastors, as they read and teach the Bible, can leave themselves out of the text and application. Peter consciously included himself as the target of his own admonitions (v. 1). He appealed to fellow pastors of every century because he had been there.

What is so remarkable about his advice to pastors is that this fiery, hair-trigger-temper, self-serving Peter advocated gentle and selfless leadership for pastors (vv. 2–4). When you think of Peter, invariably words like "over-confident," "headstrong," and "proud" come to mind. Don't think for a second that Peter didn't realize this. God worked in this area of his life also, prompting his comments on humility and pride in this chapter (vv. 5–7). How amazing is this transformation in Peter's life!

Proud people tend to be self-sufficient and certain that they can work things out themselves. When this doesn't happen, they can often degenerate into intense anxiety and worry. This works against our ability to trust in God. Peter was quick to counter this approach to life (v. 7).

Still, this is not just a chapter on human relationships and attitudes. A far more significant element lurks here—the presence of Satan (vv. 8–9). The Christian believer is easily lulled to sleep regarding his or her expectations of Satan. Not wanting to be preoccupied with Satan and evil, we swing the other way and ignore his presence. This invites temptation and often causes us to fall into sin. Even in the midst of this spiritual battle, we should lift high the providence and care of God (vv. 10–11).

The final word that 1 Peter leaves with us is the one word that we should never forget—**grace**. Undeserved, unwarranted, unprecedented grace. As Christians, we should always be increasing in our awareness and appreciation of the grace of God in our lives (vv. 11–13).

V. PRAYER

Thank you, Lord, for this letter, written so long ago, but rippling with the reality of life. I will pray harder and longer for those who lead our churches. Give them courage and grace to be the kinds of leaders who will honor you by their lives and leadership. I must also pray for those who sit under their leadership. What an awesome assignment we have together—to honor you and your kingdom through our cooperation. Give those of us who follow our spiritual leaders the grace and humility we need so that our lives, too, will be an example for those who are looking our way. Dear Lord, may we never forget who our real enemy is. May we never forget who our true King is. Help us to resist our enemy and trust our King. Amen.

VI. DEEPER DISCOVERIES

A. Not Greedy for Money (v. 2)

This statement has implications for every follower of Christ, not simply pastors. Rarely, however, does the average Christian think through a theology of money or even a Christian philosophy related to money. Several principles related to money are important for believers as we determine the influence of money in our lives.

First, the Bible recognizes that money is necessary for survival, but it warns against the love of money (see Matt. 6:24; 1 Tim. 6:10; Heb. 13:5). Money can be dangerous because it lures the believer into thinking that wealth is the easiest way to get everything we want. As a result, we often grow lax in our trust of God and trust our financial assets instead.

Second, the love of money is often a barrier between us and God. Money often becomes the barometer by which we measure our success. We talk about being "a self-made man." Invariably this reflects our material wealth. We never say we are "a God-made man." We invariably link the money and possessions that we have to our own efforts, leading us to pride. This type of attitude erects a spiritual barrier between us and God.

Third, money can be a tremendous vehicle of ministry in the lives of others as we give it to churches and organizations that serve the kingdom of God. We must constantly ask ourselves, What does my money really mean to me? Will I use my money and possessions for the benefit of others? Would I be willing to take a lower salaried job if God called me to it? Can I live at my current income level and give my future raises to the work of the Lord?

Our reaction to questions like these will demonstrate our attitude toward money, whether we use it to serve others or whether we have already become its slave or servant.

The fourth principle that must be grafted into our minds is that money is not necessarily a measurement of our standing with God or a demonstration of his special favor in our lives. Although many believers enjoy material prosperity, as did individuals in the Bible (for example, Abraham, Job, Priscilla, and Aquila), many others live in hardship and poverty (see Heb. 11:36–39). Wealth is not necessarily a sign of faith or partiality on God's part.

B. Your Enemy the Devil Prowls Around (v. 8)

A correct understanding of the person and work of Satan is vital for the believer. Many misconceptions and false teachings revolve around this subject. In general terms, Satan's activities include:

- seeking to provoke us to sin (1 Chr. 21:1),
- ranging the world to find victims (Job 1:7),
- causing some of the earth's physical illness (Job 2:7),
- spiritually blinding unbelievers (2 Cor. 4:4),
- shooting flaming arrows (Eph. 6:16),
- hindering (1 Thess. 2:18),
- seeking to devour (1 Pet. 5:8),
- undermining the Word of God (Matt. 13:19),
- wanting to take advantage (2 Cor. 2:11), and
- transforming himself into an angel of light (2 Cor. 11:14).

At the same time, Satan's activities are limited:

- He must receive permission from God (Job 1:12).
- His head has been crushed by Christ (Gen. 3:15).
- He can be resisted (Jas. 4:7).
- He can be overcome (1 John 2:13).
- He is overcome by the blood of the Lamb (Rev. 12:11).

- He cannot touch those begotten of God (1 John 5:18).

In addition, Scripture describes Satan's destiny:

- He will be crushed by the God of peace (Rom. 16:20).
- Jesus destroyed his power of death (Heb. 2:14).
- The Son of God destroyed his works (1 John 3:8).
- He will be bound for one thousand years (Rev. 20:2).
- He will be cast into the bottomless pit (Rev. 20:3).
- He will be cast into the lake of fire (Rev. 20:10).
- He will be doomed to everlasting fire (Matt. 25:41).
- He will be cast from heaven (Luke 10:18).
- He will be judged by God (John 16:11; see House, 78).

C. She Who Is in Babylon (v. 13)

Scholars differ about the meaning of this term.

1. Some believe it refers to a place in Egypt called Babylon, near the modern city of Cairo. This is unlikely since the Babylon in Egypt was on a small Roman military outpost. It is improbable that many Jews lived there or that the apostles started a church there this early in the first century.

2. Others believe it refers to Babylon on the Euphrates River. This Babylon was still large enough at this time to be a place of some importance and would fit the most literal reading of the word. The writers of the New Testament letters were accustomed to mentioning the real and literal place of writing when they identified such. Furthermore, church traditions indicate that the apostles often traveled in the east, and it would have been natural for some of them to visit the city of Babylon. Others suggest that this could not be the true identity of Babylon because the city had faded in size, importance, and influence by this time in history. Additionally, it is unlikely that Peter, Silas, and Mark were ever together in the city of Babylon. No tradition suggests this. Finally, it would have been very difficult for Peter to hear of the persecutions in Pontus and the other areas mentioned in 1:1 if he was in the eastern city of Babylon.

3. Some interpreters believe the reference is to the city of Rome. This interpretation was universal both in the east and west until the Reformation. In Revelation 17 and 18 Rome is called Babylon, and it does not appear to be used there for the first time. Babylon is found as a name for Rome in the Apocrypha. The wealth and universal vices of Rome parallel the city of Babylon. In the case of 1 Peter, discretion may have determined the use of the symbolic name, as the letter may have had to pass the censorship of government officials.

VII. TEACHING OUTLINE

A. INTRODUCTION

1. Lead Story: Satan on the Prowl
2. Context: The church, but especially those undergoing suffering, must have strong, godly leadership in the form of pastors who can care for and strengthen the believers. At the same time, complete dependence by the people of the church must always be on the Lord. Humility and trust before him are essential in the battle of faith.
3. Transition: The church rises and falls on the spiritual quality of its leaders. If the leaders are immature or unruly, the congregation often replicates this pattern. Before saying good-bye to his friends, Peter challenged their pastors (elders) who set the tone in the church.

B. COMMENTARY

1. Leadership in the Church When the Heat Is On (vv. 1–4)
   a. Peter's identification with leaders (v. 1)
   b. The motives and methods of leaders (vv. 2–4)
2. The Responsibilities of Those Being Led (vv. 5–7)
   a. An attitude of submission (v. 5a)
   b. An attitude of humility (vv. 5b–6)
   c. An attitude of trust (v. 7)
3. Rallying Together in Resisting Satan (vv. 8–11)
   a. A call to attention (v. 8)
   b. A call to resistance (v. 9)
   c. A call to remember (vv. 10–11)
4. Final Greetings (vv. 12–14)

C. CONCLUSION: FORGIVEN SOULS

VIII. ISSUES FOR DISCUSSION

1. What does it mean to share in the glory to be revealed? Do you expect to share in this glory? Why or why not?
2. Describe the qualities you think God requires of anyone who would serve as pastor of a church.
3. What does it mean to be humble? Can you be humble as the Bible directs and still be successful in your occupation?

4. Describe personal experiences that have impressed on you the reality and power of Satan. What feelings do you have about Satan? What keeps you from being frightened of Satan?

5. What is meant by the true grace of God? In what ways have you experienced this grace? What does it mean to you? to your church?

2 Peter 1

Faith's Arithmetic

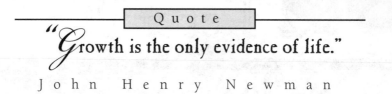

"Growth is the only evidence of life."

J o h n   H e n r y   N e w m a n

BOOK PROFILE: 2 PETER

- Sent to first-century Christians living in a variety of locations in the northern part of Turkey or Egypt. Although some internal indications might suggest the targeted audience is the same as 1 Peter (see 2 Pet. 3:1), it is more likely that the address of the readers is unknown.
- The audience seems to include those from both Jewish and Gentile backgrounds.
- The letter has three primary purposes:
  (1) to alert the readers to the dangers of false teachers (1:12–13);
  (2) to remind the readers that their personal faith should not remain static (1:8–10; 3:17–18); and
  (3) to encourage the believers in their faith and in the fact and expectation of the Lord's second coming.
- Probably written from the city of Rome shortly after 1 Peter and before Jude, about A.D. 65–67.
- First Peter's primary theme is *suffering*, while 2 Peter focuses more on *false teachers and false teaching*. The tone of 1 Peter is more directed toward *comfort*, while 2 Peter leans toward *confrontation and warning*.
- Uses "know" sixteen times, possibly lending credibility to the argument that the letter addressed an early form of Gnosticism, with its preoccupation with special knowledge.

AUTHOR PROFILE: PETER

- Simon Peter, the author of 1 Peter, wrote this letter shortly before his death. He may have been in prison.
- Peter mentions some familiar events that lend credence to his authorship:
  (1) This letter has the only reference to the transfiguration of Jesus outside the gospels (1:16–18).
  (2) 2 Peter 1:14 repeats Jesus' prediction that Simon Peter would die a martyr (John 21:18–19).

(3) 2 Peter 3:10 reminds us of Jesus' saying that he **will come like a thief.**

(For additional information about the author, see the Author Profile notes on 1 Peter.)

IN A NUTSHELL

*G*reetings to all believers whose faith in Jesus Christ provides them with an invaluable faith, like ours. Be encouraged when you realize that God's power can transform your life and direct it toward virtues that will have a positive and productive impact on others. Since my time on earth is short, may I point out to you that what I tell you is not made up. I was an eyewitness. If that is not enough, we have the Old Testament writings God gave us to study and learn from.

Faith's Arithmetic

I. INTRODUCTION

You Can Be Transformed

*W*hen Joey Barrow was a teenager, his schoolmates labeled him the class sissy. At eighteen, while the other guys were involved in more "masculine" activities, Joey was taking violin lessons. One day, they called him "sissy" one time too many. Joey smashed the boy who made fun of him smack on the head with (you guessed it) his violin. It didn't help. The story simply brought another round of laughter from Joey's classmates.

One boy did not laugh. Big, strapping Thurston McKinney decided it was time Joey got involved in something with a little more muscle. Thurston exercised regularly at a local gym and asked Joey to come along. As always, Joey had his violin with him. "If you want to work out with me," said Thurston, "you'll have to rent a locker." Locker rental was fifty cents. The only money Joey had was what his mom had given him for that week's violin lesson. So Joey borrowed some gym trunks and some old tennis shoes from Thurston, rented the locker with his violin money, and put the violin inside.

The first time Thurston invited Joey to spar with him, Joey clobbered him. Flattened him. The dazed response of Thurston McKinney, himself already a Detroit Golden Gloves Champion, was, "Boy, throw that violin away!" With the money his mother had intended to finance weekly violin lessons, Joey kept a permanent locker. In five years, Joey Barrow would turn twenty-three and be the heavyweight boxing champion of the world!

The anthologies of athletics say little about Thurston McKinney, but he took Joey Barrow under his wing. Joey dropped his last name, Barrow, so his mother wouldn't know the newspapers were talking about her son. The world knew for years before she did that sissy Joey Barrow had been transformed into the unbeatable "Brown Bomber," Joe Louis.

Another transformed man wrote 2 Peter. His name is Simon Peter. His transformation did not produce a fighter, but just the opposite. Peter was transformed from a fighter into a servant of Jesus Christ. So dramatic was the change in Peter's life that he wrote this letter to remind his readers that Christian faith was never intended to remain unchanged or static. Christian faith always adds something. It is always growing. Christians continually experience change or transformation in their lives.

Second Peter 1 helps us to begin to see the character of this transformation. It reminds us that we do not pursue this change simply on our own, with only our own power. Our transformation is a cooperative venture that unites God's power with our sincere and positive efforts at change. Furthermore, the direction of our change is not something that we simply pull out of the air, but it is grounded in the unchanging character of the Scriptures.

II. COMMENTARY

Faith's Arithmetic

MAIN IDEA: *Change and transformation in the Christian life are fueled by the combination of human responsibility and divine power. Jesus Christ and the Old Testament Scriptures show us the truths behind God's divine arithmetic that adds change, transforming our lives into eternal kingdom lives.*

A Greeting (vv. 1–2)

SUPPORTING IDEA: *Through his righteousness revealed in Jesus Christ, God gives his people a faith that brings grace and peace to life.*

1:1. Unlike his opening in 1 Peter, where he identifies himself simply as Peter, here Peter chose to introduce himself with his full name, **Simon Peter.** In doing so, he suggested the transformation that had occurred in his own life. Simon was his old name before he became a follower of Christ. Peter was his new name, a name given to him by Christ (see Matt. 16:18) and identifying the transformation in Simon's life. "Peter" means "man of rock." That is the kind of character God ultimately built into Simon's life as he followed Christ. He became rock-like—courageous, steady, persistent, and bold for Christ.

The new Peter mentioned two changes in his life when he described himself **as a servant and apostle.** "Servant" is actually the term "slave" (*doulos*). Simply put, this means that his desire is to obey Jesus Christ and be his willing follower. It is a description of submission. At the same time, it was often used in the Old Testament of a position of honor or authority. That authority is reinforced in his second term of description, "an apostle." (see explanation in notes on 1 Pet. 1:1). When Simon first became a disciple, he often bragged that he would serve Christ longer and more zealously than the other disciples. At the same time, he seemed regularly to be looking for a position of authority among the disciples. Writing decades later, he had been transformed into a humble servant and authoritative apostle.

In greeting his readers, Peter did not specifically identify their geographical location. Some interpreters suggest they are the same group addressed in 1 Peter (Christians living in Turkey). Others have suggested Egypt as the destination. It would be better to conclude that he wrote to a group of Christians whose address is not made known. Wherever they lived, their faith was under attack, and some of them were vulnerable to that attack. Some of them were being influenced by false teachers to doubt their faith, so Peter wasted no time in reassuring them of the validity of their faith, introducing at the end of verse 1 the wonderful expression, **a faith as precious as ours.**

"Faith" means the trust or belief that brings a person to embrace Jesus Christ as personal Savior from sin. We place our faith and trust in Christ for eternal salvation. "Precious" means that their faith is equal in honor, privilege, and standing. "Precious" was used to describe foreigners in a country who asked for and then received equal citizenship in that country. Christians have been given equal rights of citizenship in the kingdom of God; our faith is on the same footing as the faith of the apostles, like Peter. Our faith is as precious in the eyes of God as the faith of the apostles.

The reason for this is because our faith is **through the righteousness of our God and Savior Jesus Christ.** "Righteousness" frequently refers to the righteous act of God in Christ which brings salvation to us through the cross and identifies us as righteous in his sight because of Christ's death. However, Peter in this verse and elsewhere used "righteousness" as an ethical term, referring to the fairness or justice of God. The righteousness or fairness of God refuses to make distinctions among those who receive his grace. God does not play favorites with his grace. Everyone is given the same opportunity of grace through Christ.

1:2. This is the same word of greeting that Peter used in 1 Peter 1:2, with the addition of the phrase, **through the knowledge of God and of Jesus our Lord.** This knowledge is not an academic or theoretical knowledge. It is a personal knowledge. It is a knowledge that grows because a person begins to know someone fully and to understand that person's heart. As we grow in personal knowledge of God and Christ, as we experience God the Father's unconditional acceptance through Christ, a transformation begins. We begin to experience **grace and peace in abundance,** not only in our relationship with God, but also in our relationships with one another.

ⒷEffective and Productive Lives (vv. 3–11)

> **SUPPORTING IDEA:** *God's power enables us to make every effort to add transforming characteristics to our lives which in turn enable us to lead effective and productive lives for Jesus Christ.*

1:3. The same one who calls us, that is, who invites us by grace to be a part of his kingdom, also enables us to change or to grow spiritually. **Life and godliness** together are best understood as referring to a godly life. This is the destination toward which the transformation will take a follower of Christ. A godly life includes two primary ideas. First, it describes an attitude of reverence in the presence of one who is majestic and divine. Secondly, a godly life

describes actions of obedience. At the heart of godly living and spiritual transformation is an attitude of reverence toward God and actions of obedience.

The source of strength that enables the believer to move in this direction
is **His divine power.** These words describe the work of God's Holy Spirit in
the life of the believer. He provides the believer with gifts and the ability to
use those gifts. God's design is that through the power of the Holy Spirit, the
believer is assisted in living a godly life.

This process is assisted **through our knowledge of him who called us.** As
in verse 2, this refers to the believer's personal knowledge of Jesus Christ and
to a growing relationship with him. The more we come to know Jesus Christ
in a personal way, the more we begin to understand who he really is and what
he has done for us. As we grow in this kind of understanding, we begin to
appreciate his divine power that assists us in growing spiritually.

1:4. **His very great and precious promises** refers to the promises Jesus
gave during his earthly life, particularly the promises he made regarding the
enabling and purifying ministry of God's Holy Spirit in the life of the believer
(see John 14:15–17a; 16:7; Acts 1:4–5,8). In John's Gospel Jesus promises the
believer the continual presence of the Holy Spirit to assist in obedience. In
fact, the common designation of the Holy Spirit as the "Counselor" affirms
that understanding since the term "Counselor" (*paraclete*) means "the one
called alongside to help." In some places the word was an ancient warrior's
term. Greek soldiers always went into battle in pairs, so that when the enemy
attacked, they could draw together back to back, covering each other's blind
side. The soldier's battle partner was called the *paraclete,* or the helper.

So too, God does not send the believer into the battle alone or unarmed.
Jesus Christ promises his followers the presence of the Holy Spirit in our lives.

This promise is assured because of the character of the one making the
promise. The promises of the Holy Spirit come **through them,** the characteristics of Jesus Christ mentioned at the end of verse 3 as **his own glory and
goodness.** These words describe who Christ intrinsically is. They describe
the majesty of his nature. The point of the verse is that the promises of
Christ, related to the ministry of the Holy Spirit in the believer's life, can be
counted on because his character remains stable and constant.

As a result of the ministry of the Holy Spirit in the life of the believer, we
**may participate in the divine nature and escape the corruption in the world
caused by evil desires.** That is, we are able to move closer to God and further
away from the sinful culture. Participating in the divine nature simply means
that as believers, through the power of the Spirit, we begin to change positively and demonstrate more and more of the character of God in our lives.
At the same time, we demonstrate less and less of the character of the culture.
As a result, we escape the internal decay or rottenness that accompanies so
much of the evil desires of the world.

1:5–7. These verses describe in more specific terms what participating in the divine nature should look like. Such participation exhorts us to **make every effort** to change our lives. Verses 3–4 lay out the incredible gift of God in allowing his power, his Spirit to be a part of the believer's life as a divine helper in the process of transformation. Verses 5–7 show that each believer also has a role to play in this transformation. A resolve, a desire, a commitment to growth and transformation must be part of the individual believer's life if the Holy Spirit is to be effective.

The characteristics in verses 5–7 describe in overview the nature or essence of godly living introduced in verse 3. We see here that the letter is addressed to believers who are asked to **add to** [their] **faith.** The beginning point of transformation is salvation that Peter assumes his readers have experienced. The characteristics of godliness can be attained only by saved people:

Goodness speaks of moral excellence.

Knowledge concentrates on practical knowledge or knowledge that is lived out. This kind of knowledge makes a distinction between what is true and what is not true. It is able to discern what is right versus what is wrong and what is encouraging versus what is hurtful.

Self-control describes the inner strength to control one's desires and cravings. The believer, through the enabling power of the Holy Spirit, is not to be a prisoner to any sinful desire or craving.

Perseverance in its most literal rendering means "to walk under the load." This refers to the courage to deal with the difficult times in life, perhaps a veiled reference to the dominant theme of suffering in 1 Peter.

Godliness is the virtue heralded in verse 3, and it means "reverence and obedience."

Brotherly kindness translates one Greek word, *philadelphia,* a common word used to describe relationships of love with a family. According to Green, brotherly kindness involves "bearing one another's burdens, and so fulfilling the law of Christ; it means guarding that Spirit given unity from destruction by gossip, prejudice, narrowness and the refusal to accept a brother Christian who is what he is in Christ" (Green, 79).

Love (*agape*) is a deliberate desire for the highest good of the person loved. It demonstrates itself in sacrificial action for that person's good.

These last two characteristics, "brotherly kindness and love," are supremely the characteristics of Jesus Christ. His mission in life was to sacrifice himself for humanity's good. The transforming process of God's Holy Spirit is to take each individual believer toward this direction—becoming Christlike (cf. Rom. 8:28–29).

It is most difficult to model reverence toward God and continued obedience when your life is under siege from people or circumstances. Yet, with the enabling of the Spirit and the personal resolve to pursue such a course, this becomes another mark of transformation in the growing believer's life, a life continually reflecting "brotherly kindness and love."

1:8. This transformation does not occur in one blinding flash, nor is it something that a person can consider completed or look back to and conclude, "Now, that's finished." The phrase **Possess these qualities in increasing measure** points to the ongoing, never-finished aspect of the transformation. "In increasing measure" translates a present participle whose tense implies that spiritual growth must be a constant and ongoing process. To determine your effectiveness and productivity spiritually, you need to assess honestly whether these characteristics are present and increasing in your life.

1:9. In contrast, if you do not have these characteristics increasing in your life, you are spiritually sick, suffering from shortsightedness, blindness, and forgetfulness. Someone who is blind cannot see at all; someone who is short-sighted cannot see in the distance; and someone who has forgotten cannot remember the grace of God in their past. One interpreter points out, "In their blindness, short-sightedness and forgetfulness, they no longer understand their past sins, their present disobedience or their future condemnation" (Stott, 62).

1:10–11. This section concludes with a word of challenge and encouragement. False teachers attacked the faith of the original readers of 2 Peter. Some of them were beginning to doubt their faith. Peter, particularly in verse 2 above, went out of his way to reassure them of the validity of their faith. Thus, the expression **make your calling and election sure** must not be construed to suggest that God has any doubts regarding their faith or calling. The problem of doubt or questioning is one the readers struggled with, not God.

As you begin to see changes and transformations occurring in your life, this should reassure you that God has called you to himself. These changes serve to "make your calling and election sure." The opposite is also true. If your life shows no positive changes and this causes you no concern, then you should wonder and question whether you are a true believer in Jesus Christ.

If you respond positively to the challenge, you will find encouragement in the words, **you will never fall.** This does not mean that you will never have a problem or that you will never sin again. The picture is that of a march, and the point here is that the true believer will never fall out of the march to heaven. You will never be left behind, but you can be assured of a glorious welcome into your eternal home. God will never change his mind about you, nor will he alter the means by which you get to heaven. True believers can be assured that God will never send us away from heaven because we are not good enough.

C Reminders and Reassurances (vv. 12–21)

SUPPORTING IDEA: *This truth of God's transforming salvation based on Jesus' power and grace is no human invention. It rests on eyewitness testimony confirmed by Scripture's prophecy.*

1:12–15. Three times these verses talk about reminders or remembering spiritual truths. Thirty-plus years prior to this time, Jesus informed Peter that one day he would die as a martyr (see John 21:18–19). Apparently, some time recently, the Lord had revealed again to Peter, in a special revelation, that he would soon die as a martyr. As a result, Peter wrote with urgency (v. 13). Peter hoped his writing would help believers remember spiritual truths even after he died (v. 15).

Even firmly established believers need reminders. Those who are mature in their faith need to be warned against complacency. They can benefit from a reminder to grow in grace and apply further the spiritual lessons they have already learned. Some Bible students suggest that verse 15 may be a veiled reference to the Gospel of Mark, where Mark recorded much of Peter's testimony and view of Christ.

1:16a. Later (vv. 19–21), Peter will give an extended defense of the written Scriptures in terms of their authority and accuracy. First, he went out of his way to display the glory of the Lord. The order of his presentation suggests that we will never appreciate or value the reminders of Scripture, the Word of the Lord, until we value and worship the Lord of the Word.

False teachers labeled the truths that Christians believe as make-believe, fiction, or simply stories. They claimed the incarnation of Jesus Christ, the resurrection, and his coming kingdom were only invented stories. Peter responded that he was speaking and writing about spiritual truths and certainly was not embellishing the facts or inventing a story.

1:16b. In this verse, Peter revisited the transfiguration of Jesus he had witnessed some thirty years earlier: **but we were eyewitnesses of his majesty** (v. 16b). This event was the most supernatural event in the ministry of Christ. It provided a preview or picture of the Second Coming when Christ will return in glory. If Peter is wrong here, then everything is wrong—a myth just as the false teachers claimed. The transfiguration of Jesus Christ declares who he is, speaking of the glory and the majesty of the character of Christ. If his character is flawed, then his word is flawed. "Majesty" refers to the splendor and grandeur of Christ. It points to the very nature of Jesus.

1:17. On the mountain of transfiguration Peter had the unique experience of being present when Jesus **received honor and glory from God the Father.** *Honor* describes the exalted status of Jesus Christ. *Glory* refers to the brilliance of the light that radiated from Christ at that moment—the same brilliance and honor that belong to God alone. This light or glory radiated from within the person of Christ and put into a visual aid the perfect character of Christ. In the Old Testament, the word *glory* originally expressed the idea of weight. From there it came to be applied to any characteristic of a person that makes that individual "weighty" in other peoples' eyes and prompts them to honor that person. The glory of Christ is the perfection of God in Christ.

God the Father affirmed this essential nature of Jesus Christ. The **Majestic Glory** is another way of describing the very presence of God—a presence that Matthew's Gospel indicates demonstrated itself in "a bright cloud" (Matt. 17:5) descending upon the mountain. In that moment, God the Father solemnly affirmed the divinity of Jesus his Son. The scene was forever burned into Peter's memory: God the Father, meeting with God the Son, in the presence of eyewitnesses and declaring to them all the majesty, glory, and perfection of Jesus Christ.

1:18. Peter's reiteration of his participation in this moment as an eyewitness underlines his authority in teaching about the person and work of Christ. If readers doubt the character of the messenger, they will certainly doubt the character of the message. Peter's testimony leaves no doubt about the character of the messenger and his message.

1:19. The section from here to the end of chapter deals with the false teachers. Despite such teachers, we can know the truth about God. **The word of the prophets** refers to the writings of the entire Old Testament, not simply the prophets. In making reference to this, Peter expressed his complete confidence in the Old Testament Scriptures. Peter has just described his incredible experience of seeing Jesus Christ in all of his glory on the mountain of transfiguration. That experience was a preview of what it will be like to see Christ at his second coming. Yet here, when Peter notes that **we have the word of the prophets made more certain,** he essentially says to his readers: "You do not have to rely only on my experience. We have another source of assurance about Christ that is even more reliable—the Scriptures."

So confident was Peter of the reliability and authority of the Scriptures that he counseled us to use the Scriptures as our guide until the Second Coming of Christ. **Until the day dawns** refers to the day of the Second Coming (see Mal. 4:2). **The morning star** is a picture of Jesus Christ at his Second Coming (see Luke 1:78, Eph. 5:14; Rev. 22:16). We are to walk by the torchlight of Scripture until the second coming of Jesus. One commentator suggests: "We are on a pilgrimage throughout our lives in this dark world. God has graciously provided us with a lamp—the Scriptures. If we pay attention to them for correction, warning, guidance and encouragement, we shall walk safely. If we neglect them, we shall be engulfed by darkness" (Green, 100).

Until we see Christ face-to-face, we have an authoritative source of spiritual truth. Scripture introduces us to God and a way of life that honors him. Why do we neglect to "pay attention" to it? Some in Peter's day were so influenced by the false teachers that they were beginning to fail to give serious attention to the Scripture.

1:20–21. The Old Testament writers did not invent or make up their material. The Old Testament prophets were the communicators, in written form, of God's message. **Carried along** was used of a sailing ship carried along by the wind. The metaphor pictures the cooperation of the Holy Spirit with the individual writer. The prophets raised their sails, and the Holy Spirit filled them and carried their craft along in the direction he wished. Through their own unique personalities, styles of writing, and vocabularies, God moved each of them by his Spirit to communicate his truth.

> **MAIN IDEA REVIEW:** *Change and transformation in the Christian life are fueled by a combination of human responsibility and divine power. Jesus Christ and the Old Testament Scriptures show us the truths behind God's divine arithmetic that adds change, transforming our lives into eternal kingdom lives.*

III. CONCLUSION

Exhibiting God's Love

What an encouraging chapter! Peter outdid himself in reminding us of our exalted standing in Jesus Christ. As a result of our personal relationship with Jesus Christ and the indwelling of the Holy Spirit, each of us has the wonderful privilege of growing up in the faith and being transformed into people who truly reflect the character of our Savior. The Scriptures reflect the voice or word of God regarding the wonderful position every believer enjoys.

An anonymous interpreter has written fitting words summarizing 2 Peter 1: "In the Cross we may see the dimensions of Divine love. The Cross is not the cross of a man, but the exhibition of the heart of God. At the back of the wall of the world stands God with his arms outstretched, and every man driven there is driven into the arms of God. The Cross of Jesus is the supreme evidence of the love (and grace) of God."

PRINCIPLES

- Every believer in Jesus Christ enjoys a precious faith.
- The Holy Spirit indwells and enables a Christian in spiritual transformation of life and character.
- Godliness involves reverence for and obedience to God.
- Jesus Christ promised the presence of the Holy Spirit in the believer's life.

- Sanctification or transformation in the Christian's life is an ongoing and continuing process.
- The second coming of Jesus Christ is a promised reality.
- The deity of Jesus Christ is affirmed by God the Father.
- The Old Testament Scriptures are reliable and accurate.

APPLICATIONS

- List the positive changes or marks of transformation that have appeared in your life as a direct result of your relationship by faith to Jesus Christ.
- Be confident of the presence and power of the Holy Spirit in your life.
- Ask the Holy Spirit to reveal to you characteristics of the culture that he wants to take out of your life. Pledge your cooperation with him in conforming your life to Christ and not to culture.
- Review where you might have gone and who you might have become had it not been for the intervention of the grace of God in your life.
- Write down the basic gospel truths you have learned by studying Peter's writings. Develop a plan to live out these truths.
- Reject the teaching of anyone who denies the majesty and glory of the character of Jesus Christ.
- Study and pay attention to the authoritative Scriptures. If you do not know the truth, you will be easily fooled by error.

IV. LIFE APPLICATION

He Is Everything

One evening the great conductor Arturo Toscanini conducted Beethoven's Ninth Symphony. The audience loved it. At the conclusion they clapped, whistled, and stomped their feet. Toscanini bowed and bowed to the audience. He then signaled the orchestra, whose members stood to acknowledge the wild applause. Eventually the applause began to quiet. With the quieting applause in the background, Toscanini turned, looked intently at his musicians, and almost uncontrollably exclaimed, "Gentlemen! Gentlemen!"

The orchestra members leaned forward to listen. Why was the maestro so disturbed? Was he angry? Had someone missed a cue? Had the orchestra flawed the performance in some way? No. Toscanini was not angry. He was stirred to the very core of his being by the sheer magnificence of Beethoven's music. Scarcely able to talk, he whispered fiercely, "Gentlemen, I am nothing!" This was an extraordinary admission since he was blessed with an enormous ego. "Gentlemen," he added, "you are nothing." That was hardly news. The members of the orchestra had often heard the same message in rehearsal. "But Beethoven," said Toscanini in a tone of adoration, "he is everything, everything!"

Peter would have us adopt this same attitude toward Jesus Christ. When the orchestration of our life is coming to a final conclusion, he would whisper fiercely to each of us, "Ladies and gentlemen, I am nothing! You are nothing! But Jesus Christ—he is everything, everything!"

How do we show that Jesus is everything in everyday life? First, we remember how valuable we as followers of Jesus Christ are to God the Father. He shows no hesitancy in his love for us, no second-guessing, no conditional offers. He recognizes no second-class citizens in his kingdom. What a tremendous assurance this should be for us as we endeavor to follow Jesus. Still, we often struggle. We become passive onlookers rather than active participants in the journey of faith. That can change. How? Through wonderful cooperation between the Spirit of God activated in our lives and our own desire or spirit moving us toward the goal of character and lifestyle transformation.

Allowing this transformation to happen is the second way we show Jesus is everything in our lives. How seriously do we take this process? How committed to it are we? How honest have we been in evaluating our progress? Too many of us would rather coast home. We feel safe and secure, and with that safety net we lie down and get comfortable. As strong as the encouragement and the assurances of this chapter are, the warning is just as strong: if we as followers of Christ have little inclination or energy for spiritual growth and transformation, we may be Christians in theory, but not in fact. At the very least, we have forgotten exactly what it is that Jesus Christ has done for us.

This letter keeps bringing us back to that central truth, reaffirmed and attested by the transfiguration of Jesus Christ and the sure and certain word of the Scriptures. If we follow the majestic and glorious Christ whom Peter presents in this chapter, and if we take seriously the Spirit-crafted Scriptures, then our mandate is clear. Our eyes are to be on our glorious Savior; he is the one we are to follow and live for.

V. PRAYER

Lord, how difficult it is for us to see that our faith is precious to you. How easy it is to believe that we are worthless in your sight. Thank you for giving your Son on our behalf that we might, through faith in him, be seen as precious in your sight. Thank you also for the promise of the Holy Spirit, who in cooperation with our spirit, enables us to be transformed into the likeness of your Son. Help us, dear Lord, to regularly and continually turn to the light of

Christ as revealed in the light of the Word of God so that we might continue on our journey of spiritual growth and transformation. Amen.

VI. DEEPER DISCOVERIES

A. Simon Peter (v. 1)

The authorship of 2 Peter is keenly debated among New Testament critics. Did the apostle Peter really write this book? The style and tone of writing in 1 Peter is so different from 2 Peter that many scholars think it unlikely that the same person authored both letters.

In spite of this, a great deal of evidence, both internally and externally, supports Petrine authorship.

1. Internal. The writer identifies himself as Peter, and the charge that someone merely inserted his name to lend credence to the book cannot be validated. Furthermore, the autobiographical allusions are true to the facts. For example, the writer talks about the overpowering scene of the transfiguration of Jesus in the tone of an awed spectator (1:16–18), classifying himself among the eyewitnesses and quoting word for word: **This is my Son, whom I love; with him I am well pleased.** In doing so, he claims to have personally heard this testimony.

   Additionally, Peter clearly alludes to the prediction Jesus made about his martyrdom (John 21:18): **as our Lord Jesus Christ has made clear to me** (1:12–14). This letter was written prior to the Gospel of John where this prediction was recorded, indicating that only a person who witnessed the conversation between Jesus and Peter could have talked about it with such firsthand knowledge. The writer seems to have a personal familiarity with the apostle Paul as an inspired writer of New Testament Scripture (3:15–16). Rather than an evidence of a much later authorship and of composition after the canonicity of Paul's letters by the church at large, these appreciative statements are what one would expect if Peter journeyed to Rome a few years after Paul did. His Roman readers would certainly expect and appreciate his comments on the work of Paul.

2. External. There appears to be an early attestation to 2 Peter in the epistle of Jude. It is unlikely, as some suggest, that one borrowed directly from the other, or even that one influenced the other. More likely, both Jude and 2 Peter were written in the same time period, and both dealt forcibly with the problems raised by heretics who were infiltrating the Christian community. The dramatic difference in style and tone of 1 and 2 Peter is easily understood by their different

declared purposes. First Peter was written to comfort and encourage believers who were undergoing persecution. Second Peter consists of stern and urgent warnings against false teachers and doctrine. The two purposes require different styles and tones.

Since 1 Peter utilized Silas as amanuensis or secretary in writing the letter down, some stylistic differences could also be anticipated. Silas may have been responsible for the simplicity and ease of expression in which 1 Peter is composed. Second Peter was probably written by Peter in a Roman jail without the help of an amanuensis like Silas. Thus, 2 Peter displays a more intense and rugged style (see Archer, 426–427; Thiessen, 287–289; Geisler and Howe, 537–538).

B. Make Your Calling and Election Sure (v. 10)

Second Peter 1 seeks to bring assurance and hope. It does not want to bring false hope. God does the calling and the electing, but such election implants the Holy Spirit in the heart of the elect. That heart then produces the good works of the arithmetic of faith described in verses 5–8. This is not a Christian option. People of faith will not stand still. The nature of faith is to grow. Through such growth, Christians confirm their salvation experience. The calling to salvation that God extended becomes a reality in our lives. Our election as children of God cannot be doubted. The teaching of 1 John 2:3 operates in our lives: "We know that we have come to know him if we obey his commands."

Second Peter joins the rest of Scripture in affirming that people can know they are saved. Our continuing growth in faith and in daily actions mirrors for us and the world the faith we have in our heart and proclaim with our lips. Thomas Schreiner describes the reality:

> Those who do not keep God's commandments are not really Christians at all. They reveal their true allegiance by their disobedience. . . . Second Peter asserts that believers "confirm their calling and election" (1:10) by practicing the character qualities in 1:5–7. These good works do not constitute an earning of salvation, but good works confirm that one really belongs to the elect community. Those who turn back to "the corruptions of the world" (2:20) and do not follow Jesus Christ to the end will not experience salvation but judgment (2:20–22) (*The Law & Its Fulfillment*, Baker, 1993, 207).

C. No Prophecy of Scripture Came About (v. 20)

God has chosen to reveal divine truth through the Scriptures. The extent and limits of this revelation have produced significant debate resulting in several theories of inspiration:

- *The Natural Theory.* The writers of the Bible were inspired much like William Shakespeare.
- *The Mechanical Dictation Theory.* God used the writers of the Bible like secretaries in the sense that he audibly dictated the actual words they were to write down.
- *The Content (or Concept) Theory.* God inspired only the ideas in the Bible, but not the words.
- *The Partial Theory.* God inspired only certain sections or parts of the Bible.
- *The Spiritual-Rule-Only Theory.* Only those parts of the Bible that refer to spiritual matters are inspired by God; all others are not (for example, science, history, etc.).
- God inspired all of the Bible (plenary), and the very words used (verbal).

This writer holds to *The Plenary-Verbal Theory.* This view implies:

- All parts of the Bible are equally inspired but not equally important (e.g., John 3:16 is more important that the final personal greetings in the letters of Paul).
- No guarantee is placed on the inspiration of any modern version or ancient translation of the Scriptures.
- Scripture contains no false teaching but does record the lies of others (for example, Satan to Eve).
- No historical, scientific, or prophetic error is permitted.
- Biblical writers did use extrabiblical sources (for example, Paul in Acts 17:28 and Titus 1:12).
- God did not overwhelm the personality of the human writer. Paul sounds like Paul, and John like John.
- God inspired the use of pictorial or symbolic language. Scripture must be interpreted by recognizing the various styles of language and figures of speech.
- Uniformity is not required in all details of events described in the Bible.
- God has accurately transmitted in the Bible all that he wishes us to know.

VII. TEACHING OUTLINE

A. INTRODUCTION
1. Lead Story: You Can Be Transformed
2. Context: When you feel isolated and rejected, you are an easy target for false teachers. Knowing his readers felt this way, Peter spent a

great deal of time in 2 Peter countering the error of these self-proclaimed teachers. He lifted high the person and work of Jesus Christ and held him out to his readers with confidence. He wanted them to be sure to recognize that Christ is going to return at the Second Coming and that this hope is firm.

3. Transition: When people feel isolated from God and others, they often need someone to come alongside of them and affirm them. This chapter does exactly that while at the same time challenging us to live out our identity in Christ with trust in the perfection of his person and his word.

B. COMMENTARY

1. Greeting (vv. 1–2)
   a. Author: Simon Peter (v. 1a)
   b. Recipients: Christians of no known address, but whose faith in Jesus Christ is precious (v. 1b)
   c. Greetings (v. 2)
2. Effective and Productive Lives (vv. 3–11)
   a. The target: godly living (v. 3)
   b. The enablement: the Holy Spirit (vv. 3b–4)
   c. The effort necessary (v. 5a)
   d. The effects demonstrated (vv. 5b–9)
   e. The assurance and confidence (vv. 10–11)
3. Reminders and Reassurances (vv. 12–21)
   a. Urgent reminders (vv. 12–15)
   b. Powerful reassurances (vv. 16–21)
      (1) Personal testimony (vv. 16–18)
      (2) Absolute certainty (v. 19)
      (3) Divine inspiration (vv. 20–21)

C. CONCLUSION: HE IS EVERYTHING

VIII. ISSUES FOR DISCUSSION

1. In what ways is your faith in Christ precious to you?
2. What have you received through God's divine power?
3. What qualities need to be added to your Christian life in order for it to be the transformed life Christ wants it to be? Who will cooperate with you in accomplishing this arithmetic of faith?
4. What do you need to do to make your election and calling sure?
5. Describe what the phrase "inspiration of Scripture" means to you.

2 Peter 2

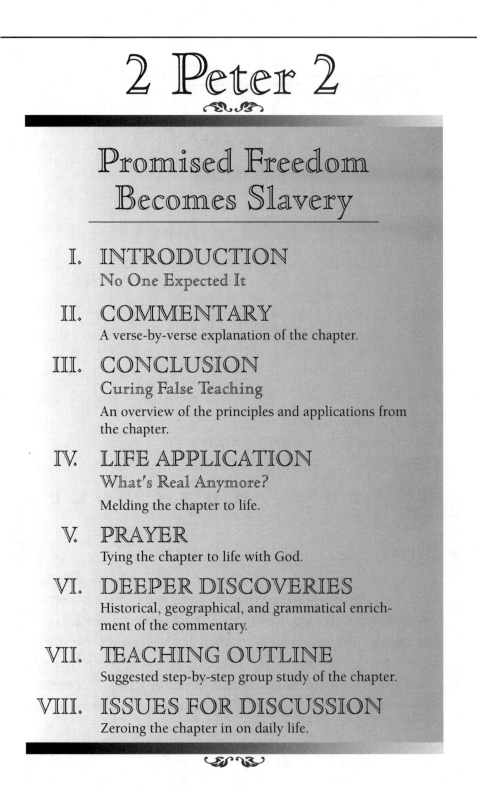

Promised Freedom Becomes Slavery

Quote

"*The heresy of one age becomes the orthodoxy*

of the next."

Helen Keller

 IN A NUTSHELL

Be careful out there! False prophets and teachers are always around. They are greedy. Their eternal punishment stands fixed by God. Arrogantly they feed you false teachings and model a pleasure-driven lifestyle totally opposed to Christ. These smooth talkers are particularly good at entrapping new Christians who don't know better. They promise freedom but deliver slavery. Mouthing the right "church" words, they have never been changed or transformed by Christ. As a result, they inevitably return to their dark and filthy ways. What a tragedy!

Promised Freedom Becomes Slavery

I. INTRODUCTION

No One Expected It

*N*o one ever expected it would happen, especially with this model congregation. They provided a heated swimming pool for underprivileged kids, horses for inner-city children to ride, gave scholarships for deserving students, and provided housing for senior citizens. They even had an animal shelter, medical facility, an out-patient care facility, and a drug rehabilitation program.

Walter Mondale wrote that the pastor was "an inspiration to us all." The secretary of health, education, and welfare cited the pastor's outstanding contributions: "He knew how to inspire hope. He was committed to people in need; he counseled prisoners and juvenile delinquents. He started a job placement center; he opened rest homes and homes for the retarded; he had a health clinic; he organized a vocational training center; he provided free legal aid; he founded a community center; he preached about God. He even claimed to cast out demons, do miracles, and heal."

Lofty words. A lengthy resume for what appeared to be a mighty spiritual leader and his church. Where is that congregation today? What is it doing now? The church is dead . . . literally.

Death occurred the day the pastor called the members to the pavilion. They heard his hypnotic voice over the speaker system, and from all corners of the farm they came. He sat in his large chair and spoke into a hand-held microphone about the beauty of death and the certainty that they would meet again. The people were surrounded by armed guards. A vat of cyanide-laced Kool-Aid was brought out. Most of the members drank the poison with no resistance. Those who did resist were forced to drink.

First, the babies and children, about eighty in number, were given the fatal drink. Then the adults, women and men, leaders and followers, and finally the pastor. Everything was calm for a few minutes. Then the convulsions began; screams filled the sky; mass confusion broke out. In a few minutes, it was over. The members of the Peoples Temple Christian Church were all dead. All 780 of them. So was their leader, Jim Jones.

Mark it down, and be on your guard: religious hucksters inhabit God's house. Don't be fooled by their looks or dazzled by their words. They are phonies, and they are poisonous. That was as true in 1978 with Jonestown as it was in the first century for Peter and his readers.

Peter devoted more than a full chapter to this problem because within three decades after the resurrection and ascension of Jesus Christ, the early church was being rocked by false teachers. Peter wrote to disarm them and to alert his Christian friends to their insidious presence.

II. COMMENTARY

Promised Freedom Becomes Slavery

MAIN IDEA: *The church is always subject to the heresy of smooth-talking false teachers. Christians must understand who these false teachers are and how they operate. We must understand God's verdict on such people and be alert for their presence within the body of Christ.*

A Exposing the Error (vv. 1–10a)

SUPPORTING IDEA: *If you do not know truth, you will be easily fooled by error. If you are not able to discern the methods and teachings of false teachers, you will be easy prey for them*

2:1. Jewish history was replete with false prophets who pretended to speak for God. False teachers repeated the pattern in the early church. **Introduce** means they smuggled in their ideas. Being smooth operators was the primary identifying mark of these false teachers. The ideas they smuggled were **destructive heresies**. These false teachers indoctrinated people with information that was not simply neutral or harmless. It was destructive to true faith.

The focal point of their heresy was Christological. They were **denying the sovereign Lord who bought them**. They may have denied Christ's ability to save or his second coming. Beyond that, they denied his claim over them as Savior and Lord. Although they claimed to love and serve Christ, what they did and taught denied him. Scripture labels such people as unsaved, not being Christians. "The sovereign Lord who bought them" does not suggest that these false teachers were at one time believers, and now were not. It means even though Christ's death on the cross provided for their salvation, they had not personally by faith trusted Christ as their Savior.

They pretended to be followers of Christ, but in their lives and in their teaching they consistently denied him. As a result, they bring **swift destruction on themselves**. This refers to an everlasting state of torment and separation from God. It is "swift" because it will come upon them very suddenly either at their death or at the second coming of Jesus Christ.

2:2. Despite this, many people will be attracted to these false teachers and will follow after their **shameful ways.** These words translate a single strong Greek word that means "reckless and hardened sexual immorality." These false teachers convinced themselves that sexual activity outside of marriage was acceptable and honoring to God. They borrowed the prevailing opinion of the Greek culture and smuggled it into the church. The impact of this false teaching and immoral living was to lure Christians into similar paths of immorality and thus to bring discredit upon Christ and true Christianity.

Bring . . . into disrepute translates the Greek verb *blasphemeo,* literally, "to injure the reputation of someone." The reputation of Christ and the Christian way of truth is brought to discredit when those who say they identify with Christ involve themselves in obvious immoral behavior. This discrediting occurs in the eyes of other Christians. Most importantly, those who do not know Christ will be influenced negatively. Immoral living by people who are identified with Christ's church raises a potential barrier, preventing unbelievers from embracing Jesus Christ.

2:3. These false teachers were interested only in personal gain. **Greed** involves going after selfish gain at the expense of others. Overtones of extortion are inherent in its meaning. These teachers were interested only in making their religion a money-making enterprise. For them, religion was something to be commercialized. They would buy and sell, trade in and exploit people. With fabricated stories, they fleeced the sheep. **Exploit** pictures a traveling mercenary who habitually cheats others for his own gain.

Having identified the approach and tactics of these false teachers, Peter turned to their future and how God views their activities. God has already decided on the verdict. He has condemned them. Their punishment is **destruction** (see v. 1 for explanation).

2:4. Verses 3–9 give three illustrations to prove that God has judged in the past and will judge again in the future. The examples gradually reduce in scale, from the cosmic (**angels**), through the worldwide (**flood**), to the local (**cities of Sodom and Gomorrah**). These illustrations concentrate on the pride and rebellion of the angels, the apathy and disobedience of the people of Noah's day, and the sheer sensuality of the men of Sodom, precisely the characteristics of these false teachers.

The first example gives an intriguing but partial glimpse into the world beyond our human experience—a world of angelic beings. At one time before the creation of the universe as we know it, they served God the Father. Even in that context, they rebelled against him. As a result, God judged them.

This verse makes two major points: (1) No one is exempt from judgment, not even angels. The arrogant, false teachers claimed, among other things, that they were beyond God's judgment. No one, not even the most glorious and powerful of those who stand against God, can avoid his judgment.

(2) Judgment, although delayed, is still very real. The angels sinned in the past and are only being held in the present time. Be assured that final judgment awaits them in the future. Built into the way that God runs the universe is the principle that punishment does not necessarily follow rebellion immediately, but it is certain to come.

2:5. The second illustration is the Genesis flood. The people of Noah's day rejected God. Because they rebelled against him, punishment and judgment resulted. At the same time, the principle of the protected and saved remnant is woven throughout this illustration, for God's grace is always available to those who believe him.

2:6. The third and final illustration focuses on Sodom and Gomorrah. Whenever these cities appear in the Scripture, they represent sin and rebellion at its highest level. Their particular sin was sexual sin, specifically homosexual practices. Coupled with this was their complete disregard for God and his law. As a result, God brought destructive judgment against the cities. This judgment was designed to serve as an **example** of how God will deal with the ungodly in the future. "Example" means "a pattern."

These illustrations describe an inevitable pattern of events: sin, unconfessed and unforsaken, will lead to judgment and destruction. The God of the Bible is the God of justice. His character is just. For God to allow the scales of justice to remain forever out of balance would be for him to compromise his own integrity. That God will not do.

2:7–8. At the same time, grace is always available. Although God's judgment on a sinful creation is inevitable, it is not inescapable. God protected Noah and those who believed his message (cf. v. 5). He rescued **righteous** Lot from the judgment on Sodom. Note that "righteous" appears three times in these verses to describe Lot's character. This may seem surprising to our ears. The Lot who was prepared to sacrifice his daughters to the sexual whims of Sodom, the Lot who chose the best land rather than leave it for his uncle Abraham, and the Lot who drank himself into a stupor—could this be the Lot who is now highlighted for his righteous character?

God knew something about Lot's heart not recorded in the Old Testament record, but revealed to the apostle Peter by the Spirit. While he lived in Sodom, Lot endured a daily struggle in his heart against the evil he was witnessing. He was worn down by the filth he saw every day to the point that he was **tormented** by it. The term can also be translated "tortured." Its imperfect tense pictures the continual nature of the torment. Such was the heart of Lot, to the point that he is now remembered for being "righteous."

2:9. Lot's rescue emphasizes God's promises **to rescue godly men from trials.** This may suggest present trials in the life of the believer. God can and does rescue believers from trials and difficulties; however, this is certainly not the norm, nor is it the biblical promise (see Jas. 1:1–2 and the commentary on 1 Peter). Such an interpretation misses the point of Peter's illustration. His emphasis is on God's final judgment of the ungodly (cf. v. 6).

"Trials" (*peirasmou*) literally means "the test." Consistently, the New Testament views the second coming of Christ as the final test. Then the Lord will rescue his true followers, but the ungodly will face judgment, for the Lord knows how to **hold the unrighteous for the day of judgment.** "To hold" literally means "to keep or to guard." It suggests that God is in control of judgment and people; he will have the final say.

While continuing their punishment in the NIV represents a rigid translation of a Greek present participle that most likely has a future meaning here, so the NIV translator's note is probably preferable: "until the day of judgment" (see the discussion of Bauckham, WBC 50, 253–254). An intermediate state of punishment or purgatory is not in view. The entire context points to the final judgment of rebellious angels, people, and teachers.

2:10a. A final postscript to this section makes it clear that the false teachers (see v. 1) are included in the judgment of God. This verse is an apt summary of the character of these false teachers. They are fueled by the corrupt desires of their nature and have so exalted their opinion of themselves that they **despise authority.** *Despise* means "to think down upon someone." In the case of the false teachers, this primarily refers to their rejection of the rule of the Lord Jesus Christ over them and their denial of the power and majesty of Christ.

Ⓑ Turning Up the Heat (vv. 10b–22)

> **SUPPORTING IDEA:** *False teachers are bold and arrogant beasts who will pay the price for their evil deeds. These immoral smooth talkers try to get others to fall into their own immorality. They promise freedom but deliver slavery.*

2:10b. Bold and arrogant identifies the general attitude of these false teachers. They are presumptuous and self-willed. They respect no one, and nothing seems to restrain them. One who is "bold" rides roughshod over the rights, opinions, and interests of others, whether they be human or divine. One who is "arrogant" goes further; they cannot be reasoned with. No amount of conversation or dialogue will stop them from doing or teaching just as they please. They assume they are right and everyone else is wrong.

This assumption is fleshed out in the last part of this verse: they are **not afraid to slander celestial beings.** Interpreters disagree about the precise identification of these "celestial beings." Peter is probably saying: "These false teachers, with their overinflated view of themselves, are not afraid to speak against God's angels or perhaps God himself. They seem to make light of the unseen spiritual powers and, at the same time, speak disrespectfully of celestial beings. They are guilty of dismissing spiritual activities in the realm of the angels."

2:11. An illustration of contrast underlines the audacity of such behavior. God's angels, who are superior to human beings, do not speak critically about other angels, even the evil, fallen angels against whom God has already pronounced judgment.

The false teachers were free with their slanderous insults against angels and God, but the angels of heaven so reverence their Lord that it never occurs to them to allow slanderous, insulting language to pass their lips, even though it would be deserved.

2:12. Despite their claims to a higher level of knowledge and spirituality, these false teachers speak out of their own ignorance, acting much like irrational animals. For all their claims to a higher level of spirituality, they are really in completely over their heads. They do not have a clue about true spirituality.

Their actions will not go unpunished. They will **perish.** This may simply refer to their inevitable death after living animal-like lives, or it may be a reference to their eternal punishment apart from Jesus Christ.

2:13–14. The initial statement of this verse is open to the same double reference as verse 12. In the overall view of this section (see v. 17 especially), these references seem to speak of eternal punishment in hell. This judgment is validated by graphic details of the actions and activities of these false teachers. Even the pagan world generally practiced its deceit under the cover of darkness, but these people were without shame. They began their parties before dark and apparently turned the church's fellowship meals and communion gathering into a drunken celebration.

According to verse 14, these false teachers went well beyond that. **Eyes full of adultery** literally reads, "Their eyes are full of an adulterous woman." The problem is not that they noticed beautiful women. The problem is that they lusted after every woman they saw and could not look at a woman without fantasizing about her sexually. They succeeded to some degree in that they were able to **seduce the unstable.**

Added to their drunkenness and sexual addictions, they were **experts in greed.** A more literal translation is, "They have a heart exercised or trained in greed." "Experts" (*gymnadzo*) is a term borrowed from the athletic world, and it describes the well-trained athlete. These false teachers had trained themselves well. They had worked out for long periods of time. They had exercised to the point of exhaustion in an effort to become well-toned experts in "greed," which simply means "a desire to have more." These false teachers were out for what they could get out of their religion. As such, they were **an accursed brood!** They rested under the curse of God, which is eternal punishment in hell.

2:15–16. An Old Testament story illustrates this emphasis (see Num. 22–24). Balaam, who was supposed to be a prophet of God, loved money more than God. He was willing to pursue fame and fortune instead of obeying God. He also taught immorality. As a result, he was rebuked by God through a donkey. For a donkey to rebuke the prophet's madness reflects not only on the foolishness of Balaam but also on that of all false teachers.

2:17. These false teachers give nothing of substance because they have nothing to give. They are like a dry well. They cannot deliver what they promise. Even if they could, it would be only temporary, like a mist or fog that disappears when the wind comes up. Far worse, **blackest darkness is reserved for them.** This is hell. The darkness of hell is not merely a room with the lights turned off, but a thick, fierce, comfortless isolation that endures throughout eternity.

2:18–19. The empty, boastful words of these false teachers were enticing enough for some believers to be ensnared by them. This was particularly true of new Christians who were just emerging from the clutches of sexual license practiced in the non-Christian culture. The false teachers, aware of this, twisted the concept of Christian freedom into something it was not. They taught that freedom is the license to do whatever a person desires. In fact, Christian freedom is the ability to do what is right, based on God's Word. The false teachers told these new Christians that religious freedom was freedom from all the authority and moral demands of Christianity. The irony of their religious rhetoric is that the entire time these people raised the flag of personal freedom, they were slaves to their sexual habits and addictions.

2:20–22. The New Testament distinguishes clearly between people who are in the church and people who are actually followers of Jesus Christ. They are not always the same people. This distinction is seen clearly with this group of false teachers. They were not followers of Jesus. The **knowledge** of Jesus mentioned in verse 20 was simply a head knowledge, not a knowledge of the heart. They knew all about Christ and Christianity; this is how they were able to offer a counterfeit. Because of their association with true believers in the church, they had escaped some of the **corruption of the world** simply because true believers move away from this behavior.

However, knowing about Jesus Christ and being associated with Christians does not mean that they had embraced Jesus Christ as their Savior. Since they were worse off at the end than they were at the beginning, these people had never reached full, saving faith.

Worse off at the end than they were at the beginning aptly summarizes what Peter went on to explain in verses 21–22. They were worse off because those who give themselves to the pursuit of greed and sexual immorality ultimately become so corrupt that they lose the ability to enjoy themselves. Like a sick dog, they wallow in their own vomit (v. 22). They were worse off, secondly, because they deliberately chose to reject the truth they had learned (v. 21). They rejected the way of Christ, the way of forgiveness for their sins, the way of heaven. As a result, they chose hell over heaven and confirmed the judgment already confirmed upon them (see v. 17).

> **MAIN IDEA REVIEW:** *The church is always subject to the heresy of smooth-talking false teachers. Christians must understand who these false teachers are and how they operate. We must understand God's verdict on such people and be alert for their presence within the body of Christ.*

III. CONCLUSION

Curing False Teaching

This chapter sounds a sober warning to all believers. Just because we are in a church does not guarantee that we will not be exposed to those who teach error. Lies, disguised as the truth, are regularly presented for consumption. Many Christians, unable to tell the difference, gobble up these tasty morsels and then find themselves getting sick from what they ate. The prescription against error is knowing the truth ahead of time so we can distinguish between the real and the phony. This chapter exposes the practices and premises of false teachers in the first century and the eternal consequences that accompany their lifestyle and doctrines. The warnings of the first century ring true in our time as well.

PRINCIPLES

- Biblical heresy is always destructive.
- Most heresies focus on the person and work of Jesus Christ.
- Immoral sexual activity is not consistent with Christian morality.
- Heretics are often motivated by money and selfishness.
- God's future judgment will come, and it will be final.
- The Bible teaches the reality of angels.
- The character of God requires his response of judgment.
- The judgment of God does not dilute the availability of the grace of God.
- False teachers do not possess a "secret" knowledge of God and his ways.
- The Bible affirms the reality of eternal punishment in hell. It does not teach annihilation.
- Christian freedom is not unbridled license.

APPLICATIONS

- Be discerning in your assessment of biblical teaching.
- Reject any teacher who advocates a lifestyle or doctrine clearly contrary to the Word of God.
- Develop your own understanding of doctrinal purity. Write out your own doctrinal statement.
- Examine your own life for greed and selfishness.
- Be wary of any teacher who uses the Bible or the pulpit as a means to gain personal wealth.
- Look for opportunities to speak to others concerning the truth about Jesus Christ.
- Cultivate moral purity. Be a part of an accountability group or have a Christian friend to whom you are accountable.
- Guard your sexual purity.
- Make the study of God's Word a priority in your schedule, applying its truths to your own life.

IV. LIFE APPLICATION

What's Real Anymore?

Lewis Grizzard was a Southerner, with a capital *S*. He was also a writer, a funny guy. In *The Last Bus to Albuquerque* he reminds us of a question we need to ask in the church.

For weeks, I had been seeing a television commercial for this certain chain of restaurants. The commercial claimed the restaurant served home cooking, "The kind mom used to do." Now, I grew up at a fried chicken, pork chops, pot roast and fresh vegetable table, with corn bread or Mama's homemade biscuits on the side. I must have this sort of food at least once a week or be struck by the dreaded bland-food poisoning. So I gave this chain a try. I walked into one of its restaurants and looked over the menu. There was no fried chicken or pork chops. But there was country-fried steak and pot roast. I decided to go for the pot roast. "Can I get mashed potatoes and gravy with the pot roast?" I asked the waitress. "Sure," she answered. The pot roast was so-so. The gravy was suspect. One bite of the mashed potatoes, and I knew. I called the waitress back over. "I would take it as a personal favor if you would be perfectly honest with me," I said. "These mashed potatoes came out of a box, didn't they?" The waitress dropped her eyes for a brief second. Then she looked up and said apologetically, "Yes, they did."

I hate mashed potatoes that come out of a box. When God created the mashed potato, I am certain the Bible points out somewhere, he had no intention of anybody goofing around and coming up with mashed potatoes from a box. He meant for real potatoes to be used. You peel them, you cut them into little pieces and put them in a pot of boiling water. You put in some salt and pepper, and then you add some butter and maybe even a little sour cream, and then you beat them and stir them and you've got biblically correct mashed potatoes.

So, when I paid my bill I did have a word with the assistant manager, (but he) took my money anyway. "May the Lord forgive you . . . you potato ruiner," (I said on my way out). Mashed potatoes from a box. That's what's wrong with this country. That and canned biscuits, soybean anything, frozen French fries, fake flowers, tanning salons. What's real anymore?

Peter addressed not what is wrong with the country, but what is wrong with the church. He challenged all of us who truly follow Christ to know exactly what and who is real. The answer is, Jesus Christ.

So much of what we face each day is artificial—not the real thing. It's a copy or a replica, maybe even a limited edition, but not the original—not the genuine article. Increasingly, this is true in religion and in the church. Whether we think of leadership in the church or laypeople in the church, it cuts across all levels. Of all the places where descriptive words like "genuine," "legitimate," and "real" should apply, there seems instead to be an increase in phoniness, imitation, and frauds in the church. It leaves you scratching your head asking, "What or who is real anymore?"

This question bothered Peter deeply. Into the church had slithered a lot of phoniness in the form of false teachers or religious hucksters. They did everything they could to confuse Christians by selling them an imitation of the real thing. They were creating havoc. That's why this chapter is so important. Peter came down hard on these false teachers, describing them in exacting detail without mincing his words.

We must learn from church history that "new truth" is often old error in new disguises. The same voices are being heard in the church today. We are told to surrender our old-fashioned morality, to lighten up and enjoy the ride. We are challenged to find the "real" Jesus, to search for him and then rejoice when he emerges entirely differently than the Jesus of the Gospels. We are invited to pursue wealth as the "king's kids" and to take all that money back from the devil.

People regularly whisper to us to believe in heaven, but to discard the old-fashioned idea of hell. A God of love could not possibly entertain the idea of eternal punishment. We are being seduced by the same voices that confused the first-century church; we just don't know it. Worse, if we do, we don't protest. This chapter presents the eternal seriousness of falling for heresy in doctrine and lifestyle. It is a call to the church to return to the purity of the gospel and the glory of Jesus Christ.

V. PRAYER

Lord, it is too easy to be fooled, to be led astray. Sometimes we just put our guard down. We stop thinking. We stop trusting your word. Lord, help us to be strong in the faith, without becoming hard and brittle to others. Allow our minds to be continually renewed by your Spirit so we might know your word. Allow our hearts to remain soft so we might communicate your word with love and gentleness. May we never lose sight of the fact that people are going to spend eternity apart from you in hell unless they accept you as Lord and Savior. May we always hold on to you and hold you out to others. Amen.

VI. DEEPER DISCOVERIES

A. If God Did Not Spare Angels When They Sinned, But Sent Them to Hell (*Tartarus*) . . . (v. 4)

At issue here is "When did these angels sin?" and "Where or what is Tartarus?"

When did these angels sin? The two main viewpoints are: (1) these angels sinned prior to creation and specifically at the original fall of Satan, or, (2) these angels are frequently connected to the story of the "sons of God" in Genesis 6:1–4, so that their sin involved cohabiting with human women and producing a race of unredeemable demon men (see Jude 6).

Where or what is Tartarus (translated as "hell")? This word is only found in this verse in the New Testament and here in a verbal form rather than the noun. Tartarus was the name in classical mythology for the subterranean abyss in which rebellious gods and other such beings as the Titans were punished. However, the word was taken over into hellenistic Judaism and used in the book of Enoch (20:2) in connection with fallen angels.

In the New Testament, another term (*abussos*) is used to refer to the abode of demons. It occurs nine times in the New Testament and is most often translated as "the bottomless pit" or "the deep" (see Rom. 10:7; Rev. 9:1,2,11; 20:5). The word literally means "unfathomably deep" and most often describes a place of imprisonment for disobedient spirits. Tartarus and the bottomless pit would seem then to refer to a place of confinement for demons until the final judgment. Greek sources connect punishment with the imprisonment. It is not certain that Peter meant anything more than imprisonment until the time of final judgment and torment.

B. Did Not Spare Angels When They Sinned . . . Putting Them into Gloomy Dungeons to Be Held for Judgment (v. 4)

This raises the question, "Are fallen angels bound or are they free to tempt human beings?" Explanations vary, but two opinions are usually offered. The first explanation is that Peter is speaking of the ultimate destiny of fallen angels (demons), not their actual and immediate status. That is, while they are already sentenced by God to eternal damnation, they have not yet actually started serving their term, although they know that their time is coming (Matt. 8:29; Rev. 12:12). A second explanation suggests that there are different classes of fallen angels or demons:

1. The first class is the permanently bound demons (cf. Jude 6). These indulged in some great sin (see above) that caused God to consign them permanently to the abyss.
2. Temporarily bound demons (Rev. 9:1–3). They are bound only temporarily because they are released from the abyss during the tribulation period described in the Book of Revelation. These demons are not the same as the first class of demons since Peter makes it clear that they are being held for judgment. There is no suggestion of release.
3. Free demons. These are the fallen angels who currently assist Satan in his work throughout the world. Why this group has not been bound is not made clear in the Bible. What is made clear is that some demons roam freely over the earth, oppressing and even possessing people (cf. Matt. 12:22; 17:14–17; Acts 16:16–18; Rev. 16:14).

C. Hold the Unrighteous for the Day of Judgment (v. 9); They Are Born Only to Be Caught and Destroyed (v. 12); and Blackest Darkness Is Reserved for Them (v. 17)

Will the unrighteous be annihilated (destroyed), or will they suffer eternal punishment in hell? The debate on this issue has become more intense in recent years. Those who adopt an annihilation viewpoint teach that all people continuing in sin and apart from faith in Christ are completely annihilated, that is, reduced to nonexistence. To support this point of view, they argue that for God to allow eternal torment is inconsistent with his love; that the cessation of existence is implied in certain terms applied to the destiny of the wicked, such as the words *destruction* (Matt. 7:13; 2 Thess. 1:9) and *perishing* (John 3:16). They also teach that since God alone has immortality (1 Tim. 1:17; 6:16), any other immortality attached to humanity is a special gift connected with redemption in Jesus Christ (Rom. 2:7; 1 Cor. 15:52–54; cf. House, 139).

Those who argue against annihilation and for eternal punishment in hell offer the following arguments. The rich man who died and went to hell was in conscious torment (Luke 16:22–28), and there is no suggestion that the torment was going to stop. Jesus spoke often of the people in hell as "weeping and gnashing [their] teeth" (Matt. 8:12; 22:13; 24:51), which indicates consciousness. Hell is said to have the same duration as heaven, "eternal" (Matt. 25:41; 2 Thess. 1:9). The beast and the false prophet are to be thrown alive into the lake of fire at the beginning of the thousand years (Rev. 19:20), and they are to be found there, conscious and alive, after the thousand years (Rev. 20:10). The Book of Revelation also affirms that the devil, the beast, and the false prophet "will be tormented day and night for ever and ever" (Rev. 20:10). Jesus referred to hell as a place where "the fire is not quenched" (Mark 9:48), where the bodies of the wicked will never die (cf. Luke 12:4–5). It makes no sense to have everlasting flames without anyone to experience the torment (see Geisler and Howe, 493–494).

It is the clear picture of the New Testament that eternal punishment, in addition to what is mentioned above, involves separation from God and his glory (2 Thess. 1:9); different degrees of punishment (Matt. 11:21–24; Luke 12:47–48), and the final state where no second chance is provided or offered (Mark 9:44–48; Matt. 25:46). It is this writer's position that the Bible clearly teaches eternal punishment in hell for anyone who dies without having embraced by faith the gospel of Jesus Christ.

VII. TEACHING OUTLINE

A. INTRODUCTION

1. Lead Story: No One Expected It
2. Context: In an environment where new revelation and wisdom were highly valued, the church stood in a vulnerable position. Unorthodox but appealing teachers enticed them into beliefs and behaviors contradictory to the Scriptures and to the life of Jesus Christ. Peter boldly exposed the errors of the false teachers and spelled out clearly their doom apart from Christ.
3. Transition: Honoring and reverencing the person of Jesus and the Word of the Lord (1:17–21) is helpful and beneficial only if it allows you to discern error that is being proclaimed. In this chapter Peter courageously allowed the Scripture to expose the errors of these false teachers. As he did so, he exhorted the Christians to be alert to the destruction being wielded by these people.

B. COMMENTARY

1. Exposing the Error (vv. 1–3,10a)
   a. In general terms (v. 1a)
   b. Specific characteristics (vv. 1b–3)
      (1) Destructive denials (v. 1b; cf. v. 10)
      (2) Shameful ways (v. 2; cf. v. 10)
      (3) Exploiting methods (v. 3)
2. Describing Final Outcomes (vv. 4–9)
   a. Destruction, judgment, and punishment (vv. 4–9)
   b. Protection and rescue (vv. 5,7–8,9)
3. Further Explanations (vv. 10b–16,18–19)
   a. Fearless arrogance (vv. 10b–12)
   b. Unbridled selfishness (vv. 13–16, 18–19)
      (1) In morality (vv. 13b–14, 18–19)
      (2) In greed (vv. 14b–16)
4. Final Consequences (vv. 12b–13a,17,20–22)
   a. Eternal punishment (vv. 12b–13a,17)
   b. Present distress (vv. 20–22)

C. CONCLUSION: WHAT'S REAL ANYMORE?

VIII. ISSUES FOR DISCUSSION

1. Describe false teachings that plague the church today. How can you be sure that you do not fall prey to such teachings?
2. What do you believe about the second coming of Jesus? Why?
3. What biblical illustrations can you give to show that God punishes sinners? Do you think such punishment is merely during this lifetime? Does it involve annihilation but not eternal punishment? Does it involve eternal suffering in hell?
4. What connection do you expect between what a person teaches and the way a person lives?
5. How do you define Christian freedom?

2 Peter 3

Follow No Detours

"*G*od of glory, Lord of love, hearts unfold like flowers before thee, opening to the sun above."

Henry Van Dyke

IN A NUTSHELL

*D*espite the confusion that exists today, be assured that the Lord is still in control. He has promised in the past that he will return; he will keep that promise. So don't despair, and don't give up living lives that honor the Lord. Many people will continue to attempt to detour you from the path that you are on. Resist them, but never stop loving them and others. That will be the case as you continue to grow in your appreciation of the grace of your Savior, the Lord Jesus Christ.

Follow No Detours

I. INTRODUCTION

It's a Good Idea

A little six-year-old girl told her mother her favorite Bible story was Jesus turning water into wine at the wedding. Her mother, a little puzzled by her daughter's choice, asked, "Well, what did you learn from that story?" The little girl responded, "What I learned from the story is that when you have a wedding, it's a good idea to have Jesus there."

As it describes the church, the New Testament uses a brilliant metaphor, painting the church as "the bride of Jesus Christ." That picture says we who are followers of Jesus, and, therefore, part of the church, will one day see Christ as individuals and as a corporate body. For us, that day will be a celebration, a wedding of sorts. When you have a wedding, it is a good idea to have Jesus in attendance. The church will be the bride, and Christ will be the bridegroom.

For those who are not followers of Christ, no wedding is planned. No celebration is in the works—only judgment and punishment. On that day, Jesus Christ will also be present.

It is that day, the day of the Lord, the day of the Second Coming that now occupies Peter's thinking. The nearness of Jesus Christ gripped Peter. His promised coming was nearer as Peter wrote this chapter than when he began the letter. He pushed his readers to look past the errors of the false teachers and to concentrate on the hope and assurance of Christ's return, when all will be made right. As we look forward to this sure hope, this hope motivates us to continue to live godly lives and to influence others.

II. COMMENTARY

Follow No Detours

MAIN IDEA: *False teachers in the church will always be a pressing problem for Christians, but the promised presence of our returning Savior, Jesus Christ, looms bright on the horizon, superseding any human presence that now assaults us. To him we must continue to look, and for him we must continue to live.*

A The Thief in the Night (vv. 1–10)

SUPPORTING IDEA: *In the midst of uncertainty and struggle, believers in Jesus Christ must never lose sight of the certainty and hope of the future that bring meaning to the present.*

3:1. Most of this concluding chapter of 2 Peter is devoted to the second coming of Jesus Christ. The emphasis here is not that Christians wait passively for that event, but that we are to live differently as we wait. **My second letter** seems naturally to refer to 1 Peter, but it probably refers to an otherwise unknown letter. First and 2 Peter were most likely written to different audiences, and 1 Peter was certainly not written in the form of a reminder.

Peter's purpose here is to **stimulate you to wholesome thinking.** "Wholesome" means "sincere, uncontaminated or unmixed." Peter's words of encouragement and warning should produce such thinking and keep us from letting false teachers lure us into unwholesome thinking with their beliefs. False teachers must never distort the biblical truth we have come to embrace. Their teaching only contaminates our thinking.

3:2. This verse introduces two potential areas of contaminated thinking. The first is encircled by **the words spoken in the past by the holy prophets.** This refers primarily to the sections of the Old Testament that spoke of the promise of the second coming of the Messiah, Jesus Christ. This subject was a favorite target of the false teachers. Essentially, Peter said don't overlook that emphasis in the Old Testament writings. Do not allow the influence of false teachers to persuade you that the Second Coming will not occur.

The second area that needed protection from the contamination of the false teachers is addressed in these words: **and the command given by our Lord and Savior through your apostles.** The "command" refers to the moral demands of the Christian faith, primarily Jesus' command of love reaffirmed by the apostles (cf. John 13:34; 15:12; Rom. 12:10; 13:8–9; Heb. 10:24; Jas. 2:8; 1 Pet. 1:22; 4:8; 1 John 3:11). Christ's followers are to love one another as we await Jesus' second coming.

3:3–4. Most people in Peter's day (and ours) follow false teachers and consider biblical beliefs, especially belief in the Second Coming, to be foolish. **In the last days** refers to all the days between the first advent of the Messiah and the second advent. Characteristic of that time frame, however long it will be, is the fact that people will make fun of the doctrine of the Second Coming. **Scoffing** means "to make fun of someone." It describes the characteristic attitude of the day toward the Second Coming. False teachers argued that the promise of the Second Coming had been delayed so long that we may safely conclude that it would never happen. As far as they could see, the world was going on just as it always had—people lived and died, but nothing really changed. They concluded that God's promises were unreliable and that the universe was a stable, unchanging system where events like the Second Coming just don't happen.

Their argument, although convincing to some people, was in reality a smoke screen for their pursuit of **their own evil desires** (v. 3). This expression describes two characteristics of people: (1) they are cynical about life and people in general, and (2) they are preoccupied with themselves and their own needs. These kinds of people with these attitudes are the ones the Bible encourages us to love as we await the second coming of Jesus Christ.

3:5–7. This section points out that although these false teachers knew the Old Testament Scriptures, they chose to ignore them. They chose to deny God's intervention in past history. They denied, for example, his positive intervention in the creation of the world (v. 5) and his negative intervention in judgment at the time of Noah and the Flood (v. 6). Despite their scoffing and unbelief, the divine Word that created the heavens and the earth and then called forth the deluge to destroy them will again call forth destruction at the Second Coming (v. 7). The Old Testament consistently teaches that the cosmos is a moral universe created by God and that God will not let sin go unpunished forever. God is not only the creator of the universe; he is also the judge. The God who created the beginning of all things has the power to end them.

3:8–9. In light of this impending judgment, Peter's reminder regarding Christ's command to love is especially crucial. As we extend love even to difficult people who oppose the gospel, we may become the human instrument in bringing them to saving faith in Jesus Christ. We must not forget that God has a different perspective on time. He stands above time. When time is seen in light of eternity, a single day could be like a millennium, and a millennium could be viewed as a single day. God's apparent delay in fulfilling the promise of the Second Coming is partially understood as an issue related to his perspective on time versus humanity's perspective. Beyond that, the apparent delay of the Second Coming is also related to God's incredible love for humankind. His desire is that no one perish, **but everyone come to repentance.**

According to Green, "The plain meaning is that, although God wants all people to be saved, and although He has made provision for all to be accepted, some will exercise their free-will to exclude God. And this He cannot prevent unless He is to take away the very freedom of choice" (Green, 148).

God's apparent delay is not caused by inability to perform or indifference; it is prompted by his grace.

3:10. This is excruciatingly plain to see in light of the ultimate destination the universe is headed for. **The day of the Lord** is another description of the second coming of Jesus Christ which is entirely consistent with the imagery of the Old Testament Scriptures which Peter regularly points back to (cf. 3:2). The Old Testament basically sees time in terms of two ages—this present age and the age to come, the age of God. The transition from one to the other would not come by human effort or evolution, because the world is headed for destruction. The transition would be by the direct intervention of God.

The time of that intervention was called the day of the Lord. It was to be a time when the universe would be shaken to its foundations. It was to be a time when the judgment and punishment of sinners would occur. Despite all the warning of the Old Testament, people still did not (and do not) believe and are not prepared for the world-ending day of the Lord. Thus Jesus taught, and Peter here reaffirms, that his coming will be as unexpected as the coming of a thief at night.

Christ's unexpected though predicted coming will bring the destruction of the present creation. The **heavens** likely refer to the galaxies and solar systems beyond the earth's. The **elements** could refer to the earth's solar system, or the elements of earth, air, fire, and water, or to the atomic particles which are the basic structure of nature. The **earth** describes the planet we inhabit. All of these things will **disappear,** be **destroyed by fire, laid bare,** and **melt in the heat** (cf. v. 13).

All of these expressions are meant to emphasize that God's final judgment will be total and complete—nothing will escape. The exact methodology of God's intervention should not be pressed from the terminology of destruction that Peter uses. The point being made is that everything that God has created and everything that humankind has made will be laid bare before Almighty God. Then God will create a new heaven and a new earth (see 3:13; cf. Rev. 21:1).

Ⓑ Living in Light of His Coming (vv. 11–18)

> **SUPPORTING IDEA:** *The final destiny of the universe ought to motivate followers of Jesus Christ to live lives that honor and reflect well upon the person of Jesus Christ.*

3:11–13. What is going to happen at the end of the age, as **the day of the Lord** arrives? What impact will this teaching regarding the day of the Lord have on our lives? **What kind of people** (v. 11) suggests that God's people should demonstrate an outstanding quality of character in their lives as they live with the belief that Jesus Christ will return some day. The injunction **to live holy and godly lives** defines what that character should include. These terms are both plural and literally mean "in holy forms of behavior and godly deeds." Peter is not specific at this point, but suggests that holiness and godliness should impact the lives of the followers of Jesus Christ in many ways. Verse 14 specifically elaborates on these terms (see below).

Verse 12 adds a puzzling statement: **as you look forward to the day of God and speed its coming.** The timing of the second advent is, to some degree, dependent upon the character of believers' lives. How can we speed the day of God? Peter seems to suggest, *by living in the light of the day of the Lord.* Our life on earth as followers of Christ is not intended to be a passive waiting for the final events of prophecy. It is intended to be a time of active cooperation with God in the salvation of the world. In some mysterious way, not entirely explained by Scripture, as the character of Christians' lives shines in the culture, it impacts the day of the Lord.

New mention of the Second Coming leads Peter to repeat his earlier description of the impending destruction that awaits the world (see comments on 3:10). Here he added the positive hope that at that time, the new heaven and earth will be the eternal home of the believer, or in Peter's more generic term, **the home of righteousness.** Actions of righteousness find their expression in the holy and godly lives of the followers of Christ, the inhabitants of the new heaven and earth.

3:14. Peter now encouraged his readers to apply themselves diligently to the process of their salvation. We are not passive agents in God's character-shaping endeavors. We are to **make every effort to be found spotless, blameless and at peace with him.** "Spotless and blameless" should be understood together. They describe the character of Jesus Christ as seen in the lives of believers (see 1 Pet. 1:19 where these same terms are used to describe Jesus Christ). These terms do not suggest that the follower of Christ will live a perfect life, as did Christ; rather, they mean that what drives the Christian in our behavioral choices is a desire to be like Christ.

3:15–16. Peter borrowed the authority of the apostle Paul for his emphasis by reminding us that Paul, in his writings, has made the same point. Peter observed that Paul's letters contain some things that are difficult to understand, but they still contain the same authority as **the other Scriptures.** Peter's point of contact with Paul's writings is simply this: all through Paul's letters he, too, challenges Christians to live godly lives in light of the day of the Lord. That much is not difficult to understand. It could not be missed, unless deliberately. That is exactly what the false teachers have done. They have distorted or twisted the teaching of Paul, along with other parts of the Scriptures. Primarily, these teachers refused to submit their lifestyles to the scrutiny of Scripture, but instead twisted the Scriptures in order to condone their sinful lifestyles.

3:17. Knowing this common tactic of false teachers, we should be sufficiently warned. We must be on guard against this kind of teaching. In essence, Peter advised his friends: "Don't fall for them. You know that they are among you; now it is your responsibility to watch and to guard yourselves against their lies. You have been adequately warned and prepared so there is no reason to be swept off your feet by them. You have been firmly grounded in the Scripture; now stay there."

Fall from your secure position should not be understood in reference to salvation. "Secure position" describes the fact that they were stable, or firmly grounded in the Word of God, unlike the false teachers who were unstable and not grounded in the Scripture.

3:18. Peter's letter concludes with words reflecting the opening statements of chapter 1. This encourages us to "keep on growing." No true Christian believes, "I have arrived." The Christian life is a continual, growing life and was never intended to stand still. That growth finds its focus in an ever-increasing awareness and understanding of the person and character of Jesus Christ. To him belong all praise and glory.

> **MAIN IDEA REVIEW:** *False teachers in the church will always be a pressing problem for Christians, but the promised presence of our returning Savior, Jesus Christ, looms bright on the horizon, superseding any human presence that now assaults us. To him we must continue to look, and for him we must continue to live.*

III. CONCLUSION

Recognizing God's Grace

As Peter concludes this brief but powerful letter, we sense his intensity increasing, especially as he brings to the forefront the subject of the second coming of Jesus Christ. Any teaching that denies this hope is scandalous and is to be repudiated at all costs. When the Lord does return, it will be in glory and judgment. A new heaven and a new earth are promised to the believer, but before that promise is fulfilled, the destruction of the present cosmos will occur as part of God's judgment. Until such a time, we should recognize God's gracious hand in the apparent delay of his coming, and with that mindset, pursue the course of godly living that the Bible consistently outlines for us.

Life Application

PRINCIPLES

- The second coming of Jesus Christ is taught clearly and literally in the Bible.
- The Old Testament Scriptures are an accurate word from God.
- All Christ's followers are to exhibit love to others.
- The universe was created by God and will be judged by him.
- God desires that everyone be saved.
- The present cosmos will be destroyed by God.
- The believer is assured that God will create a new heaven and earth.
- The doctrine of the Second Coming should impact the way believers live today.

APPLICATIONS

- Avoid teachers who deny the literal second coming of Jesus Christ. Be alert to false teaching in this area.
- Be a student of the entire Bible, including the Old Testament.
- Be prepared to be laughed at because of your belief in the Second Coming.
- Since the Lord's "delay" provides opportunity to further extend the gospel message, look for occasions to share the good news of salvation.
- Make grace a dominant factor in your Christian growth.

IV. LIFE APPLICATION

Make Me a Holy Man

At the closing service of the World Congress on Evangelism in Berlin, West Germany, in 1966, Dr. Billy Graham spoke on the need in Christian work for a life marked by gentleness, kindness, love and forgiveness, a life that will mark us as different from the world. He added, "The Christian minister is to be a holy man."

He illustrated his point with the story of the conversion of Dr. H. C. Morrison, founder of Asbury Theological Seminary. Many years ago Morrison, a farm worker, was cultivating a field. Looking down the road, he saw an old Methodist circuit rider coming by on his horse. The young plowman had seen the preacher before, and he knew him to be a holy man. As he watched the saint go by, he felt the power of his godly presence way out in the field. Such a sense of conviction for sin came over Morrison that, fearful for his soul, he dropped on his knees. There between the rows of corn, alone, he made a resolve to give his life to God.

As he concluded the story, Billy Graham earnestly prayed, "Oh, God, make me a holy man—a holy man" (cited by Robert E. Coleman, *Nothing to Do But Save Souls,* Zondervan Publishing House, 1990, 94–95).

Second Peter consistently encourages us to become holy people—to represent Jesus Christ through our character and behavior. At times, this means fighting off the destructive influences of those who would teach contrary to the Word of God, especially as it relates to the person and work of Jesus Christ. At other times, it means being courageous enough to stand up and be ridiculed for beliefs that others consider foolish. For the follower of Christ, the hope of the literal second coming of Jesus Christ is not to throw us into a panic or create skepticism.

Furthermore, it is not presented so that we can set the date. It is presented to offer hope for the believer and motivate us to extend the love of Christ to others. It motivates and empowers us to witness through our lives and words to the power of Jesus Christ to transform and forgive. The hope of the Second Coming calls us to be holy people.

How tragic that the very doctrine that is presented with such positive goals has become an issue that divides the church. In some circles, a person's salvation is even questioned if he or she does not see eye to eye on every detail of the Lord's return. In other places, the newspaper is read into the Scriptures, sensationalizing the Second Coming. This draws disrepute upon the name of Jesus Christ.

It is time for the church to grow up in our understanding and application of this doctrine. The Word of God presents the teaching of the Second Coming to offer future hope and to motivate us to live lives to the honor and glory of Jesus Christ. Certainly our in-house debating and hair-splitting do neither. We spend more energy fighting opposing points of view than we do presenting and living for the person of the Second Coming—Jesus Christ.

We have a mandate from Scripture to spread the word. Allow your voice and your actions to speak in a powerful way for Jesus Christ. Rejoice as people respond to the amazing grace of our Lord and join us in anticipation of his return. Be holy as he is holy.

V. PRAYER

O Lord, how easy it is to lose hope, to begin to apply our limited view of life and eternity to you. How foolish of us to doubt your promise, your faithfulness. Lord, we confess that in doing that we have not loved others as we should. We have not communicated your love to those who do not know you. And yet, it is your very heart of love that prompts your delay. How could we have missed that! How like you to be patient. How like us to be impatient. Lord, as we await your coming, by your Holy Spirit allow us to apply ourselves to godly living. Help us to grow even more in our appreciation of your grace. Make us holy people. We pray this in the name of our wonderful Savior, Jesus Christ. Amen.

VI. DEEPER DISCOVERIES

A. Where Is This Coming? (v. 4), The Day of the Lord Will Come Like a Thief (v. 10)

All commentators agree that the **coming** that Peter refers to is the long-promised second coming of Jesus Christ. There remains, however, a great variety of opinions as to details of that coming. Briefly described, these views fall under the following titles:

1. Historic Premillennialism. This view holds that the return of Christ (the coming of v. 4) will be preceded by certain indicators or signs. The Second Coming will be followed by a period of peace in which Christ will reign on earth in person.

2. Dispensational Premillennialism. This view holds to a two-stage description of the second coming of Christ. Proponents suggest that Christ will come *for* his church at the Rapture and then *with* his church after a seven-year period of time called the tribulation.

3. Postmillennialism. This view holds that the kingdom of God is now extended through teaching, preaching, evangelism, and mission activities. The world is to be ultimately Christianized, ending in a long period of peace and prosperity known as the millennium. After this period, Jesus Christ will return.

4. Amillennialism. This view teaches that between the first and second coming of Jesus Christ, a continuous growth of both good and evil will occur in the world. The kingdom of God is now present in the world through God's Word, his Spirit, and the church. At the end of this growing period, Jesus Christ will return (cf. House, 133–136).

Verse 10 mentions **the day of the Lord.** "Day" refers to a time when God deals directly with man. Therefore, the day of the Lord would be a time in which God deals with humankind in some way. Comparing the use of this expression throughout the Bible, one concludes that the day of the Lord is a time of judgment upon the wicked just prior to Christ's second coming. It is unlikely, in Peter's letter, that he had any other eschatological details in mind than this. To insert a rapture or millennial chronology into Peter's words is to read too much into his statement, and this would violate his primary message of hope. To construct a chronology of end times, one must look elsewhere in the Bible for those details. Peter does not provide them.

B. Long Ago by God's Word the Heavens Existed and the Earth Was Formed (v. 5)

This statement affirms the creative power and action of God. Such an open statement creates some conflict with those who wish to debate and/or reconcile the arguments for creation versus evolution. Obviously, in the scope of this commentary, the debate will not be concluded. However, it is worthy of further study and reading. One scholar offers this significant paragraph to prompt our thinking:

> Who created and sustains the universe? Why was it created? What is the nature of the Creator-creature relationship? These are the sorts of questions that the Bible addresses when it treats the topic of creation. Such queries are essentially theological in nature. Therefore, the juxtaposition, by some modern interpreters, of scriptural assertions about creation with scientific evidence and theories regarding origins often results in fruitless comparisons of different, although equally relevant, bodies of knowledge. At the risk of oversimplifying the issue, one might say that the Scripture deals with the who, why, and what questions posed above, whereas science investigates the problems of when and how the observable universe came into existence and continues to function (Robert J. V. Hiebert, "Create, Creation," in *The Evangelical Dictionary of Biblical Theology*, 132).

C. The Lord Is Patient with You, Not Wanting Anyone to Perish, But Everyone to Come to Repentance (v. 9)

This verses raises the debate regarding the extent of the atonement. In essence, two main viewpoints have been articulated throughout modern church history, particularly since the Reformation. Although a simplification, they are best described as a limited atonement versus an unlimited atonement.

Those who hold to a limited atonement, also called particular redemption, assert that Jesus' death is solely for the elect, not for the lost. Another way of saying this is that those who hold that the atonement is limited in extent teach that Christ died to save only those whom the Father had predestined to eternal life. Therefore, the atoning work of Christ is applied in due time to all for whom it was accomplished. Still further, this position has been stated in the following manner. The coming of Jesus Christ was not to provide salvation for all humankind, but to render certain the salvation of the elect.

Those who hold to an unlimited atonement teach that Christ's death was sufficient for all people. This does not mean that all people will be saved, but it does emphasize, without qualification, that the sacrificial offering of Christ satisfied the claims of God's law and holiness and therefore made salvation a possibility for all. The provision of Christ in his atonement is for everyone; it is sufficient for everyone to be saved.

In summary, the limited atonement view teaches that God determined that Christ would die for all those whom God elected. Since Christ did not die for everyone, but only for those who were elected to be saved, his death is completely successful.

The unlimited atonement view teaches that Christ died for the entire human race, making all humankind savable. His death, however, is effective only in those who believe.

VII. TEACHING OUTLINE

A. INTRODUCTION

1. Lead Story: It's a Good Idea
2. Context: Peter's readers faced an onslaught of false teaching regarding Jesus Christ and his work. Additionally, false teachers ridiculed them for holding to their beliefs about the second coming of Jesus Christ. It had become so bad that these Christians entertained some doubts as to the validity of their beliefs and behaviors. Was what they believed really true? Was the price they were paying worth it, after all?
3. Transition: Being aware of false teachers and false teaching is one thing (chap. 2), especially when those teachers scoff at the doctrine of the Second Coming (chap. 3). It is yet another thing to continue to live a godly and holy life in the midst of such ridicule, with the hope that your life will turn such people to Jesus Christ. This chapter pushes the believer in such a direction.

B. COMMENTARY

1. The Thief in the Night (vv. 1–10)
   a. Some important reminders (vv. 1–2)
      (1) Wholesome thinking (v. 1)
      (2) Living in love (v. 2)
   b. People to be aware of (vv. 3–7)
      (1) Those who ridicule (vv. 3–4)
      (2) Those who follow evil (v. 3b)
      (3) Those who deliberately forget God (vv. 5–7)
   c. Truths not to forget (vv. 8–10)
      (1) The timing of God (vv. 8–9a)
      (2) The patience of God (v. 9b)

(3) The judgment of God (v. 10)
2. Living in Light of His Coming (vv. 11–18)
    a. Holy and godly lives (vv. 11–14)
    b. Guarded lives (vv. 15–17)
    c. Growing lives (v. 18)

C. CONCLUSION: MAKE ME A HOLY MAN

VIII. ISSUES FOR DISCUSSION

1. What is "wholesome thinking"? What would lead you to any other kind of thinking?
2. Have people scoffed at you for your beliefs? How have you responded?
3. What do you know for certain about the Second Coming? How does this affect your daily living?
4. What is your record of witnessing to others about Jesus Christ, his salvation, and his second coming?
5. Describe your view of the atonement.

1 John 1

God Requires Repentance for Fellowship

"*F*allen man is not simply an imperfect creature who needs improvement; he is a rebel who must lay down his arms. . . . This process of surrender—this movement full speed astern—is what Christians call repentance. Now repentance is no fun at all. It is something much harder than merely eating humble pie . . . It means killing part of yourself, undergoing a kind of death."

C . S . L e w i s

BOOK PROFILE: 1 JOHN

- Sent to Christians in Ephesus, in Asia (western Turkey), possibly circulated to churches throughout Asia
- The date is uncertain. Some believe between A.D. 60 and 65, while others believe later, between A.D. 80 and 90.
- Written to encourage and strengthen believers and churches in their Christian life
- Uses themes of light and darkness as metaphors for good/truth vs. bad/falsehood
- Focuses on the love of God for us and our need to love one another as proof of our love for God
- Emphasizes the need to obey God's commands
- Refutes false teachers who perhaps suggested that spirit was good and flesh was bad (Gnosticism) and perhaps that Jesus' humanity was not real and that he only appeared to have a physical body (Docetism)
- A highly personal letter in which John refers to his "little children" and his deep concern for their welfare

AUTHOR PROFILE: JOHN

- The apostle John, one of the original twelve disciples of Jesus, who also wrote the Gospel of John
- The disciple whom Jesus loved (John 21:20,24)
- One of the two sons of Zebedee; the brother of James
- Along with James, nicknamed "Sons of Thunder" (Mark 3:17)
- Formerly a follower of John the Baptist
- Wrote this epistle (letter) in his old age
- Known as the "Apostle of Love," since the theme of love is so prominent in his writings

CITY PROFILE: EPHESUS

- Population estimated at three hundred thousand
- Capital city of the province of Asia, in modern Turkey
- A leading trade center in the Roman Empire
- Center of worship of the pagan goddess Diana; the temple of Diana was one of the Seven Wonders of the Ancient World.
- A beautiful city, very sophisticated, wealthy, and pagan

 I N   A   N U T S H E L L

We proclaim truth to you about the word of life . . . truth that we have heard, seen, and touched. God is light, without any darkness, and his children should walk in light, not darkness. However, when we do sin and then confess our sin, God will forgive us and restore us to his fellowship.

God Requires Repentance for Fellowship

I. INTRODUCTION

Engel's Confession

*M*ichael Christopher's play, "The Black Angel," tells the story of Herman Engel, a German general during World War II. The Nuremberg Court sentenced him to thirty years in prison for the atrocities committed by his army. The play tells the story of a French journalist, Morrieaux, whose entire family had been massacred by Engle's army. For years Morrieaux had nurtured his hatred, and he hungered for vengeance. Upon Engle's release, Morrieaux had stoked up the fanatics who had also lost family and friends at Engel's hand. They established a plot to burn down the cabin that Engel was living in and to shoot him and his wife.

Morrieaux, however, wanted to get to Engel beforehand. He wanted to hear the whole story. He wanted Engel to confess to the wrong he had done. He arrived at the cabin early and spent the afternoon grilling Engel, trying to fill in the gaps. Engel's feeble humanity confused Morrieaux, for he seemed less like a monster and more like a tired old man.

So it was that doubt began to blur Morrieaux's vengeance, and the purity of his hatred was contaminated. But the wheels had already been put into motion. In a short time, the fanatics would be coming to burn the cabin. Finally, driven by his doubts, Morrieaux blurted out the plan and offered to lead Engel out of the woods and save his life.

Engel slowly replied, "I'll go with you on one condition."

A condition for having life saved? wondered Morrieaux to himself.

"I will go with you on the condition that you forgive me!"

Forgiveness! What a profound thing it is! If we are to experience a normal, satisfying life, we must be forgiven our wrongs. Unless we understand the power of this most unnatural act, our life will get bound up, like an overloaded washing machine, and become unable to continue normal motion. We get so constricted by unconfessed sin that we cannot relate properly to God and we cannot relate properly to others.

The first chapter of 1 John talks about the necessity to repent and be forgiven so that we can fellowship with God and other people. It tells us how we can be cleansed from our sins and freed to relate to God and others in close fellowship.

II. COMMENTARY

God Requires Repentance for Fellowship

> **MAIN IDEA:** *Jesus was a real man through whom we have fellowship with one another and with God. We must walk in his light, and we must confess our sin when we fail.*

A John's Testimony Regarding Jesus (vv. 1–4)

> **SUPPORTING IDEA:** *Complete joy comes through witnessing personally to our fellowship with God the Father and his Son Jesus Christ.*

1:1. Verses 1–4 form a prologue for 1 John, telling us that throughout the rest of the book John will proclaim to us what he has observed about Jesus, the Word of life. It begins in an odd way. He said he had **heard, seen,** and **touched** the **Word of life.** Why would John talk about hearing, seeing, and touching Jesus? The answer seems to be related to false teaching that his readers were hearing. More than likely, false teachers were suggesting that Jesus' physical body was not a normal body; or that he was an angel, not a man; or that his physical body was an illusion; or some other erroneous speculation. John met this false teaching head-on by saying that he had firsthand experience with Jesus, and based on that experience, he is telling us what he knows about Jesus.

That which was from the beginning might refer to Jesus' eternal coexistence with the Father, or to the beginning of creation (Gen. 1:1; John 1:1), but in light of the context, John was probably referring to the beginning of Jesus' ministry. It seems that false teachers had spread bad information about Jesus. However, John was with Jesus from the very beginning of his ministry on earth. Based on that firsthand experience, John determined to set the record straight. The false teachers, whom John called "antichrists," brought new ideas about Jesus, not ideas that could be verified, firsthand, from the beginning of Jesus' ministry. These false teachers apparently denied the incarnation (God's taking on human flesh in the person of Jesus), a fact that could easily be refuted by eyewitnesses, of whom John was one.

The Word of life might be a name or title for Jesus, as the translators of the NIV decided (since they capitalized Word), or it might mean "the message about life." Either interpretation is possible.

1:2. This life is **eternal**, was originally **with the Father**, and now has appeared on earth. This supports the historic Christian teaching that Jesus is coequal and coeternal with God the Father (as well as the Holy Spirit, who is not mentioned in this passage).

1:3. John proclaimed what he knew about Jesus **so that you also may have fellowship with us**. Since John made it clear in 2:12–14 that the readers of this letter were already believers, he was not referring to the fellowship with other Christians that begins at salvation. Rather, he was referring to the ongoing fellowship of people who are already believers. They needed to be sure of who Jesus was and of their salvation. If they doubted their salvation, their fellowship with the Father and Son would be limited. If Christians are not in fellowship with God, they cannot be in full fellowship with other devout Christians. Christian-with-Christian fellowship is rooted in fellowship with the **Father and with His Son, Jesus Christ**. Apparently, the false teachers had called into question the salvation of the readers, so John was reaffirming their faith.

1:4. The prologue concludes by linking John's own joy with the spiritual welfare of his readers. He reaffirmed these truths so that their joy could be made complete. John was so concerned about their welfare that he could not experience complete joy himself as long as they were struggling with doubt created by these false teachers. If the readers had their salvation reaffirmed, their joy would be made full, and in their joy, John's joy would be made full.

B The Foundation of Fellowship Is Repentance (1:5–2:2)

SUPPORTING IDEA: *Because God is light, his children must walk in light. If we claim to be without sin, we deceive ourselves; but if we confess our sins, we will be forgiven and purified.*

1:5. The message John declared is that **God is light** and **there is no darkness** in him at all. The word pictures *light* and *darkness* are common in John's writings. John 1:4–5 mentions Jesus as light: "In him was life, and that life was the light of men. The light shines in the darkness, but the darkness has not understood it." In a number of places, Jesus referred to himself as light (John 9:5; 12:35–36,46). John 8:12 gives his most direct statement: "I am the light of the world. Whoever follows me will never walk in darkness, but will have the light of life." Light is a picture of truth, knowledge, and righteousness, while darkness is a picture of falsehood, ignorance, and sin. John declared that God is light (truth, knowledge, and righteousness) and in him there is no darkness (falsehood, ignorance, and sin).

1:6. Since God is light and there is no darkness in him, no person can claim that he is living in full fellowship with God while walking in sin at the same time. If anyone makes that claim, he lies and is not living according to the truth.

1:7. On the other hand, when we walk in the light (live in light of truth, knowledge, and righteousness), two things happen. First, **we have fellowship**

with one another. Some commentators teach that the fellowship is with other Christians. If so, the sense would be, "If we walk in truth, knowledge, and righteousness, we have full fellowship with other Christians who do the same." On the other hand, other commentators reject that interpretation for grammatical reasons. The Greek pronoun for "one another" (*allelon*), they say, would normally refer to the two parties named in the first part of the statement (God and the Christian). If so, the sense would be, "If we walk in truth, knowledge, and righteousness, we have fellowship with God who is light and has no darkness."

The second thing that happens when we live in the light is that **the blood of Jesus, his Son, purifies us from all sin.** This strengthens the interpretation that the fellowship is between God and the Christian. It seems less connected to suggest that when we walk in the light, we have fellowship with Christians and the blood of Jesus purifies us from sin. It seems more natural to suggest that when we walk in the light, we have fellowship with God and are cleansed by God from every sin. It would certainly also be true that if we are walking in the light, we would have fellowship with other Christians, so no great doctrinal truth is lost regardless of which way this verse is interpreted.

To be "purified from all sin" does not suggest that if a believer does not walk in the light, his sins are not forgiven in the judicial sense. Nor does it mean that all believers are completely freed from all sin. Rather, the verb is in the present tense, suggesting a continuous and progressive action. It might include the forgiveness and purification from all past sin at the moment of salvation. But because of the present tense, it goes further to suggest that those who are walking in the light have sin's defilement removed and that they experience a progressive sanctification—a progressive character transformation into the image of Jesus.

All sin means every kind of sin and shows there is no limit to the categories of sin that Christ is willing to forgive. His sacrificial death made every type of sin forgivable.

1:8. We do not know if the false teachers were suggesting that the Ephesian believers were without sin, or if that is an error the Ephesian believers fell into by themselves. Either way, it needs to be corrected. A person might not be conscious of sin, but this does not mean he or she is free from it.

There are two kinds of sin—doing those things we ought not to do and not doing those things we should do. The longer we walk with Christ, the more likely it is that we will put aside more and more of the things we ought not to do. If we came to Christ as adults, we might be successful in putting away many of the overt sins we committed during our non-Christian days. We might no longer smoke and get drunk and curse and treat others abusively. We might go through a day or more in which we are not aware of committing an obvious sin.

On the other hand, when we grasp that we are to do all the things that Jesus would do if he were in our shoes, we fail continually. None of us loves perfectly as Jesus did. Therefore, we sin, because a failure to love perfectly is a sin. If we think we are without sin altogether, we are deceived and we live a lie.

1:9. John comforts us, however, with the truth that even though we have sin in our lives, we can still be purified from this sin and maintain our fellowship with God (and resultant fellowship with other believers).

Scholars offer two major interpretations of this verse. The first possible meaning is that this confession refers to the confession of sin at salvation. It is a once-for-all confession that solves the problem of eternal judgment for sin. The reasoning is that if it referred to sins we commit after salvation, we might die after we commit a sin but before we confess it. Therefore, that sin would be unforgiven, since this verse teaches that we are not forgiven until we confess. If so, we would go to hell. Since the Bible doesn't seem to allow a person to lose his or her salvation, the reasoning goes, it must be referring to confession at salvation.

Others take this interpretation a step further and teach that a Christian does not have to confess his sins and ask forgiveness from God after he has become a Christian because a believer already has forgiveness in Christ (Eph. 1:7). Many Christians, according to this understanding, spend too much time in morbid introspection. They wonder if they have confessed all their sins and if they are in fellowship with God or not. They never experience freedom in Christ. This is needless, since Christ has already granted us forgiveness. We do not have to keep track of our sins and confess them. We just have to live under the realization that our sins are already forgiven, enjoying our freedom in Christ.

It is true that all our sins are forgiven at the moment of salvation in the sense that none of our sins after salvation will keep us out of heaven. In that sense, all of our sins are forgiven, and we will never have to pay the penalty for those sins. This is the teaching of Ephesians 1:7.

This does not mean, however, that if a person sins after salvation he will go to hell. Verse 7 says that **if we walk in the light**—if we are saved, if we are children of light—then the blood of Jesus cleanses us from all sin.

This does not mean we no longer have to ask for forgiveness from God for our sins. This interpretation seems to miss the point given to us by our Lord in the disciple's prayer (Matt. 6:11–12). Jesus taught his disciples to pray, "Forgive us our debts" (trespasses). This is a needless instruction if we need not ask for forgiveness after our salvation.

This interpretation is contrary to our human experience. Yes, in a loving relationship we often get forgiveness before we ask for it, or without asking for it. But the healthy, sensitive, intimate relationships tend to be those in which the guilty person readily asks forgiveness from the offended party, not because forgiveness must be given or else the relationship will be broken, but because it is the loving and sensitive thing to do. It is careless and insensitive not to ask forgiveness for our sin against someone else, even though we may feel assured of receiving it.

The forgiveness John talks about in 1:9 can be understood as parental or familial forgiveness, not judicial forgiveness. That is, we all receive judicial forgiveness one time when we receive Jesus as our personal Savior (Eph. 1:7; Rom. 5:6–11). We were, at that time, saved from the penalty of our sins. It is called judicial forgiveness because it is granted by God acting as a judge. After our salvation, we still sin (Phil. 3:12; Jas. 3:2,8; 4:17). This sin does not cause us to lose our salvation (Rom. 8:37–39), but it does break the fellowship between us and God, just as the sin of a child or a spouse breaks the fellowship with parents or a mate.

We confess our sin out of respect and love for the person we have sinned against. God forgives our sin, purifies us from all unrighteousness, and restores us to his fellowship. We need *judicial* forgiveness only once. We need *parental* or *familial* forgiveness whenever we sin.

The NIV translation, **will forgive us our sins**, is a valid translation, but the word *our* is not in the Greek text. Literally, it reads, "will forgive us the sins." It is possible to translate this as an article of previous reference, which contrasts "forgive us the sins" with **all unrighteousness**, which follows it. According to Hodges,

> John's thought might be paraphrased, "If we confess our sins, he ... will forgive the sins we confess and moreover will even cleanse us from all unrighteousness." Naturally, only God knows at any moment the full extent of a person's unrighteousness. Each Christian, however, is responsible to acknowledge (the meaning of "confess," *homologomen;* compare 2:23; 4:3) whatever the light makes him aware of, and when he does so, a complete and perfect cleansing is granted him. There is thus no need to agonize over sins of which one is unaware (Zane C. Hodges, *The Bible Knowledge Commentary, New Testament,* 886).

God's forgiveness of our sin under these conditions is based on his justice. He is just and will forgive our sins. We might expect that forgiveness in this instance is based on God's mercy, but it is based on his justice. God is just because Jesus paid the penalty for our sin when he died on the cross. God has promised to forgive our sins in Christ (2:2) when we confess them, and he will abide by his promises.

1:10. A number of verses in the Bible tell us that we will sin after conversion (Phil. 3:12; Jas. 2:10; 3:2,8; 4:17). Because a Christian will sin after salvation, he should not deny his sin. If he does, he makes God out to be a liar.

When a Christian realizes, through the convicting ministry of the Holy Spirit, that he has sinned, he should agree with God about his sin, confess it, and receive the restoration to fellowship that is promised in the previous verse.

2:1–2. Most Bible teachers agree that the first two verses of chapter 2 conclude the discussion of chapter 1. John does not change subjects until verse 3. Therefore, we will deal with those verses in this chapter.

We see in this chapter a delicate balancing act between feeling forgiven and feeling free to sin. The apostle John says in 1:9 that if we confess our sins, we will be forgiven. We have no reason to be buried with guilt because of our inability to eradicate sin in our lives. Just because Jesus is willing to forgive our sins doesn't mean we can feel free to keep on sinning. This Scripture is written so we won't sin. "Do your best not to sin," we might paraphrase, "but if you do, you have help."

Dear children signifies a fond affection for the people to whom John wrote this letter. The exhortation to **walk in the light** encourages us not to sin. But we will. All is not lost when we do sin. Jesus is our advocate, one who speaks to the Father in our behalf, as a defense attorney would argue our case before a judge.

The advocate speaks with extraordinary authority before the judge, however, because his defense for us is that he, the defense attorney, has already paid any price the judge could impose. The willingness of the judge to forego judgment is not based on the life of the one on trial (us), but rather on the merits of Jesus' sacrifice. Jesus sacrificed his life in our place. He paid the price for our sin with his death. He is our atoning sacrifice (sacrifice that pays the price and allows forgiveness).

Jesus' atoning sacrifice is sufficient not only for our sins, but also for the sins of the whole world. Does this mean that everyone is saved? No, the Bible makes it clear that not everyone will be saved (Matt. 7:14; 1 Cor. 6:9; Gal. 5:21). But anyone who hears the gospel can be saved if he or she wants to be (Rev. 22:17).

> **MAIN IDEA REVIEW:** *Jesus was a real man through whom we have fellowship with one another and with God. We must walk in his light, and we must confess our sin when we fail.*

III. CONCLUSION

You Are Sick unto Death

C. S. Lewis wrote about our need to repent and our need for forgiveness:

> If the universe is not governed by an absolute goodness, then all our efforts are in the long run, hopeless. But if it is, then we are making

ourselves enemies to that goodness every day, and are not in the least likely to do any better tomorrow, and so our case is hopeless again.

Christianity tells people to repent and promises them forgiveness. It therefore has nothing (as far as I know) to say to people who do not know that they need any forgiveness. It is after you have realised that there is a real Moral Law, and Power behind the law, and that you have broken that law and put yourself wrong with that Power—it is after all this, and not a moment sooner, that Christianity begins to talk. When you are sick, you will listen to the doctor (C. S. Lewis, *Mere Christianity*, 38–39).

This chapter of 1 John says, "You are sick. You need a doctor. If you don't get one, you will die!" In other words, you are a sinner. You must repent. Jesus will forgive your sins. He will make you well. To deny this is to make God a liar. There is little doubt about the need for repentance. It is the foundation for all relationships, human and divine.

PRINCIPLES

- Christianity is not founded on speculation but on historical events (we have heard, seen, touched the Word of life).
- Fellowship with God and other Christians is based on a correct understanding of who Jesus is.
- Light equals truth, knowledge, and righteousness. Darkness equals falsehood, ignorance, and sin.
- Christians are to walk in light, not darkness.
- If we claim to be without sin, it is a sign that we are walking in darkness.
- Confession of sin allows us to continue to walk in light.

APPLICATIONS

- Base your commitment to Christ on credible historical events (the life of Jesus, his resurrection, the spread of the church, etc.).
- Commit to walking in the light, not the darkness (Rom. 12:1–2).
- Confess the sin that the Holy Spirit convicts you of.
- Accept and rest in the forgiveness that God offers you.

IV. LIFE APPLICATION

Corrie's Cold Heart

To confess our sins means, literally, "to say the same thing" (*homologeo*: *homos* = same; *lego* = to speak) that God says about them. When the Holy

Spirit convicts us of sin, we agree that it is sin and that we should forsake it. This is the basis of fellowship with God and other Christians. A powerful example of this is seen in the life of Corrie ten Boom, a Christian woman who lived in Holland during World War II and whose family was involved in hiding Jews fleeing from the Nazis in Germany.

Corrie and her family suffered terribly at the hands of the Nazis. Her sister died in a Nazi concentration camp, and Corrie herself spent many harrowing years in the same camp. When she was released, she committed her life to spreading the message of forgiveness through Jesus to all people. In her book, *Tramp for the Lord,* she records a powerful example of how lack of repentance and forgiveness allows walls to exist between Christian and Christian and between a Christian and God.

Corrie went to Munich with the message that God forgives, a much-needed message in that defeated and disillusioned nation. After speaking in a basement room, with solemn faces staring back at her, not quite daring to believe this unbelievable message, she saw one of the most cruel guards in all the prison camp coming toward her. In an instant, her mind was flooded with flashbacks of a blue uniform and a visored cap with the skull and crossbones, a huge room with harsh overhead lights, a pathetic pile of dresses and shoes in the center of the floor. Following hard were a flood of emotions . . . the shame of walking naked past this man. She could see her sister's frail form ahead of her, ribs sharp beneath the parchment skin. Finally, this former prison guard stood in front of her, his hand out in friendship.

"A fine message, Fraulein!" he declared. "How good it is to know that, as you say, all our sins are at the bottom of the sea!"

Corrie continued the story, in her own words:

> And I who had spoken so glibly of forgiveness, fumbled in my pocketbook rather than take that hand. He would not remember me, of course—how could he remember one prisoner among thousands of women?
>
> But I remembered him and the leather crop swinging from his belt. I was face-to-face with one of my captors and my blood seemed to freeze.
>
> "You mentioned Ravensbruck in your talk," he was saying. "I was a guard there." No, he did not remember me.
>
> "But since that time," he went on, "I have become a Christian. I know that God has forgiven me for the cruel things I did there, but I would like to hear it from your lips as well. Fraulein"—again the hand came out—"will you forgive me?"

And I stood there—I whose sins had again and again to be for-given—and could not forgive. Betsie had died in that place; could he erase her slow terrible death simply for the asking?

It could not have been many seconds that he stood there—hand held out—but to me it seemed hours as I wrestled with the most dif-ficult thing I had ever had to do.

Corrie knew that she would have to forgive. Jesus said, "If you do not for-give men their trespasses, neither will your Father in heaven forgive your trespasses." She knew this, not only as a command, but as an utter necessity. The victims of Nazi brutality who were able to forgive their tormentors were able to heal and get on with life, no matter how bad the physical scars. Those who didn't, couldn't.

She knew that forgiveness was an act of the will, not of the emotions, so she prayed for help. Then, she lifted her hand, woodenly, mechanically. As she did, the Lord filled her heart with forgiveness and love for her former captor. Warmth filled her heart as tears filled her eyes. "I forgive you, brother!" she cried. "With all my heart" (Corrie ten Boom, 55–57).

Yes, we must forgive if we are to retain our fellowship with God and with other Christians who have wronged us. But we must also forgive if we are to keep from drying up spiritually. If we do not forgive, we lose three ways. We lose our fellowship with God; we lose our fellowship with other Christians; and we lose our own spiritual vitality. How important it is when the Bible tells us that when we confess our sins, God is faithful and just to forgive our sins and to purify us from all unrighteousness.

V. PRAYER

Dear Father in heaven, help us to accept your grace to confess our sins, to repent of them and walk in the light. Help us to accept the truth when your Holy Spirit convicts us of sin, and to take the only way out . . . to accept the only remedy—forgiveness. Thank you for your mercy, that you do not leave us to wallow in our sins, but you lift us up out of the "miry clay" to walk in fellowship with you and others. Amen.

VI. DEEPER DISCOVERIES

A. Gnosticism

Gnosticism may have had a significant role in the writing of the First Epistle of John. Gnosticism was a heresy in its infant stages during the years when the New Testament was written, and a number of books in the New Testament spend some time refuting Gnosticism or the teachings that led to

Gnosticism in later years. Therefore, an overview understanding of this false teaching can be very helpful in understanding not only 1 John but other books in the New Testament as well.

- "Gnosticism" comes from the Greek word "to know."
- The teachings of the Gnostics had two major features:

  (1) Salvation was found in a higher, spiritual knowledge. Those who entered into this knowledge were considered "enlightened ones." Ordinary people, even Christians, did not have this knowledge. They had to get it through mystical ways.

  (2) Spirit and flesh were thought of as separate entities. Spirit was good; flesh was bad. The spirit was untouched by fleshly influences, no matter what the flesh did. Therefore, the flesh could sin at will if it desired, and the spirit was unaffected. Therefore, a Gnostic could live a very immoral lifestyle and still claim to be a spiritual person.

Gnosticism was rooted in ancient Greek philosophy (Plato and Philo). When the church spread from Jerusalem to Greece, it inevitably encountered this philosophy. Gnostics did not see how a good God could have created an evil physical world, so they concocted a worldview that absolved God of any responsibility for this world by separating the spiritual world from the physical world.

Another teaching, Docetism, was related to Gnosticism. "Docetism" comes from the Greek word "to seem." Docetics taught that it was impossible for God, who was spirit (good), to take on a physical (bad) body, so they asserted that Jesus did not have a real physical body, but only *seemed* to have a physical body. Still others believed that the power of Christ came upon Jesus when he was baptized and departed from him before his death on the cross. So it was simply the man Jesus who died, not God in the flesh.

Whatever form of Gnosticism or variation existed, it struck at the very heart of the Christian faith by denying the physical death and resurrection of Jesus, the God-Man. Therefore, salvation did not come through the substitutionary atonement of Christ for our sins, but through gaining the mystical, special knowledge of God.

B. Light/Darkness (vv. 5–7)

Light and darkness are prominent themes for the apostle John. They are powerful pictures of the warfare between good and evil waged in every human heart. In the Bible, light is always used as a picture of God and his truth, understanding, and righteousness. Psalm 27:1 says, "The LORD is my light." Psalm 104:2 describes the Lord who "wraps himself in light." Jesus said, "I am the light of the world" (John 8:12).

These references make it clear that God is the ultimate source of truth, understanding, and righteousness. The Word of God is a "lamp to my feet and a light for my path" (Ps. 119:105). When we walk in physical darkness, we are in danger of stepping into a hole or bumping our heads or getting lost. Just a little light from a flashlight (modern lamp) lets us avoid all these dangers. The same is true with God and the light his Word sheds in our lives. We can avoid accidents or getting lost by doing what the Bible says (that is, walking in the light).

"Light has come into the world, but men loved darkness instead of light because their deeds were evil" (John 3:19). When we walk in darkness, we live in falsehood, misunderstanding, and sin. However, this passage teaches us that if we remain in darkness, it is because we do not want to walk in the light. The light exposes our motives and actions for what they are. We do not like this because we want to continue in our sin. Each person is confronted many times daily with opportunities to choose to walk in light (truth, understanding, and righteousness) or darkness (falsehood, misunderstanding, and sin).

C. Fellowship (vv. 3,6,7)

Fellowship is a prominent theme in chapter 1 of John's first epistle. Such fellowship may take place both between a Christian and God and between a Christian and another Christian. "Fellowship" (*koinonia*) means to share in common, to participate, to experience unity.

Other Scriptures refer to our fellowship with God. First Corinthians 1:9 tells us that we have fellowship with Jesus Christ our Lord when we are saved. First Corinthians 9:23 tells us that when we dedicate ourselves to sharing the gospel as effectively as we know how, we share (have fellowship) in the blessings of the gospel. Believers also fellowship with the Holy Spirit (2 Cor. 13:14), which is important for spiritual unity in the church (Phil. 2:1–4). Finally, we commune (have fellowship) with the body and blood of Jesus in the Lord's Supper (1 Cor. 10:16). When we participate in the Lord's Supper, we enter into communion or participation with the death and resurrection of Jesus.

The fellowship we have with the Lord is intended to produce fellowship with other Christians: "Because there is one loaf, we, who are many, are one body, for we all partake of the one loaf" (1 Cor. 10:17). Since we are one with Jesus, as symbolized by communion, so we are one with all other Christians. One loaf is a symbol of one body.

Fellowship with other Christians means more than just having coffee and donuts together. Fellowship involves practical considerations. First, it brings basic doctrinal agreement and interpersonal peace (Eph. 4:1–6). Second, just as Jesus gave himself completely for the sake of his body, the church, so are we to give ourselves for the sake of one another (Col. 1:24). Finally, we are to share financially with one another—and by implication, whatever we have to share with others in need. Paul used *koinonia* to refer to the financial contribution he was collecting from Gentile Christians for the sake of needy Christians in Jerusalem (2 Cor. 8:4; 9:13). "For if the Gentiles have shared in the Jews' spiritual blessings, they owe it to the Jews to share with them their material blessings" (Rom. 15:27).

We see from these references that fellowship—which means participation or to share in common—is much broader than the American concept of fellowship, in which we get together in a social setting to enjoy one another's company. Rather, Christian fellowship means we share in one another's lives. It is a matter of the will rather than our emotions. For example, the apostle Paul said, concerning James—the Lord's brother—Peter, and John that they "gave me . . . the right hand of fellowship" (*koinonia*), and this happened right after a hotly debated controversy involving legalism and the status of Gentiles in the church (Gal. 2:1–10). Fellowship is serious business in the church.

D. Confess (v. 9)

Confess (from two Greek words, *homos,* "the same" and *lego,* "to speak") means, literally, "to speak the same thing." It carries the idea of agreeing with, or admitting to. To confess our sins means we are to say the same thing about the sin as God says—to agree with God about the sins—that they are wrong and need to be abandoned. True confession calls sin the same thing God calls it: envy, jealousy, lust, hatred, deceit, greed. In confession we admit with God that sin is wrong. We agree with God that we must abandon the sin. We recognize with God that this sin *by itself,* if there had been no other sin in all the world, would have been enough to drive the nails through Jesus' hands and feet and hang him on the cross.

Confession is no small thing. It is not a matter of praying a poetic prayer or making excuses about our lives. We do not pray, "O Lord, if I've done anything that is wrong, I'm sorry." Rather, we pray, "O Lord, I have sinned by (name the sin). This sin cost Jesus his life. I accept your judgment about it, that it is wrong, and I need to turn from it. Please forgive me and restore me to fellowship with you. Thank you for your mercy, grace, and love."

Confession is a reality check. It connects us with our inability to save ourselves, with God's gracious willingness to do so, with the enormous price that had to be paid in order to do so, and with the gratitude that should flow as a result.

VII. TEACHING OUTLINE

A. INTRODUCTION

1. Lead Story: Engle's Confession

2. Context: The first chapter of 1 John tells us that, contrary to claims by false teachers, John had seen, heard, and touched Jesus. John, not false teachers, can give us an authoritative account of Jesus' life and ministry. John proclaims this Jesus, so that we can have true fellowship with God and with other Christians who accept the truth about Jesus. The beginning point of fellowship with God and other Christians is recognizing that we need to walk in light rather than darkness. If, however, we do sin, when we confess our sins, God is faithful and just and will forgive our sin.

3. Transition: As we look into this chapter, we will get a picture of our need to walk in light and keep short accounts with God. We can know the joy of fellowship with God and other Christians based on a pure heart.

B. COMMENTARY

1. John Gave His Testimony About Jesus (vv. 1–4)
2. The Foundation of Fellowship Is Repentance (1:5–2:2)

C. CONCLUSION: CORRIE'S COLD HEART

VIII. ISSUES FOR DISCUSSION

1. What convinces you that Jesus really lived as a human being on this earth?
2. Define Christian fellowship. With whom do you have such fellowship? What does it mean to your life?
3. What does it mean to you that God is light?
4. How can you walk in the light? Does this mean you will never sin?
5. What is involved in confessing sin? What results from true confession?

1 John 2

Faithful Christians Must Accept God and Reject the World

I N   A   N U T S H E L L

If you know God, you must obey him and live as Jesus did. You must also love your Christian brother. Anyone who hates his brother is still walking in darkness. On the other hand, you must not love the world, which is passing away. Nor are you to listen to false teachers, antichrists, who deny the Son. Cling confidently to the truth.

Faithful Christians Must Accept God and Reject the World

I. INTRODUCTION

The Grumpy Monk

*I*t is very difficult to avoid the "lure" of the world. It encroaches on us even when we have made a concerted effort to resist its pull. A man who had grown weary of the constant pressure to "keep up with the Joneses" decided to get away from it all, so he joined a mute monastery. It was a very demanding commitment. Monks could only say two words every five years. For the first fifteen years, monks were on trial. If they were successful in meeting the requirements of the monastery during this fifteen-year trial period, then they could take final vows.

Perfect, the man thought. *No phones to ring. No clients to call on. No credit cards to pay off. This is just what I need.* So he joined as a novitiate (someone on trial) and for the first five years didn't say a word. At the end of that time, he was called into his superior's office where he was told he could say two words.

"Bad food!" he complained.

"Thank you, I'll make a note of your observation," his superior said, rather stiffly.

The man went back to his duties as a novitiate and for another five years didn't utter a word. At the end of that time, his superior asked him if he had anything he would like to say in two words.

The man replied, "Hard bed!"

For another five years he said not a word. His superior called him in and asked him if he had anything to say and if he were ready to take his final vows.

The man stood up and said, "I quit!"

His superior replied, "Well, I'm not surprised. You've done nothing but complain since you got here!"

Even joining a monastery to get away from all temptation doesn't protect us from the world. Our desire for the world is in our hearts, and the outside temptations only give opportunity for the heart to reveal itself. If we are going to conquer worldliness, we must do so from the inside out.

The second chapter of 1 John addresses the issue of worldliness, indicating that we must love God and we must not love the world. They are different sides of the same coin of Christian faithfulness.

II. COMMENTARY

Faithful Christians Must Accept God and Reject the World

MAIN IDEA: *Those who claim to know God must obey him and live as Jesus lived. What's more, they must demonstrate their love of God by loving their Christian brothers. On the other hand, they must not love the world, and they must reject false teachers who deny the Son.*

A Those Who Know God Must Obey Him (vv. 3–6)

SUPPORTING IDEA: *We demonstrate that we know God when we keep his commandments.*

2:3–4. To understand this letter, we must be continually reminded that it seeks to correct problems of belief and behavior of Christians in Ephesus. Every word of the letter comes in response to something that the church needed to hear. Verse 3 tells believers how we can know if we are, indeed, Christians. We know we are Christians **if we obey his commands**.

Apparently, some people in Ephesus claimed to know God, but they made no effort to keep God's commands. The religion that came to be known as Gnosticism prided itself in knowing God through mystical enlightenment, though that knowledge had no bearing on their moral behavior. They had no understanding that sin was a barrier to their relationship with God. John set them straight about this claim: "If you know God, you keep his commandments, and if you make no effort to keep his commandments, but still claim to be a Christian, you are a liar."

This distinction is comforting when we look at extreme sin, assuming we are not involved in extreme sin. It makes it plain that those who clearly live like the devil can make no claim to be Christian. However, it is very discomforting when we consider more subtle sin. How obedient do we have to be? I violated one of God's commands just last night. Am I a Christian, or am I a liar? Must we obey all commands perfectly? If that is the case, are any of us saved?

Clearly, the Bible is not saying that we have to exhibit perfect obedience. First John 1:8 just told us that if we claim to be without sin, we deceive ourselves and make God out to be a liar. The issue appears to be whether or not we take God's commandments seriously and are trying to keep them. We may not keep them perfectly. We may not even have a perfectly consistent desire to keep them. But if we are truly born again, we will not live our lives in disregard for God's commands. The Gnostics, it can be assumed, weren't even trying to keep God's commands. It is their behavior that the Bible condemns. (See Deeper Discoveries for a fuller discussion of this issue.)

2:5–6. The apostle now reassures us. If we take seriously the commands of God and desire to keep them, we can be sure we know God. Then **God's love is truly made complete** in us.

Bible teachers disagree about the meaning of **God's love.** Does it mean the love of God for the Christian, or the Christian's love for God? Either interpretation is possible, and neither dramatically changes the understanding of the passage. **Made complete** probably means "mature," not "perfect" as some people have concluded. John Wesley, the founder of the Methodist denomination, believed it meant that a Christian could grow spiritually to the point where he or she loved perfectly. Others believe that the strongest evidence against this interpretation, besides our own observation of the lives of Christians, seems to be 1 John 1:8 where the apostle has already said we will continue to sin.

The verse concludes: **This is how we know we are in him**. Unfortunately, we don't know if "this" refers backwards to "God's love being made complete in us," or forwards to "walking as Jesus walked." Again, it doesn't make much difference. The NIV has translated it so that it refers forward, and that is certainly an acceptable interpretation.

Ⓑ Those Who Know God Must Love Their Brother (vv. 7–11)

SUPPORTING IDEA: *Anyone who claims to live in the light but still hates his brother is not living in the light but in darkness.*

2:7–8. The apostle now reminds us of a new/old commandment, making a potentially confusing play on words. One command is at the same time both old and new. The command is that we should love one another. This command is found in the Old Testament (Lev. 19:18) as well as in the Gospels (John 15:12; 13:34). In that sense, it can be understood as an old command. However, the same command can also be understood as a new command in the sense that there is now new evidence and new power to fulfill it. The new *evidence* is that Jesus has died, been buried, and risen again. We have seen the complete example he came to show us (1 Pet. 2:21), and now we have a better understanding of what love looks like than we did in Leviticus or the Gospels.

The new *power* is the Holy Spirit indwelling true believers, helping them to live out the commands of Scripture. In addition, the church has now gathered together to help stimulate one another to love and good deeds. Through the love Christians can show for one another, we demonstrate to the world that the light which Jesus brought into the world continues to shine in the darkness.

2:9-11. The imagery of light and darkness continues, stating that a person cannot walk in light and darkness at the same time. If he **hates his brother**, he walks in **darkness**. If he **loves his brother**, he walks in **light**. This is not claiming that we need to be fond of every other Christian or emotionally bonded to all believers. Love (*agape*) can be understood as the steady direction of the will for the good of another. We are not commanded to "feel" a certain way toward others, but only to "act" properly toward them. Understood this way, when we act properly toward our Christian brothers, out of a desire to be obedient to God, we love them.

Some interpreters have accused John of less than Christian values for not teaching here that we ought to love not just our Christian brothers but even our enemies, as Jesus taught. John certainly didn't disagree with Jesus' teaching. His point in this book, however, was specifically to address a situation which the Ephesian Christians faced—a person claiming to be a Christian but refusing to love his fellow Christians.

C Those Who Love God Must Not Love the World (vv. 12-17)

SUPPORTING IDEA: *Your sins have been forgiven, and you have overcome the evil one. Do not love the world, for if you love the world, the love of the Father is not in you.*

2:12-14. These verses are difficult to understand, and they do not have a strong connection with what went before or what comes after. After the stern warning up to this point, these verses seem to be reassuring us that we are in fact Christians. They contrast the spiritual status of the believers with the assessment of the self-praising false teachers. Apparently, these teachers claimed that ordinary believers did not really know God because they had not received special knowledge of him through mystical means. If so, the following warning not to love the world (vv. 15-17) might also be prompted by these same false teachers who did love the world.

John addressed three sets of readers, **dear children**, **fathers**, and **young men**. Some believe this to be a division by chronological age, and others think it to be a division by spiritual maturity. Still others find both of these interpretations inconsistent, since "fathers" is out of expected sequence, being in the middle. Elsewhere the letter addresses all readers as "children" (2:1,28; 3:7,18; 5:21). As a result, many Bible teachers believe that each of the terms refers to all the readers. They were all "dear children," "fathers," and "young men."

This interpretation has more support. Often, when a Bible author contrasts ages (young/old), he does so as a figure of speech to denote young, old, and everyone in between. Joel, quoted by Luke in Acts 2:28, speaks of old men dreaming dreams and young men seeing visions—a poetic way of saying that dreams and visions will be experienced by young, old, and everyone in between. If this principle of interpretation is accepted for verses 12–14, then whatever is said of each age category is intended to be true for all believers.

If so, then like children, all of them had experienced the forgiveness of sins and all of them had known their heavenly Father. Like fathers, they had all known him who is from the beginning. That is, they had truly known and experienced fellowship with God. Like young men, all of them had engaged in spiritual warfare and had overcome the evil one, the devil, and had grown strong, perhaps *because* of the Word (**you are strong, and the word of God lives in you**).

2:15–17. To summarize, John seems to make it clear that his readers were Christians. They were **my dear children** (2:1) and **dear friends** (4:1). Verses 12–14 again call them dear children, fathers, and young men, who have experienced forgiveness, knowledge of God, and victory in spiritual battle. Far from calling into question their salvation or expressing dissatisfaction with their spiritual growth, John seems to reassure them of their salvation. Having reassured them, he then warned them against false teaching and dangers from the world.

Not only are they to love God and their brothers; they are not to **love the world**. The *world* (*kosmos*) in this context refers to the attitudes and values that disregard God or are blatantly against God. It certainly does not refer to God's natural creation or even humanity (we are to love the people in the world for whom Christ died, as God does, John 3:16), but to that part of human affairs that are under the authority of the devil (John 12:31; 1 John 5:19; Eph. 2:1–2). We love the people of the world, but we do not love the sinful attitudes and values they may embrace.

If we love the world, the love of the Father is not in us. This is a difficult statement. Does it mean that if we do love the world, God does not love us (love of the Father = the love which God has for us), or does it mean we do not love God (love of the Father = our love for God)? Good Bible students stand on both sides of this question. The context leads me to favor the latter. If we love the world, we are not loving God. We cannot love the world and love God at the same time. This interpretation is strengthened by James 4:4, "Friendship with the world is hatred toward God."

2:16. The reason we are not to love the world is that the world's values are in opposition to God. **The cravings of sinful man** are the sinful interests and desires that draw us away from God. **The lust of** [the] **eyes** refers to sinful desires that corrupt us. The eye is often used as a figure of speech to refer to sinful passions (Matt. 5:28).

When Eve looked at the forbidden fruit, it was "pleasing to the eye." David's sin with Bathsheba started when he looked on Bathsheba taking a bath (2 Sam. 11:2). It might be translated, "the desires that originate in what we see." **The boasting of what he has and does** refers to the arrogance and pride that can overtake us as we try to "get ahead of the Joneses" and when we rely on ourselves rather than God for our material possessions and worldly positions.

These values are foolish for two reasons. First, they do not come **from the Father**. Therefore, they interfere with our fellowship with the Father. Second, we are all going to die, and what we are living for will come to nothing. The well-known saying of slain missionary Jim Elliot seems appropriate here: "He is no fool who gives up what he cannot keep to get what he cannot lose."

We might paraphrase this whole passage: "Do not embrace the world's ways or goods. When you do, it squeezes out your love for God. When you live for 'getting your own way,' and for 'getting everything you want,' and for 'looking good compared to others,' you are not living for God but for the world. This is foolish because it suffocates your relationship with God, and in the end, it will all go up in smoke anyway."

D Those Who Love God Must Reject False Teachers (vv. 18–29)

> **SUPPORTING IDEA:** Antichrists (those who deny that Jesus is the Christ) are in the world now. You have an anointing of the Holy Spirit and don't need to listen to their lies. Just continue to listen to what you have heard from the very beginning, and you will be all right.

2:18–19. It is **the last hour**. This is the only time this phrase occurs in the New Testament, and it is not clear what it means. A strong likelihood is that "the last hour" refers to the time between the first coming of Christ and his second coming. Some believe it means there was only a little time left before Jesus would return, in which case John would have been mistaken.

Therefore, it seems preferable to equate the "last hour" with the "last days," in which God's plan of salvation directly through Christ is inaugurated (Acts 2:17; Joel 2:28; Mic. 4:1). From these passages we learn that the end has come, but the end is not a short period of time. Rather, the end is a distinct period of time of uncertain length. The time of Adam was not the last hour. The time of Abraham was not the last hour. Nor was the time of Moses, or the time of David, or the time of Ezra the last hour. The time between Jesus' first coming and second coming is the last hour.

The readers knew about the predicted coming of the Antichrist. John warned them about the coming of many who would display the same hostility and opposition to Jesus. Not only is the Antichrist coming, but many antichrists (people who embrace his values and agenda) are already here.

The fact that the antichrists have come proves that the **last hour** had begun. Some people in the church followed the antichrists, leaving the church. This proved that they had never been Christians. If they had been, they would not have left. Apparently, they had made a profession of faith that was not genuine.

2:20–23. We have an **anointing from the Holy One**. This anointing might be either the Holy Spirit, or the Word of God, or some body of information/knowledge passed down to the elders in the church from apostles.

The first impulse is to understand the anointing to be the Holy Spirit. After all, Jesus was anointed by the Holy Spirit, and the Gospel of John teaches us that Jesus will send us the "Spirit of truth" (John 14:17) who "will teach you all things" (John 14:26).

The second impulse reveals some significant problems with this interpretation, however. It does not tell us how the Spirit enables us to understand all things. Is it by some inner guidance, an internal, subjective experience? This seems a little out of harmony with the context, because John has appealed all along to hard facts that they have been taught from the beginning. In addition, it would invite the false teachers to counter that their own inner, subjective experience was just as valid. Plus, this interpretation does not explain the tremendous disagreement that exists among professing Christians regarding what is true and what is not true. If the anointing is inner guidance from the Holy Spirit, would he not guide us to be a little more united in this matter?

Other Bible teachers suggest that this anointing refers to the Bible, or a body of teaching passed down to the church leaders. This has the advantage of correcting the problem in the first option, eliminating the danger of spiritual subjectivism. Plus, the Word of God can be understood to "remain in you." It has the disadvantage that the Word of God is not usually understood to be an anointing. Perhaps it is a subtle combination of the two ideas. The anointing could be understood as God's Word, "not as preached externally in the community, but as it is received by faith into men's hearts and remains active, thanks to the work of the Spirit" (I. Howard Marshall, *The Epistles of John,* [Grand Rapids: Eerdmans, 1978], p. 155). If so, the antidote to false teaching is the Word of God, administered and confirmed by the work of the Holy Spirit.

No tidy answer presents itself. I prefer this latter explanation, cumbersome as it is, because of the problems created if it is understood to be the Holy Spirit. As Stephen Smalley concludes:

John is deliberately using the idea of *chrisma* [anointing, consecration] to signify *both* the Spirit and the word of God. The faithful, that is to say, are those who have (inwardly) received the gospel of truth, and made it their own *through* the activity of the Spirit (cf. 1 Thess. 1:5–6); thereby they possess the antidote to heresy. . . . It is possible that some of the heretical and schismatic members of John's church had appealed directly to the teaching of the Gospel on the Paraclete [John 14:17; 15:26; 16:13], as the Spirit of truth, precisely in order to support their own claims to possess the right knowledge of Jesus and his gospel. If so, John is indicating that the objective word of God's truth cannot be detached from the interior testimony of the Holy Spirit, present in the believer (WBC 51, 107).

When we as believers have received this anointing, then **all of you know the truth**. This phrase strengthens the option that the anointing is the Word of God. If we have a mature knowledge of the Bible, it can be said that we know the truth. Admittedly, there is plenty of disagreement about things in the Bible, but there is also much more agreement. The truth is not available only to a select few, as the Gnostics taught, but to everyone. This is not a promise of total knowledge. Anointed believers do not know all the truth there is to know. Rather, they know the truth about the inaccurate information the false teachers were spreading. They know the truth regarding the disputed issues. They need no further insight, as the Gnostics claimed.

This reinforces the truth that truly anointed Christians already believe. The false teachers (antichrists) are liars because they deny that **Jesus is the Christ**, that is, they deny that Jesus is the divine Son of God. This denial also constitutes a denial of the Father. Their claim to be in fellowship with the Father cannot be true since they are not in fellowship with his Son. A person cannot have the Father without having the Son, nor can he or she have the Son without having the Father. To accept or reject one is to accept or reject the other.

2:24–25. The false teachers have brought forth radically new teaching based on their "secret" knowledge. That is unnecessary. John's word is nothing new but what they have heard from the beginning. He challenges us to hold fast to the tried and true Word of God delivered once and for all to the saints. If we do, we will remain, or abide (in the sense of fellowship) in the Son and in the Father. Only then can we rest in the promise of eternal life.

The issue here is not a concern about losing our salvation. We can be certain that we possess eternal life (2:1–6; 5:9–13,20). The issue is reassurance in face of the false teaching they were receiving. False teaching brings questions about our salvation; true teaching based on God's Word from the beginning reassures us of our salvation.

2:26–27. I am writing these things to you about those who are trying to lead you astray: Apparently, the false teachers denied that the readers of John's letter were actually saved. Such false teachers can be disregarded. Believers gain reassurance and confidence of salvation through the anointing received from God. It remains in us and is sufficient to confirm us in the truth.

They **do not need anyone to teach** is not suggesting that they had no teachers, or that they knew everything and didn't need to be taught. Rather, it means that, as a congregation, they did not need anyone to teach them again the essentials of the faith that the false teachers were denying. They already had the truth (the anointing) and did not need anyone else (Gnostics, who claimed special inner knowledge) to tell them what was true.

The Bible includes two more verses (28–29) in this chapter, but most Bible teachers include these verses at the beginning of chapter 3.

MAIN IDEA REVIEW: *Those who claim to know God must obey him and live as Jesus lived. What's more, they must demonstrate their love of God by loving their Christian brothers and sisters. On the other hand, they must not love the world, and they must reject false teachers who deny the Son.*

III. CONCLUSION

Filling the Vacuum

What is in the heart will eventually come out: "Out of the overflow of the heart, the mouth speaks" (Matt. 12:34). If the love of God is in our hearts, it will show itself by our love for others. If we do not love others, the love of God has not yet gained control of our hearts. It does not necessarily mean we are not Christians. It just means that our attitude toward others has not yet been changed.

When we do not love others, it is much easier for the world to get a grip on us. Thus, the command to love our brothers (2:7–11) is followed with a warning not to love the world (2:15–17). The vacuum in our lives will be filled, either by living to please God and others, or by living to please only ourselves. Pleasing only ourselves will occupy our time and give us temporary satisfaction, but in the end it is emptiness and futility.

A stanza from Robert Burns' poem, *Tam o'Shanter,* says it well:

> But pleasures are like poppies spread;
> You seize the flower, its bloom is shed
> Or like the snow falls in the river,
> A moment white, then melts forever.

PRINCIPLES

- We verify what we believe by how we act.
- Love, for both God and others, is the central responsibility of the Christian.
- Love for the world suffocates and squeezes out love for God.
- People who defect from the faith were never part of the true faith.
- The spirit of antichrist is to deny the deity and sonship of Jesus.

APPLICATION

- Show your love for God by loving others and by obeying his commandments.
- Do not let personal desires, personal possessions, or pride get in the way of your love for God and others.
- Hold fast to the conviction that Jesus is the divine Son of God.
- Do not let anyone lure you from the historic Christian faith.

IV. LIFE APPLICATION

Worldliness

This chapter contains the central passage in Scripture on worldliness but gives no technical definition of worldliness. The best we can do is create descriptive definitions. *The Evangelical Dictionary of Theology* says it is "an affection for that which is unlike God and contrary to his will" (1191). Warren Wiersbe writes in the *Bible Exposition Commentary*:

> Worldliness is not so much a matter of activity as attitude . . . [It] not only affects your response to the love of God; it also affects your response to the will of God. "The world passeth away . . . but he that doeth the will of God abideth for ever" (1 John 2:17, KJV).
>
> Doing the will of God is a joy for those living in the love of God. "If you love Me, keep My commandments." But when a believer loses his enjoyment of the Father's love, he finds it hard to obey the Father's will.
>
> When you put these two factors together, you have a practical definition of worldliness: anything in a Christian's life that causes him to lose his enjoyment of the Father's love or his desire to do the Father's will is worldly and must be avoided (Wiersbe, 492).

We are to put a barrier between us and the world (2 Cor. 6:17). James 4:4 says that "friendship with the world is hatred toward God." Scripture tells us that while we cannot avoid being *in* the world (1 Cor. 5:10), we are not *of* the world (John 17:16). How to erect this barrier is complicated and unclear. In times past Christians have constructed lists of things not to do, which often included things such as don't go to movies, don't dance, don't smoke or drink, don't play cards, don't listen to secular music, don't let your hair grow long (men), and don't wear makeup or jewelry (women). These lists contained some wise safeguards, no doubt, but they didn't touch the attitudes. It was possible not to do all these things and still be riddled with greed, anger, and pride.

We would be wise to work on our attitudes and refine the list, so that we have both godly attitudes and prudent activities. But too many of us have neither godly attitudes nor prudent activities. We have become worldly.

It is time to reclaim true Christian distinctives in both attitudes and actions. As we do, we must realize that if we are to be spiritually healthy, some things we must do and some things we must not do. For example, if we want to be physically healthy, we must do certain things. We must eat properly, get sufficient sleep, and exercise. On the other hand, we must not abuse tobacco or alcohol, or place ourselves under relentless stress. It is not enough to do the positive. We must also avoid the negative.

The same is true spiritually. We must do the positive and avoid the negative. Concerning our attitudes, we should love the Lord our God with all our heart and all our soul and all our mind . . . and we must love our neighbor as ourselves (Matt. 22:37–39). We should not, we learn in this chapter, follow the lust of the flesh (illicit physical desires), the lust of the eyes (illicit mental desires), or the pride of life (illicit social-status desires).

Concerning our actions, we should obey God and serve others. We should avoid every kind of evil (1 Thess. 5:22), and we should neither participate in the evil things the world does, nor even speak of them (Eph. 5:12). If that is true, how vigilant we should be in guarding our hearts and minds against the things that pull us away from devotion to God! How disciplined we should be in pursuing the things that encourage us toward God.

A number of years ago I was in an informal meeting with a Christian leader of international stature. He was asked what he saw as the number one problem in the church today. Without hesitation, he replied, "Carnality." Then, a couple of years later, I was in a similar meeting with another Christian leader of international stature, and he was asked the same question. His reply, was exactly the same: "Carnality."

No matter what age we live in, we tend to conform to the society in which we live. We naturally take on the strengths and weaknesses of that society. We must encourage the natural strengths and battle the natural weaknesses. We can have direct control over some factors that contribute to our carnal condition—including television and music. I am persuaded that the secular media have gutted modern Christians of spiritual zeal, so that we have little to distinguish us from the non-Christians. It is not the total battle, but the battle would be well advanced if we simply stopped watching television and listening to godless music.

No one doubts that today's Christians are worldly. No one doubts that it is incorrect to rail against certain questionable activities without addressing godless attitudes. Yet, many times, especially in this media age, our activities contribute directly to the degeneration of our attitudes and values. When it comes to worldliness, we tend to think that somebody else is the culprit. We tend not to see our own activities as worldly. Yet, using the definition above by Warren Wiersbe, we might do well to refine our activities. Do our activities cause us to lose enjoyment of the Father's love or our desire to do the Father's will? If so, it is worldly and should be avoided.

V. PRAYER

Our Father, grant to us the discernment to see what is worldly in our lives, both in attitude and in actions. Give us the courage to take a stand against it, and the strength to be faithful to our convictions. Amen.

VI. DEEPER DISCOVERIES

A. If We Obey His Commands (v. 3)

This epistle seeks to assure us that we know God and have eternal life. For years, however, every time I read 1 John, the letter had just the opposite effect on me. I clearly did not love my brother perfectly and did not obey God's commandments with absolute consistency. I feared, therefore, that I must not be a Christian. Many people, I have learned, have had that same reaction. Therefore, we must resolve this issue before this epistle will have the reassuring and comforting effect on us that the writer intended.

The key to understanding this letter is to realize that God used the letter to address an extreme situation. The Gnostics were claiming to know God through special mystical insight, but they were continuing to live in sin with no regard for holiness. The letter makes it quite clear that these false teachers had no reason to believe they were Christians. True believers may, however, think that its message is intended for them. They need to hear that the letter does not intend to cause Christians who are sincerely trying to live the Christian life to doubt their salvation.

Other Scripture passages help us see this more clearly. First Corinthians 5:1–5 lets us know that Christians can fall into terrible sin. A Christian in the church in Corinth was living with his stepmother. Paul did not tell this person he was not a Christian. Rather, he told him that since he was a Christian, he was going to taste the fiery rod of God's discipline for his behavior. While

God will let non-Christians get away with this kind of behavior, he will not let Christians do so.

Hebrews 12:5–11 teaches us that God will chasten us to discourage sin and encourage righteous living. This chastening can be quite severe. In 1 Corinthians 11:17–33 we see that flagrant, prolonged sin on the part of Christians brought about weakness and sickness from God's disciplining hand. It got so bad that God even took the life of some people. This severe discipline does not result in the loss of salvation. Rather, as Paul wrote in 1 Corinthians 5:5, the sinning Christians will be "saved on the day of the Lord."

Paul reiterates this in 1 Corinthians 11:32, saying the Lord disciplines us so we will not be condemned with the world. If we judge ourselves and repent, we will be spared further divine chastening (1 Cor. 11:31).

We can reasonably conclude, then, that all who have truly received Jesus are saved (John 1:12). Certainly, we love and obey imperfectly, but even that imperfect faithfulness, compared to the stark unbelief and disregard for others manifested by the Gnostics, can bring comforting reassurance of our salvation, assuming it is built on faith that Jesus is the Christ, the Son of God (2:22–23).

A person who has an exemplary life but has not committed his life to Jesus can take no assurance of salvation. The basic biblical teaching is that if we believe in Jesus as the Son of God, our Savior, then we can receive assurance from the quality of our lives that we do, in fact, have eternal life.

B. Antichrist (v. 18)

The Antichrist is the "arch-opponent of God and his Messiah" (*Evangelical Dictionary of Theology*, 55). The term is found only in letters written by the apostle John. John draws on knowledge that the church at Ephesus apparently had of an evil figure called the Antichrist: **you have heard that the antichrist is coming**. This is likely the person mentioned in 2 Thessalonians who has a flagrant hatred for law (2:3) and makes a blatant claim to deity (2:4). He is "the man of lawlessness," "the man doomed to destruction," "proclaiming himself to be God."

Paul says that the day of the Lord will not come until this man of lawlessness is revealed (2 Thess. 2:3). He deceives many people through great miracles (2:9–10). He may be the evil figure referred to in Revelation 13:3 as a beast from the sea (the sea may be symbolic of the mass of humanity). His power comes from Satan. He is, of course, in opposition to Jesus, the Messiah. Christ will slay him by his breath and the splendor of his coming (2 Thess. 2:8, Rev. 19:15,20).

While this evil personage will be revealed at some time in the future, the values and attitudes that drive him were seen in many people even in John's day. This is why John says many antichrists are in the world even today. They are false teachers who deny that Jesus has come in the flesh and deny his deity (1 John 4:2–3). Second John 7 describes the antichrists as deceivers who teach that Jesus Christ did not come in the flesh. Before a person can be saved, he or she must have a correct understanding of who Jesus is. This is why Satan and his emissaries always strike at the biblical teaching of Jesus, his incarnation (becoming human), his death, and his resurrection.

VII. TEACHING OUTLINE

A. INTRODUCTION

1. Lead Story: The Grumpy Monk
2. Context: First John was written to a church under siege by false teachers. They held false beliefs and engaged in harmful activities. This chapter warns us of the dangers of both.
3. Transition: Put yourselves in John's shoes as he appeals to his dear friends to stand firm against the temptations of the world. How do you bring a warning strong enough to make them back off from false teachers, yet loving enough to assure them of their eternal salvation with God.

B. COMMENTARY

1. Those Who Know God Must Obey Him (vv. 3–6)
2. Those Who Know God Must Love Their Brother (vv. 7–11)
3. Those Who Love God Must Not Love the World (vv. 12–17)
   a. John affirms his readers (vv. 12–14)
   b. Christians are not to love the world (vv. 15–17)
4. Those Who Love God Must Reject False Teachers (vv. 18–27)

C. CONCLUSION: WORLDLINESS

VIII. ISSUES FOR DISCUSSION

1. What standard can you measure yourself by to find assurance that you are saved?
2. In what way is John's writing something old, and in what way is he writing something new? Why must it contain both?
3. Discuss the meaning of light and darkness. What shows that you are walking in light and not in darkness?
4. Do you have a relationship problem with another person or persons? What can you do to resolve the problem and restore the relationship?
5. What evidences of the Antichrist do you see in today's world? Does the Antichrist have any influence on your life?

1 John 3

God's Children Must Not Live in Sin

I. **INTRODUCTION**
Catching the Counterfeit

II. **COMMENTARY**
A verse-by-verse explanation of the chapter.

III. **CONCLUSION**
No Means of Retreat

An overview of the principles and applications from the chapter.

IV. **LIFE APPLICATION**
60 Minutes and the Judgment Seat of Christ

Melding the chapter to life.

V. **PRAYER**
Tying the chapter to life with God.

VI. **DEEPER DISCOVERIES**
Historical, geographical, and grammatical enrichment of the commentary.

VII. **TEACHING OUTLINE**
Suggested step-by-step group study of the chapter.

VIII. **ISSUES FOR DISCUSSION**
Zeroing the chapter in on daily life.

"*Truth exists. Only falsehood has to be invented.*"

G e o r g e s   F r a q u e

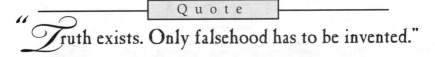

1 John

IN A NUTSHELL

God's love for us is great indeed. Those who hope to see God purify themselves, even as he is pure. The person who is born of God will not continue to live in sin. Rather, he should love his brother. As Jesus laid down his life for us, so we should lay down our lives for one another, loving not in words but in deeds.

God's Children
Must Not Live in Sin

I. INTRODUCTION

Catching the Counterfeit

*T*he United States Treasury uses a number of sophisticated techniques to keep counterfeiters from reproducing the look of paper currency. The exact makeup of paper bills is a secret, but it is widely known that the paper is made of 75 percent cotton and 25 percent linen, with red and blue flecks of silk. In addition to the high quality of the paper, United States currency also has magnetic ink, an almost invisible ink on the left side of larger bills, and an engraved "United States of America" around the face of the larger bills. The final feature that is impossible for anyone to replicate is that the paper is run through machines with high-pressure rollers that create a uniform thickness. Without these machines, this feature cannot be duplicated.

These sophisticated measures do not keep counterfeiters from trying, nevertheless, because they can get so close that many people cannot tell the difference. Deceit, of course, is the whole point of counterfeiting. Someone who does not have the real thing wants someone else to believe he has. We must be aware, alert, on guard against deceit, in regard to money as well as other things in life.

Spiritual counterfeiters had joined the church in Ephesus. They were leading people astray. In this chapter God reveals the characteristics of the bad currency and the good, so that his church can grasp the good.

II. COMMENTARY

God's Children Must Not Live in Sin

MAIN IDEA: *Those who love God must live as he wants them to live. They must not go on sinning; rather, they must love their brothers in Christ not just in words but also in deeds.*

A God Loves Us with Great Love (2:28–3:3)

SUPPORTING IDEA: *God is righteous and loves us with a great love. We who love him and hope to see him will purify our lives, as he is pure.*

2:28–29. These two verses introduce the concerns of chapter 3. **Now, dear children** seems to introduce a major new section. Christians begin by believing and trusting in Jesus. Then what? We are to **continue** (or abide) **in him** so that when Jesus comes again, we may be **confident and unashamed**. This simple statement is actually very complicated. It has several interpretations:

1. *The reference is to unsaved individuals who will be ashamed at Jesus' coming.* This seems a difficult position to sustain, since verse 28 begins by addressing Christians. This is needless instruction for those who are already saved.

2. *We are to remain in fellowship with Jesus, or we will lose our salvation and be ashamed at Jesus' coming.* One might understand this isolated verse in that sense. Taken with the teachings of the entire New Testament, the opposite meaning is true. Christian theologians have debated this for almost two thousand years. A simple description focuses on two opposing positions given in oversimplified outline. The Armenian position is that a believer can lose his salvation. The Calvinist position is that once elected and saved by God, a person can never lose that gift of salvation (see Deeper Discoveries). More complete descriptions are available in Bible dictionaries, wordbooks, or theological dictionaries.

3. *We are to remain in fellowship with the Lord, or we, as Christians, will be ashamed at Jesus' coming.* We do not normally think of Christians being ashamed at the coming of Jesus. We must remember that at the judgment seat of Christ, a Christian's works are evaluated and eternal rewards are meted out. At that time the possibility of shame exists. First Corinthians 3:10–15 says a person's works will be revealed as either perishable or imperishable: "His work will be shown for what it is, because the Day will bring it to light." On the appointed day when the Lord comes, he "will bring to light what is hidden in darkness and will expose the motives of men's hearts" (1 Cor. 4:5). Further, "we make it our goal to please him, whether we are at home in the body or away from it. For we must all appear before the judgment seat of Christ, that each one may receive what is due him for the things done while in the body, whether good or bad" (2 Cor. 5:9–10).

These passages teach us that the judgment seat of Christ will be more than a Sunday school awards banquet. Experiencing shame at living an undisciplined life might be part of what we could face. First John 2:28 reassures those who live normal Christian lives that they will not experience this shame. Only those who do not **continue in him** will do so.

That shame, should it be experienced, will be relatively short-lived. Revelation 21:4 promises that God will wipe away every tear, as the things of this world pass forever. The shame is not a perpetual thing, but is something to be avoided.

Everyone who does what is right has been born of him. Here is another difficult statement. At first impulse, we can think of plenty of people who have done what is right but were not believers in Jesus. Does this mean they were **born of him** anyway? Ghandi, for example, lived a profoundly sacrificial life, completely given over to good deeds. He treated others as he wanted others to treat him. If someone struck him on one cheek, he turned the other cheek. If he saw someone who was in need, he sacrificed all he had to help him. He lived in poverty and gave away all he had. He spoke kindly to people and lived a life filled with more Christian principles than most Christians. Does this verse mean Ghandi was born of God because he did what is right?

If we had only this verse, we might come to this conclusion. But balanced with the rest of Scripture, this impression is reversed. Scripture makes it clear that it is through Jesus—and him alone—that we receive salvation (John 14:6). A correct understanding of and belief in Jesus is necessary for salvation (1 John 2:22–23). Therefore, someone such as Ghandi, who knowingly rejected Jesus, could not be born of God.

To understand these difficult sayings, we must continually come back to their context and intent. The church had been invaded by Gnostics. They claimed to know God through special inner knowledge. They believed that the spirit was good and was untouched by the physical, which was evil (see Deeper Discoveries on 1 John 1). Therefore, the Gnostics believed they could sin flagrantly without remorse or consequence, since their spirits remained untouched by sin. They claimed to be Christian, to know God, but they hated Christians and lived sinful lives. God inspired this letter to challenge such people's claims to know Jesus. They must do what is right to validate that they are Christian. If they claim to be Christian, but do not do what is right, they are not Christian.

Does what is right can also mean "practices righteousness." Understood in this light, "doing good" is not the same thing as righteousness. Something may be good in the eyes of mankind, but not good in the eyes of God. To him, all our "righteous acts are like filthy rags" (Isa. 64:6). Our righteousness must be motivated by our knowledge that **he is righteous**. Only when our good deeds are done in response to our desire to serve Jesus—only when our acts are an expression and outworking of our faith in him—is God pleased.

3:1–3. The apostle breaks out in spontaneous wonder at the love of God in making us his children. A further wonder grasps him: **that is what we are.** The world does not **know us**, because it does not **know** our father. To "know" in this context has the sense of "accept." It appears in John 1:10–11: "He was in the world, and . . . the world did not *recognize* him. He came to that which was his own, but his own did not receive him" (italics added). The failure to recognize him was based on the fact that they did not accept him. If the world rejects God, it is no surprise that it would reject us, God's children.

Even though we are children of God, we don't grasp the full significance of what it means to be God's children. We now have only a dim perception of who we are and what we will be (**what we will be has not yet been made known**). When we see Jesus, our understanding will expand, and we will see it all. As 2 Corinthians 3:18 phrases it, "We . . . are being transformed into his likeness with ever-increasing glory." This process of transformation, which is slow and uneven here on earth, will be rapid and complete when we see Jesus.

If we begin to understand the unimaginable wonder of this fact, we will want to live pure and holy lives, for we will want to be pure **as he is pure**. Our weak commitment to absolute holiness stems in large measure from our dim perception of who Jesus is and who we have become in him. When we grasp more fully that we are now coheirs with Jesus (Rom. 8:17), we are destined to rule and reign in heaven with him. Slated for perfect holiness, united in spirit with the Creator-God of the universe, we will no longer want to fiddle around with the "mud pies" of this world. We will prefer the spotless beauty of a banquet table. One of our resources, then, for living a more holy lifestyle is pondering and meditating upon who Jesus is, who we have become in him, and what our life is likely to be when we see him.

B God's Children Do Not Live in Sin (3:3–10)

SUPPORTING IDEA: *The person who lives in sin is of the devil, and the person who does what is righteous is of God.*

3:4–6. The succession of brief statements continues. When scrutinized more carefully, they defy common understanding and lead to disagreement among Bible teachers. I have found no two commentaries that agree on what John meant in these verses. Therefore, if we have a difficult time understanding this passage, we can take some comfort in the fact that everyone seems to find it difficult. Whatever we end up believing, we must hold our opinion graciously, recognizing that other godly, well-taught people hold a differing position.

The opening statement appears obvious: when we sin, we break the law; **in fact, sin is lawlessness**. This is one of a number of biblical definitions of sin. Other biblical definitions of sin include:

- "The schemes of folly are sin" (Prov. 24:9).
- "Everything that does not come from faith is sin" (Rom. 14:23).
- "Anyone, then, who knows the good he ought to do and doesn't do it, sins" (Jas. 4:17).
- "All wrongdoing is sin" (1 John 5:17).

The Bible does not give one all-encompassing definition of sin. All these different definitions are facets of the "whole" of sin. This verse emphasizes that sin is **lawlessness**. This lawlessness is characteristic of the spirit of Antichrist. Sinners see no reason to concern themselves with God's laws. Thus, in 2 Thessalonians 2:3–4, "the man of lawlessness . . . will oppose . . . God."

The man of lawlessness does not reign. Sin is not removed from the world by simply creating a theology or philosophy that says we are above sin or incapable of sin. Sin has to be dealt with. God has dealt with our sin. **You know that he appeared so that he might take away our sins. And in him is no sin.** Jesus dealt with sin in the only way suitable to God. He lived a sinless life, and then made the ultimate perfect sacrifice. His perfect life became the model, the new creature God wants to make of all his children.

The next statement is breathtaking: **no one who lives in him keeps on sinning.** This statement is followed by an even more absolute statement: **no one who continues to sin has either seen him or known him.** To put a cap on it, verse 9 says the person who has been born of God **cannot go on sinning.**

These statements can be alarming to the Bible reader. We know we have sinned. We may be wrestling with sin that keeps cropping up in our lives. If this letter intends to comfort us with the assurance of our salvation (5:13), statements like these can have just the opposite effect. We must seek further understanding.

Our starting point is obvious: Christians do sin, as acknowledged elsewhere in this letter (1:8–2:1; 5:16–17). Repeated exhortations *not* to sin (2:1,15,29; 3:12,18; 5:21) would be needless if we *could* not sin or if we *did* not sin. Bible teachers suggest several different interpretations:

1. *The Willful-Sin Position.* According to this interpretation, the statement is referring to willful, deliberate sins, as opposed to involuntary, unintentional sins and errors.

   This interpretation raises three problems. First, even saintly people can commit major, premeditated sins. Second, distinguishing between voluntary and involuntary sins is very difficult. Third, the text gives no indication that such a limited definition of sin is meant. Rather, the text clearly talks about *all* sin.

2. *The Habitual-Sin Position.* According to this view, the text means we cannot adopt a lifestyle of willful, unrepentant sin. The verbs in these sentences are present tense, which means, as the NIV has translated it, don't "keep on sinning." We will sin. We may sin badly, as Peter did—cursing and denying Jesus, or as the Corinthians did—tolerating adultery (1 Cor. 5:1–12) and committing violations of the Lord's Supper (1 Cor. 11:23–33). We may go through a spell of "backsliding," as the churches of Asia did (Rev. 2–3).

But we will never settle down into a lifestyle that is characterized by sin. We will never adopt the extreme lifestyle of the false teachers who had blatant disregard for the standards of holiness set by Jesus. No one who practices the litany of evil deeds in Galatians 5:19–21 will inherit the kingdom of God. Any of these deeds, as individual acts, may be forgiven. But when people have no regard for holiness and claim that they are free to sin—as the antichrists in this letter seem to have done—they have indicated by their own attitude that they are not Christians.

Remember the context. False teachers claimed that Christians do not sin, or cannot sin, or are free to sin, and that if they do sin, it is of no great consequence. It is an extreme situation that calls for extreme language, so Scripture dispels this groundless teaching.

3. *The Ideal-Character Position.* Those who hold this view point out that the text's claim that a Christian does not sin states what ought to be the character of the Christian, not necessarily what is the character of *all* Christians. We ought to strive for the ideal, even if we know we will not reach it. We will be better off by trying and failing than if we had never tried at all. The extreme situation in the church required hyperbole (deliberate exaggeration) to make the point. The truth might be that you cannot keep from sinning, but the balancing truth is that you ought to try.

4. *The New-Man Position.* According to this view, Scripture teaches that the "new man" is a perfect new creation. In Ephesians 4:24 the apostle Paul says the "new self" is "created to be like God in true righteousness and holiness." The New American Standard version reads, "And put on the new self, which in the likeness of God has been created in righteousness and holiness of the truth." This is in keeping with the assertions in Romans 7:15: "[What] I want to do I do not do, but what I hate I do." But (v. 17), "it is no longer I myself who do it, but it is sin living in me."

Thus we are torn. "In my inner being I delight in God's law; but I see another law at work in the members of my body, waging war against the law of my mind and making me a prisoner of the law of sin at work within my members" (vv. 22–23). Paul concludes (v. 25) by saying, "In my mind [I] am a slave to God's law, but in my [flesh] (NASB) a slave to the law of sin." (The NIV translates the word *flesh* as "sinful nature." This is an unfortunate translation. The NASB is more accurate at this point.)

John MacArthur writes clearly about this issue in his commentary on Ephesians:

Biblical terminology does not say that a Christian has two different natures. He has but one nature, the new nature in Christ. The old
self dies and the new self lives; they do not coexist. . . . The Christian
is a single new person, a totally new creation, not a spiritual schizo-
phrenic. It is the filthy coat of remaining humanness in which the
new creation dwells that continues to hinder and contaminate his living. He is no longer the old man corrupted, but is now the new man
created in righteousness and holiness, awaiting full salvation
(Rom. 13:11) when he dies and is given a new body (p. 164).

Zane Hodges writes in a similar vein in *The Bible Knowledge Commentary:*

The regenerate life is, in one sense, an essentially and fundamen-
tally sinless life. For the believer, sin is abnormal and unnatural; his
whole bent of life is away from sin . . . Insofar as God is experienced
by a believer, that experience is sinless.

The "new man" (or "new self"; Eph. 4:24; Col. 3:10) is an absolutely perfect new creation. By insisting on this point, John was seeking to refute a false conception about sin. Sin is not, nor ever can be,
anything but satanic. It can never spring from what a Christian truly
is at the level of his regenerate being (pp. 894–895).

Because this new self, the inner man, is regenerate, there is no condemnation to those who are in Christ Jesus (Rom. 8:1), in spite of the fact that sin
might occur. It remains for our adoption to be completed by receiving a new
body (8:22–23), so that the power of sin will be completely removed from us.
Until then, we battle—the regenerate inner self with the flesh. The "flesh" does
not refer to the physical body. The body is neutral. Rather, the flesh is a spiritual gravitational pull to sin that we cannot escape until we receive a new body.

This does not answer all questions. In fact, it tells us more than we really
understand. The point seems to be that our inner man is regenerate and does
not sin. Yet, we are responsible for the sins of our whole person (Rom.
6:1–2,15). Paul says, in essence, "Heaven forbid! How can those of us who
have been born again be content to keep presenting the members of our body
as instruments to sin? It is inconceivable!"

Perhaps 1 John 3:5 applied the same principle: the person born of God
does not go on sinning. In the Romans 7 sense, that is true. The inner man, the
regenerate self, does not sin. Yet when the "filthy coat of remaining humanness
in which the new creation dwells," as MacArthur put it, "continues to hinder
and contaminate his living," he participates in the work of the devil. But the
one who is born of God (inner man) does not sin **because God's seed remains
in him,** and he cannot sin because **he has been born of God.**

There are still other positions on this passage. Most are variations of these views. The lack of consensus among Bible teachers about the meaning of this text suggests to me that whatever position we hold, we might hold it gently and without arrogance. There are good people who hold to all these differing views. Perhaps if the truth were known, elements of more than one of them might be true. We must also recognize that the problem in understanding these difficult statements in 1 John is due in large part to the historical and cultural distance that has been created with the passing of nearly two thousand years. John's readers apparently understood what he was saying well enough that he felt no need to explain himself further.

Bible teachers agree what is not said here. First John 3:6 does not say that in his everyday life, the Christian will never commit sin, or that if he does, he will lose his salvation.

3:7–10 This paragraph reiterates three points made in verses 4–6. This reiteration is set out skillfully in John Stott's commentary, *The Epistles of John* (121):

	Verses 4–7	**Verses 8–10**
The introductory phrase:	*whosoever committeth sin* (v. 4)	*he that committeth sin* (v. 8)
The theme:	The nature of sin is lawlessness (v. 4)	The origin of sin is the devil (v. 8)
The purpose of Christ's appearing:	*he was manifested to take away our sins* (v. 5)	*the Son of God was manifested, that he might destroy the works of the devil* (v. 8)
The logical conclusion:	"no one who abides in him sins" (v. 6, RSV)	"no one born of God commits sin" (v. 9, RSV).

Seeing this chart will not only help us understand the chapter, but it will also keep us from repeating ourselves excessively in explaining it.

Verse 7 warns us not to be led astray. This is probably a warning against the false teachers and antichrists who apparently felt free to sin, while denying that they were doing anything wrong. They could assert their own righteousness in the face of the facts.

Our text counters with the bold assertion that the person who **does what is right is righteous**. This revisits the problem answered in 2:29. Doing what is right does not make a person righteous. But the false teachers must recognize that if a person is righteous, he or she will do what is right. You cannot claim to be righteous, as did the antichrists, while living in open sin. It might be amplified to read, "It is the person who does what is right who is righteous, not the antichrists who claim to be righteous but do what is wrong."

He who does what is sinful is of the devil makes it clear that the sinning antichrists were not righteous, but were of the devil. This does not mean that when a Christian sins, he suddenly loses his place as a child of God and takes his place as a child of the devil. Rather, it means that the antichrists—since they claim righteousness while living in sin—are children of the devil.

Christians, who are assured of their salvation throughout the letter, need to hear the parallel implication here. When Christians sin, we are, for the moment, siding with the devil's cause and ought not to do so. All sin ultimately is satanic in nature because sin originated with the devil. Sin is his consistent practice, and he has been sinning "from the beginning" (John 8:44). To sin is to take part in the devil's plan, which automatically sets a person in opposition to God. The reason Jesus came was to destroy the work of the devil. When we cooperate with the devil by sinning, we are opposing Jesus.

Verse 9 reiterates the idea first stated in verse 6 that the person who is born of God will not sin, and then the verse goes beyond that. A person who experiences the new birth cannot sin. The options that applied to verse 6 also apply to verse 9. (The translators of the NIV have decided that it should be interpreted as **keeps on sinning** in verse 6, and **cannot go on sinning** in verse 9, and have translated it accordingly. Not all translators and Bible teachers agree with this translation.)

Sinning is impossible because of God's indwelling **seed**. The **seed** refers to one of three options: (1) the Word of God, (2) the Holy Spirit, or (3) the regenerate spirit when one is born again. We cannot be sure which of these three possibilities is meant. All three could be true and are taught elsewhere in Scripture. Scripture takes seriously the nature of believers as born-again, Spirit-filled, new creatures in Christ. It will not tolerate any casual attitude toward sin. Sin and salvation are opposites. Wanting to sin is not part of being led by the Spirit or having Christ in us. Refusal to take this warning seriously should call us to reexamine our commitment to Christ.

Christians make themselves known as children of God by doing what is right and by loving their brothers. People prove themselves to be children of the devil when they refuse to do what is right and refuse to love their brothers.

C Christians Must Love One Another in Actions and in Truth (3:11–18)

SUPPORTING IDEA: *Christians must love their brothers. Jesus showed us what this meant: he laid down his life for us. Therefore, we ought to do the same for one another.*

3:11–15. Again we hear the message of love from the beginning of Jesus' ministry (2:7). Before learning what love is, we read what love is not. We should **not be like Cain,** who murdered his brother, Abel, because Cain's actions were evil, while Abel's were righteous. Abel's righteousness apparently engendered profound resentment—anger great enough to prompt murder. Just as Cain resented Abel's righteousness, so the world will resent our righteousness. As a result, just as Cain hated Abel, so the world will despise Christians. This again counters the claims of the antichrists to be righteous Christians, while manifesting a lack of love and even a hatred toward true Christians.

True Christians, those born of God, have love for their brothers placed in their hearts by the Lord, so that we **know that we have passed from death to life, because we love our brothers.** Loving our brothers does not give us eternal life. God does that through Christ. If we have eternal life, we will manifest it by loving our brothers. We may have difficulty loving some Christians who make it hard to love them, but a fundamental desire to love them will show through our lives. Even Jesus' disciples quarreled among themselves about who would be the greatest among them. That was an unloving thing to do. It did not, however, relegate them to the realm of the unsaved.

Next in the succession of challenging declarations is that **anyone who does not love remains in death;** if anyone hates his brother, he is a murderer; and **no murderer has eternal life in him.** We must again stop to consider what John might have meant by this statement. The options are the same as the previous difficult statements.

1. *The Face-Value View.* This view takes the words at face value. If you hate your brother to the point of being willing to murder him, or if you actually murder him, you are not a Christian. This level of hatred is incompatible with the regenerate life. Does this mean that a person who has killed someone cannot be saved? History, I think, disproves that option.

2. *The Abiding View.* Zane Hodges writes in the *Bible Knowledge Commentary* that "it is an illusion to believe that a real Christian is incapable of hatred and murder" (p. 896). He cites the examples of David when he killed Uriah the Hittite and of Peter who warned his Christian readers not to let any of them suffer as a murderer (1 Pet. 4:15).

The key to this view is the word *abiding* which the NIV does not translate. We could translate more literally, "No murderer **has eternal life** abiding **in him.**" The Christian, as long as he is abiding in Christ—or living in conscious fellowship with Christ—would certainly never murder anyone. If he murders someone, it is because he is not abiding in Christ. In this sense, eternal life and Christ must be seen as synonyms.

Again, we must appeal to the context. All of us can recall times when we have not loved our brothers, or we can think of people we don't like to associate with. As a result, we can conclude that we are not Christians. This would be an overreaction. John writes in a context of extreme contrasts. He does not suggest that we are not Christian if we love imperfectly.

3. *The Continuing-to-Hate View.* The final view of these verses treats hate and murder the same as "sin" in verses 6 and 9. A Christian might hate or murder someone, but if this happened, he or she would be overcome with remorse. If a person is willing to harbor habitual hate, or have no remorse at murder, that person is not a Christian. No one whose life is characterized by hate or murder can be a Christian.

3:16–18. In stark contrast to this unspeakable hatred is Jesus' remarkable love. We can understand what love is by looking at Jesus' example. He laid down his life for us. We ought to be prepared to do the same for one another. While the necessity of laying down our lives for one another is rare, the necessity of helping meet one another's needs is not. The true test of a Christian's love is not his words (loving with **words or tongue**) but his willingness to sacrifice for the sake of his brother . . . to love **with actions and in truth**.

D Christians Can Have Confidence Before God (3:19–24)

> **SUPPORTING IDEA:** *When we do not live out our desire to love others perfectly, we should not fear that we are not Christians. God sees our heart, not just our actions, and he knows the truth regarding our salvation. If our heart does not condemn us, we may have fruitfulness in prayer and obedience to him.*

3:19–21. **This then is how we know that we belong to the truth:** This phrase probably looks back to verses 17–18 rather than forward. If so, the apostle is saying that it is by our deeds of **action and in truth** that we know that we belong to the truth. The antichrists may have been teaching that they knew the truth by special, inner insight, even though their lives were models of greed and hatred. John countered this impression by claiming the mark of truth is a lifestyle of high moral character and good deeds growing out of our commitment to Christ.

In our desire to live lives of high moral character and good deeds toward others, we will fail. We will fall short even of our own ideals, let alone God's. When this happens, our **hearts** may **condemn us**. But we can **rest in his presence**, for God **knows everything**. He knows that we believe in Christ, that we strive to love our brothers, and that we regret falling short. God does not look only at the outer facts of imperfect love, but at the inner fact of having been born of God. The human heart is not the final standard. Rather, God is! God's power keeps us secure in him. God's power and steadfastness—not our own—give us security. As Jesus said, "My Father, who has given them to me, is greater than all; no one can snatch them out of my Father's hand" (John 10:29).

3:21–22. We may silence our condemning hearts in two ways: (1) by confessing our sin (1:8) so that we are forgiven and cleansed of all unrighteousness, and (2) by resting in the fact that God knows all things, looking not just at our deeds but at our hearts. Once our hearts no longer condemn us, we can have **confidence before God.** This confidence leads us to fruitfulness in prayer. Characteristically, John states it in absolute terms: **we receive from him anything we ask.**

Some passages of Scripture seem to give assurance that we will receive anything we ask for (Matt. 7:7–8), but other passages give qualifications to answered prayer. The assurances of answered prayer seem to assume a knowledge of the qualifications. Answers to prayers are predicated on our obedience to God's commands. This same letter introduces the qualification of asking in God's will (5:14). We must ask in Jesus' name (John 14:13; 16:23,26), and abide in Jesus (John 15:7,16).

Stott (p. 148) points out that the receiving of answers to prayer is the Christian's habitual experience since the verbs are in the present tense. The conditions, along with the verb tense, suggest that John did not intend to promise a blank check for any and every prayer, but that answered prayer is the ongoing experience of the Christian. Even Jesus' request that the cup of crucifixion pass from him was not answered affirmatively (Luke 22:42). We should observe, however, that the request was followed by the statement, "Yet not my will, but yours be done."

3:23–24. What commands must we obey if we are to be fruitful in prayer? We must believe in Jesus and love one another. These two ideas stem from the same attitude of the heart, and John sees them as one command. To do one is to do the other. Those who obey God's commands live in him, or abide in him. Similarly, John 15 links abiding with obeying (15:9–10).

The way we can know that he lives in us is **by the Spirit he gave us.** There are several views on this passage.

1. *The Charismatic View.* This view sees reference here to the charismatic gifts, such as gifts of prophecy, healing, etc. (*The NIV Application Commentary,* 171). Since the letter is devoid of other clear references, this seems unlikely.

2. *The Inner Witness View.* This view says the Holy Spirit gives us an inner conviction, an inner assurance that we are true Christians. This also seems unlikely, since this would play into the hands of the antichrists who taught that secret, inner knowledge was the sign of divine enlightenment.

3. *The Life Witness View.* This phrase looks *forward* to what John is going to say—not back to what he has said. First John gives four tests of true Christianity: (1) moral character, (2) love of the brethren, (3) obedience to God's commands, and (4) confession that Jesus is God

in the flesh. Immediately after John mentioned the Spirit which God gave us, he launched into a serious warning not to trust just any spirit, but to test the spirits. He suggested a threefold test:

- Doctrine: **Every spirit that acknowledges that Jesus Christ has come in the flesh is from God** (4:2).
- Love: **Everyone who loves has been born of God and knows God** (4:7).
- Obedience: **This is love for God: to obey his commands** (5:3).

The Holy Spirit produces doctrinal purity, love for the brethren, and a spirit of obedience to God's commands. When we see these three things, we can be confident that he lives in us. They are the unmistakable signs of the Holy Spirit's presence in our lives.

MAIN IDEA REVIEW: *Those who love God must live as he wants them to live. They must not go on sinning; rather, they must love their brothers in Christ not just in words but also in deeds.*

III. CONCLUSION

No Means of Retreat

This is a very difficult chapter. Nevertheless, it is an important and valuable record of divine truth, and we must labor to understand it as well as we can. Three subjects found throughout the letter dominate this chapter: (1) anyone who has the hope of seeing Jesus purifies himself, even as Jesus is pure; (2) love one another; and (3) obey God's commands.

This call to committed living is exemplified in the story often told about the Spanish explorer, Cortez. In 1519 he landed at Vera Cruz with a small force of seven hundred men to begin his conquest of Mexico. Legend tells us he purposely set fire to his fleet of eleven ships. Presumably, his men on the shore watched their only means of retreat sink to the bottom of the Gulf of Mexico. Now they had only one direction to move—forward into the Mexican interior to meet whatever might come their way.

The Bible calls us to this kind of single-mindedness—absolute commitment to authentic Christian belief and behavior.

PRINCIPLES

- Ongoing, willful sin is incompatible with true Christianity.
- True Christian experience is revealed not just in our beliefs but in our behavior.
- Love for other Christians is a mark of authentic Christianity.
- Obedience to God's commands is a mark of our love for him.

APPLICATION

- Look forward to the wonderful change that will occur when we see Jesus and become like him. Draw encouragement, motivation, and emotional strength from the hope.
- Because Jesus came to destroy the works of the devil, commit yourself totally to following Jesus and obeying his commands.
- Be willing to help your brother if he is in need and if you have the resources to help him.
- Rest in the fact that even when you do not love others perfectly, God knows your heart, and he does not condemn those who are in Christ.

IV. LIFE APPLICATION

60 Minutes and the Judgment Seat of Christ

A fellow pastor-friend of mine once shared with me his course of action when he has difficulty deciding if some action is right or not. He envisions the 60 Minutes film crew bursting into his office and asking questions about his decision on nationwide television. This has a peculiar ability to clear his head and help him make sound decisions.

While it is sobering to consider 60 Minutes asking us penetrating questions that will be aired on television, how much more sobering it is to imagine God asking us penetrating questions that will be aired in heaven. That is just what will happen . . . not with a sordid newsreel of all our dirty secrets, but certainly an assessment of our motives.

French philosopher Montaign once said that if all our inner thoughts were made public, each one of us would deserve hanging at least ten times in his or her life. I suspect he is conservative in his estimate. "We must all appear before the judgment seat of Christ, that each one may receive what is due him for the things done while in the body, whether good or bad" (2 Cor. 5:10). Then God "will bring to light what is hidden in darkness and will expose the motives of men's hearts. At that time each will receive his praise from God" (1 Cor. 4:5). We see, then, that our motives are what God judges.

When we combine this with 1 John 2:28, which says that we may experience shame at the coming of Jesus, it seems likely that this shame would come at the judgment seat of Christ. In this verse, John is not suggesting that we must live perfect lives or else be shamed. He goes to great lengths in 3:19–20 to assure us that when we live imperfect lives, God knows our hearts and takes into account our weaknesses (Ps. 103:8–11). The common sins that come to an earnest disciple of Jesus are not thrown up in our faces to cause us shame.

A much more serious failure causes shame. First John warns us not to depart from the faith, as the antichrists have done. Their lives were characterized by (1) a lack of love toward brothers in Christ (2:9–10), (2) a love of the world (2:15–17), and (3) a denial that Jesus was the Son of God (2:23).

John says, unlike the antichrists, **see that what you have heard from the beginning remains** (*meno*) **in you** (2:24). Then he says, **continue** (*meno*) **in him, so that when he appears we may be confident and unashamed before him at his coming.** If we hold to the truth, we will not be ashamed. If we reject **what you have heard**, we will be ashamed when Jesus returns. As we remain faithful to him in the direction of our lives, we need not fear shame at the judgment seat of Christ. Our bad motives may be made public, and while those past sins will be forgiven, they will not be rewarded. Good motives, however, will also be made public, and all righteousness will be rewarded.

So if we would not want a television reporter to burst into the room and broadcast the thoughts and intentions of our hearts, we should strive to keep the thoughts and intentions of our hearts pure.

V. PRAYER

Dear Lord, help us to live our lives today in light of eternity, that our motives may bring reward to us and glory to you. Amen.

VI. DEEPER DISCOVERIES

A. Can Christians Sin? (v. 9)

The Epistle of John is a troublesome letter to understand. It contains many black-and-white statements that, if taken only at face value, seem to contradict teachings elsewhere in Scripture. By studying carefully what John is really saying, we can harmonize the epistle with the rest of Scripture.

In chapter 3, perhaps the most troublesome issue is what a Christian's sin indicates. Does sin mean a believer has lost his salvation? Is it a sign he was never saved in the first place? First John 3, especially verse 9, can be read in this way. The NIV, on which this commentary is based, reads: **No one who is born of God will continue to sin . . . he cannot go on sinning, because he has been born of God.** Other good translations (KJV, NKJV, NASB, etc.) basically translate: "No one who is born of God will sin," and "He cannot sin, because he has been born of God."

Therefore, we must look into the issue more closely to see if a Christian can sin and not lose his salvation. The answer, of course, is yes. First John admits this in 1:8: **If we claim to be without sin, we deceive ourselves and** the truth is not in us. Again in verse 10: **If we claim we have not sinned, we make him out to be a liar.**

Other Scripture passages strengthen this understanding. Peter demonstrated that we cannot sin so often or so badly that God will not forgive us. He came to Jesus, asking him how many times he should forgive someone who had sinned against him. Peter ventured a bold answer to his own question—"seven times!" (Matt. 18:22). That was a generous number in the eyes of the world. How many times would you forgive someone who insulted your wife, or drove over your lawn, or took money from you? Seven seems like a lot. Amazingly, Jesus answered, "Not seven times, but seventy-seven times."

Jesus did not intend to stop at seventy-seven, but merely to dramatize the answer by multiplying Peter's own generous suggestion. From other teachings in Scripture, it is safe to say that we should forgive as many times as we are wronged. This is not to say that we make no precautions against being wronged again, but we must always forgive, not only to be obedient to the Lord (Matt. 6:15; Eph. 4:32), but also to keep bitterness from springing up and choking out our spiritual life.

If God expects us to forgive so many times, would he hold himself to a lower standard? So we see we cannot sin so many times that God will not forgive us.

Nor can we sin so badly that God will not forgive us. Again, Peter demonstrated this by cursing and denying that he knew Jesus—about as bad a sin as anyone could commit (Matt. 26:69–74). Yet, only a few days later he was eating breakfast with Jesus on the shore of Lake Galilee, in perfect fellowship (John 21:15–19). We cannot sin so many times or so badly that Jesus won't forgive us.

If you believe in Jesus, have come to him for forgiveness, have committed your life to him, and have been born again, you are saved. No sin can separate you from the love of God (Rom. 8:38–39). When God's children sin, God chastens us. His discipline yields the peaceful fruit of righteousness (Heb. 12:5–11).

A man in Corinth was committing adultery with his stepmother (1 Cor. 5). Paul urged the Corinthian church to excommunicate him. Paul declared that, in this way, this man's body might be destroyed but his spirit would be saved (v. 5). Also in Corinth some believers were violating the Lord's Supper. Paul said that because of this, some of them were weak, some were sick, and some had even died (1 Cor. 11:30). Still, nothing Paul said indicated that they had lost their salvation.

The point is that if God is willing to save a person when he is an enemy of God, how much more is he willing to save a person once he has become a child of God (Rom. 5:10)? After we are saved and then fall into sin, we may incur God's chastening hand in our lives, but we will never be lost.

If we have no regard for righteousness, if we treat sin lightly, if our life is set in opposition to the holiness of God, this is an indication that we were never saved in the first place. The false teachers in the church in Ephesus, the antichrists, were claiming to be righteous while they were immoral at the same time. They did not love the brethren, and they denied that Jesus was God in the flesh. They claimed that they knew God by special inner knowledge, but they did not believe the truth and lived unrighteous lives. John's bold statements were designed to make it clear to everyone that these antichrists were not Christians. This was demonstrated by their lack of faith as well as their immoral and uncaring lifestyles.

VII. TEACHING OUTLINE

A. INTRODUCTION

1. Lead Story: Catching the Counterfeit
2. Context: First John 3 tries to counter the information being spread by false teachers called antichrists. They apparently claimed to know God through special, inner knowledge and claimed to be righteous, even though they loved the world, hated their brothers, and denied that Jesus is the Son of God. These extreme circumstances called for extreme words, and John was biting and direct in his condemnation.
3. Transition: As we look at 1 John 3, we see a number of parallels to our own times. The message of this chapter is a message we all need to hear and heed. It calls on us to examine our lives and renew our commitment to Christ.

B. COMMENTARY

1. God Loves Us with Great Love (2:28–3:3)
2. God's Children Do Not Live in Sin (3:4–10)
3. Christians Must Love One Another in Action and in Truth (3:11–18)
4. Christians Can Have Confidence Before God (3:19–24).

C. CONCLUSION: *60 MINUTES* AND THE JUDGMENT SEAT OF CHRIST

VIII. ISSUES FOR DISCUSSION

1. What would you say to a church member who expressed fear that he had lost his salvation?
2. How can you describe the love of God to a person who is not a Christian?
3. Describe the hope for eternity that you have in Christ. How does this affect your daily life?

4. What will you be ashamed of at the judgment seat of Christ? What do you think will happen to you there?

5. What is the strongest evidence you have that you are saved and will receive the reward of eternal life with God in heaven?

1 John 4

Test and Live the Truth

Quote

"*If* you examined a hundred people who had lost their faith in Christianity, I wonder, how many of them would turn out to be reasoned out of it by honest argument? Do not most people simply drift away?"

C . S . L e w i s

1 John

IN A NUTSHELL

We should put to the test every person and message we hear to make sure they are of God, to see if they confess the humanity and deity of Jesus, and to discern the spirit of truth and falsehood. We must love one another as God has loved us. As we do, we present a mature picture to others of God's love, and we will have confidence at the judgment seat of Christ. Whoever loves God must also love his brother.

Test and Live the Truth

I. INTRODUCTION

Canals on Mars

*A*t the turn of the century, the world's most distinguished astronomer was certain that Mars had canals. Sir Percival Lowell, esteemed for his study of the solar system, had a particular fascination with the Red Planet.

In 1877 he heard that an Italian astronomer had seen straight lines criss-crossing the Martian surface. Lowell spent the rest of his years squinting into the eyepiece of his giant telescope in Arizona, mapping the channels and canals he saw. He was convinced the canals were proof of intelligent life on Mars, possibly an older but wiser race than humanity. Lowell's observations gained wide acceptance. So eminent was he that none dared contradict him.

Now, of course, things are different. Space probes have orbited Mars and landed on its surface. The entire planet has been mapped, and no one has seen a canal. How could Lowell have "seen" so much that wasn't there?

Two possibilities: (1) he wanted to see canals so strongly that he did, over and over again, and/or (2) he suffered from a rare eye disease that made him see the blood vessels in his own eyes. The Martian "canals" he saw were nothing more than the bulging veins of his eyeballs. Today the malady is known as "Lowell's syndrome."

It is easy for us to see something that is not there, and often, not to see something that is there. Many times we simply see what we want to see. First John 4 begins by warning us not to be taken in by deceptions. We are to test what we hear against the absolute standard of God's Word. We are not to let our own desires or our own peculiar limitations get us off course, following what is not true.

II. COMMENTARY

Test and Live the Truth

MAIN IDEA: *We must learn to discern the spirit of truth and falsehood, to love one another as God has loved us, and to love our brothers. Then we will face final judgment with hope and joy.*

A Christians Must Exercise Discernment (4:1–6)

SUPPORTING IDEA: *We must not believe every spirit, for only the spirit that acknowledges that Jesus Christ has come in the flesh is from God; the one that fails to make this acknowledgment is the spirit of the Antichrist.*

4:1–3. Spirit can be interpreted in one of three ways:

1. The spirit behind the prophet who is speaking (**many false prophets have gone out into the world**), in which case it would refer to the Holy Spirit or to demons, depending on whether the prophet was of God.
2. The prophet himself, "spirit" being a figure of speech, a metaphor, meaning "the prophet."
3. The message itself, "spirit" being a figure of speech, a metaphor, meaning "the message."

All three of these interpretations are possible. Most Bible teachers prefer option 1 or option 2 because the test given for the spirits in the next verse seems personal (**every spirit that acknowledges**). Each of the options tells us not to automatically believe anyone who comes to the church to preach or teach. We are to listen carefully to their treatment of Jesus. Apparently, false prophets in the church at Ephesus were denying that Jesus is fully human and fully divine. This test was specifically set up for this situation: Does the teacher accept Jesus' full humanity and full deity. If not, his entire teaching is to be rejected.

This is not the only test a teacher must pass. An eloquent teacher of God's Word might agree to the divinity and humanity of Jesus, but have other things so out of bounds in his theology that he still might qualify as a false prophet. Jesus himself said that not everyone who called him "Lord" would enter the kingdom.

In this context, the person who acknowledges or confesses that Jesus has come in the flesh is from God. Those who don't are the spirit of the Antichrist, which John had already warned his readers about (2:18–27; see 2 John 7). Every teacher belongs in one of the two categories: true prophet of the Word or Antichrist.

4:4–6. Warnings might make us question if we have listened to false teachers and become Antichrist. No! You have overcome the antichrists, for you have successfully resisted the lure of the false prophets. The **one who is in you** (the Holy Spirit; Rom. 8:9) is greater than the **one who is in the world** (Satan; 1 John 5:19), who is called "the prince of this world" (John 12:31).

The antichrists and false prophets are cut out of the same piece of cloth as the world. As a result, they speak to the same values as the world, so the world listens to them. They are from the world, but we are from God. So when the apostles (and possibly other true witnesses) speak from God, those who are born of God listen to them. The Holy Spirit convicts of sin (John 16:8), calls to righteousness (John 16:8), and illumines the mind to the truth of Scripture (1 Cor. 2:12–14).

The world does not listen to the things of God. The person without the Spirit "does not accept the things that come from the Spirit of God, for they are foolishness to him and he cannot understand them, because they are spiritually discerned" (1 Cor. 12:14). The ministry of the Holy Spirit lets us discern the spirit of truth and the spirit of falsehood. Therefore, prayer, meditation, and spiritual sensitivity are the primary factors that protect us from being deceived by false doctrine—not raw intelligence or academic learning.

B Let Us Love One Another as God Has Loved Us (4:7–12)

> **SUPPORTING IDEA:** *Love comes from God, so if we are born of God, we will also love. God loved us first, so we must love one another.*

4:7–8. The letter returns to a subject already talked about—love—which **comes from God**. If we want to be like God, we, too, must love. Love becomes another test of believers. Only those **born of God** know how to love. They know how because they know God, the only source of love. We must admit that we see remarkable displays of sacrificial love among those who reject Christ. So in what sense can we agree that everyone who loves is born of God? It would be wrong to conclude that anybody who shows love is a child of God, regardless of whether he or she actually believes in Jesus.

This conclusion is possible only if we take this statement out of its context. John has already made the point that the true child of God both loves and believes (3:23). Yet, even those who are not true children of God can love others—sometimes even more fully than many Christians—because we have all been created in the image of God. The capacity to love comes to us as part of divine creation. Yet, true love—love that includes loving God and the full expression of love for others, namely telling them about salvation in Jesus—is characteristic only of true Christians.

Then John flipped the coin over, claiming that anyone who does not show love **does not know God**. The evidence of this? The nature of God. His very essence is love. Thus, this negative test seems easier to understand. How could someone receive divine life through Jesus, have the indwelling Holy Spirit, and not love? A person saved by love and indwelled with love must love. We may have trouble loving perfectly, but there is a big difference between not loving perfectly and not loving at all.

4:9–10. If we need to love as God loved, we might wonder how God loved. The clear answer appears in 3:16: **This is how we know what love is: Jesus**

Christ laid down his life for us. Verse 9 says the same thing from the Father's perspective. God the Father showed how he loves. **He sent his one and only Son,** knowing he would be horribly treated and ultimately crucified. This is how God loved. He sacrificed his Son so **we might live through him.**

This immeasurable gift was in no way a response to humanity's love for God. Quite the opposite. It was initiated by God. We respond to him. Jesus died on the cross to pay for our sins. God solved our problem at his expense. He made Jesus our **atoning sacrifice.** This term (*hilasmos*) appears only here and in 2:2 (related words are used in Matt. 16:22; Luke 18:13; Rom. 3:25; Heb. 2:17; 8:12; 9:5). This is language of religious sacrifice, used in Greek religion for rites designed to placate the anger of the gods. Theologians argue whether Christ's sacrificial death on the cross should be described as expiation or propitiation. Expiation emphasizes payment of a penalty to remove guilt. Propitiation speaks of appeasing or averting God's wrath.

4:11–12. God set the standard of love for us. Since we are children of God, we should love other people, especially fellow believers, just as God loved us. God has never been seen in his pure form (Exod. 33:20,23; Deut. 4:12; John 1:18; 5:37; 6:46; cf. John 12:45; 14:9; 17:24; 1 John 1:1–3; 4:14). If you want to know what God is like, you can look at what he has done for us and what we should do for one another. This invisible God actually lives in us. The love he has for us is made visible and complete as we love one another. This is the way the world sees God's love, as it is expressed by him through our lives. Only as God's love completes its purpose of reaching out to those he loves—the world (John 3:16)—is his love complete or fulfilled.

Verse 13 looks back to verse 12. How is God's love expressed and made complete through us? The Spirit does it. Our ability to love one another is dependent upon the Spirit whom he has given us. The Spirit lives in us, implants God's love in us, exercises his love through us, and thus ensures us that we live in God.

C We Must Acknowledge Jesus to Be the Son of God (4:14–21)

> **SUPPORTING IDEA:** *The true Christian who acknowledges that Jesus is the Son of God must live in love toward God as well as his brother.*

4:14–16. John's readers probably never saw Jesus in the flesh. False teachers, however, claimed to have made heavenly journeys during which they saw God in heaven. This is impossible. God cannot be seen. How do you deny the claims of these teachers and still say, **we have seen?** How, if your readers have never seen Jesus, can they testify that God sent his Son to be our Savior? First, John and his fellow apostles saw Jesus in the flesh, but the majority of those who saw Jesus did not join in the testimony. They cried for his crucifixion.

Second, such testimony is based on more than eyewitness. It comes through eyes of faith. Only after the resurrection did this testimony become real for the apostles. They testified to the church. Then the church accepted and repeated their testimony. We do the same.

Third, you do not have to see the earthly Jesus to testify about what God has done through him. You need only hear and believe in the testimony to him from Scripture and from faithful followers. Such testimony is both verbal testimony and God's love exercised through our lives. The impact God has made in other Christians—this is what **we have seen.** Based on the manifestation of Jesus in the lives of Christians, those who have witnessed it can testify that the Father sent Jesus to be the Savior of the world. That is, God sent Jesus to the cross to pay for our sins so we do not have to suffer the wages sin pays, namely, death.

Testimony about Jesus tells more than what Jesus did—save from sin. It also tells who he is—the Son of God. Again, all this goes against false teachers. They apparently claimed Jesus could not be human, thus could not die on the cross. On the other hand, Scripture claims that anyone who acknowledges this Savior they have seen is a true Christian, living in union with God.

This section concludes by repeating an affirmation made earlier—that God is love and that the person who **lives in love lives in God, and God in him.** This is the test of true Christianity in the letters of John. We must recognize the basic character of God, rooted in love. We must experience that love in our own relationship with God. Others must experience this God kind of love in their relationships with us. That's why God sent Jesus to die on the cross for our sins.

4:17–18. The judgment seat of Christ received brief mention in 2:28 and now reappears briefly to assure us we can face Christ on that day with confidence. Such confidence comes because we live in love toward God and one another. The person who does not live in love toward his brother may experience shame (2:28). However, if we live in love toward our brothers, we will have confidence when we face Jesus because in this world we are like him. No one who was like Jesus in this world can fear approaching Jesus' judgment seat. Fear expects punishment. One who loves expects to receive love.

Why? Because mature love has no fear. A Christian who fears the judgment seat of Christ shows that God's love has not yet reached maturity (been made perfect) in him. A person who lives in love toward God has nothing to fear on the day of judgment.

4:19–21. God first loved us and made a relationship with him possible. The text drives home its refutation of the antichrists and false prophets. We cannot claim we love God and then show that we hate our brothers. This only proves one thing: we are liars.

It is difficult to prove whether or not we love God based on our actions toward him because we cannot see him. Love for God is reflected in love for his children, our brothers and sisters, whom we can see. Therefore, God gave us this verifiable command: Whoever loves God must also love his brother. Jesus stated the principle in other words: whatever you did not do for one of the least of these you did not do for me (Matt. 25:40).

MAIN IDEA REVIEW: *We must learn to discern the spirit of truth and falsehood, to love one another as God has loved us, and to love our brothers. Then we will face final judgment with hope and joy.*

III. CONCLUSION

Recognizing Him

Actor Cary Grant once told how he was walking along a street and met a fellow whose eyes locked onto him with excitement. The man said, "Wait a minute, you're . . . you're—I know who you are; don't tell me—Uh, Rock Hud . . . No, you're . . ."

Grant thought he'd help him, so he finished the man's sentence: "Cary Grant."

The fellow responded, "No, that's not it! You're . . ."

Cary Grant was identifying himself with his own name, but the man didn't realize it.

John says of Jesus, "He was in the world, and though the world was made through him, the world did not recognize him" (John 1:10). Like Cary Grant, the real thing—Jesus—was presented to the church in Ephesus, but many people did not recognize him for who he was. How could this be?

Like us, the Ephesian believers lived in difficult days that required real discernment to keep on track in the Christian life. Glib worldly orators touted many options about how we relate to God. Those who did not know the Scripture well, or who were not strongly committed to truth, could be easily swayed. John warned us to be discerning and driven to live out the truth.

Those of us who, by the grace of God, do recognize him must love him and his other children, our brothers, and be faithful to him to the end.

PRINCIPLES

- You are responsible under God to test what you hear against what the Bible teaches.

- True Christians believe in both the full humanity and the full deity of Christ.
- God's Spirit in us is greater than Satan, the prince of this world.
- A person attuned to God will listen to the witness of fellow believers.
- God is love, indwells believers with love, and exercises his love through the lives of believers.
- A life dominated by hate and which shows no love is not a Christian life.
- God has proven his love by sending his son Jesus to die for our sins.
- God's love expressed through our lives gives us confidence to face the final judgment.

APPLICATIONS

- Beware of exciting new teachings and teachers. Test them carefully against Scripture.
- Be sure your daily life reflects God's love to other people.
- Check up on your hate list; it should have no entries.
- In what ways does your life testify to Jesus?
- Ask God to fill you with love so you have no fear of final punishment.

IV. LIFE APPLICATION

Spiritual Pickpockets

Dean Niferatos was riding the Number 22 CTA bus in Chicago. The bus was filled with dozing office workers, restless punkers, and affluent shoppers. At the Clark and Webster stop, two men and a woman climbed in. The driver, a seasoned veteran, immediately called out, "Everybody watch your valuables. Pickpockets are on board."

Women clutched their purses tightly. Men put their hands on their wallets. All eyes fixed on the trio, who, looking insulted and harassed, didn't break stride as they promptly exited through the middle doors.

Just as the seasoned bus driver warned the passengers to be vigilant, so the apostle John warned the church in Ephesus to be vigilant. Evil is less likely to overtake us when we are watching. In this spirit, the apostle says, in essence, "Don't believe everything you hear. Check it out. Make sure it conforms to reality."

Our days are just as dangerous, spiritually, as the days of 1 John. We confront false teachers, false prophets, antichrists, and gullible people at every turn—inside as well as outside the church. All serious Christians must be spiritually discerning of, and deeply committed to, historic Christian truth and exemplary Christian lifestyle.

First John points us to at least four specific dangers:

1. A *loss of objective truth.* Most Westerners (including Europeans and North Americans and those influenced by American and European ways of thinking) used to agree about truth in moral, spiritual, political, and scientific areas. Today our civilization argues over whether truth can be known at all. Chuck Colson has written that the confusion over truth is the fundamental crisis of our age.

   What good does it do to tell people that "the Bible says" if two-thirds of our listeners don't believe the Bible is true? What good does it do for us to say that "Jesus is the truth" if two-thirds of the American people believe there is no such thing as truth? This is not to deny that the Word of God has the power to convince even the hardest heart. But if Christians are to be heard by the modern mind and to make effective inroads into our culture, we must first develop what Francis Schaeffer called "a cultural apologetic": We must defend the very concept of truth (from "Introduction" in Ravi Zacharias, *Can Man Live Without God?* [Dallas:Word Publishing, 1994], pp. ix–x).

2. *Tolerance of anything except intolerance.* A breakdown in moral values is evident all around us. What is right for one person is not seen as necessarily right for someone else. Therefore, we must be tolerant of the views of others if we want them to be tolerant of ours. John Leo reported in the July 27, 1997, edition *of U. S. News & World Report* that some American college students won't condemn Hitler for the Holocaust. "After all, from the Nazi point of view, Hitler believed he was doing the right thing."

3. *Belief that Jesus is a way of personal salvation, but that we are intolerant to suggest that he is the way.* The current outlook of politically correct thinking can tolerate Christianity only if it is viewed as simply another path of spirituality. So we can hear this kind of praise: "Oh, that's wonderful that you are a Christian. It's great that you have found meaning in following Jesus. I, too, have found meaning. I have rediscovered my past life as a Native American shaman (medicine man) and am now into tribal chanting as my mystical path. It's so spiritual. I feel so close to God and nature when I do it. Isn't that wonderful? We're both spiritual!"

   To suggest, however, that Jesus is the right way and that all others are wrong brings indignation and rejection from many people.

4. *Separation of belief (spirit) and behavior (body).* It is widely assumed that you can believe what you want to believe and live how you want to live.

The two do not need to impinge on one another. A famous country music singer is renowned for his immoral lifestyle. He sang in a church in Austin one Sunday morning when I lived there. In a less than noble reaction, I asked, "What did he sing? 'Take Time to be Holy?'" " No," the answer came, "Amazing Grace." We all want to believe in grace, because we do not want to be held accountable for our actions. But the Bible is just as clear about judgment as it is about grace.

American culture clings to the groundless conviction that we can determine for ourselves our own truth. Many people define truth as something we believe, but which doesn't have to control our behavior.

The clash over right and wrong plays itself out daily on television talk shows. Every day guests defend practices and beliefs that would only be discussed privately—and then only rarely—forty years ago. Everything is defended by statements such as these: "Who are you to tell me what is right?" or "I'm happy in what I'm doing, and it's not hurting anybody, so why does it matter to you?"

Those of us who believe the Bible and who believe in Jesus and have committed our lives to him must be clear on the truth. What we believe is absolutely irrelevant unless God believes the same thing. Therefore, we must be alert and vigilant about what we believe. We must not be seduced by false teachers; we must not be influenced by false prophets; we must not be deceived by antichrists. Today, just as in John's day, we must (1) confess that Jesus Christ is the Son of God, (2) love God and love our fellow Christians, and (3) live a moral, ethical lifestyle. To do anything less is to allow false teachers to pick our spiritual pockets.

V. PRAYER

Father, you are love. You have shown this love so clearly by sending your son Jesus to die on the cross for our sins. Implant your Spirit in our lives. Let us love others as you love us. Let love so control our lives that others will see your love through us. May love rid our lives of all fear as we face the final judgment. Amen.

VI. DEEPER DISCOVERIES

A. Test the Spirits (v. 1)

We are living in an age of freewheeling opinions about God, truth, and spirituality. The New Age movement is having a great impact on the thinking of Americans. The many different facets of the New Age movement do not all agree with one another, but they do agree about a number of things.

They agree that they do not think Jesus is the way, the truth, and the life, and that no one comes unto the Father but through him (John 14:6). New Agers have different perspectives about how a person does come to God. Many believe that God is all things and that all things are God (pantheism). Many believe in reincarnation, and that we must try to live good lives so that we will be reincarnated in a higher life form, and eventually reach nirvana, a state in which there is permanent bliss and an end to reincarnation and suffering. Many believe that every one of us is divine, that we can tap into the divine potential within us and achieve our full potential as human beings.

Most New Agers agree that truth is relative: we can determine what is true for ourselves by what we believe and how we act. We can create our own reality, so that something that is true for you may not be true for me, and vice versa.

Many believe that we are all part of one great "whole" of existence and that whatever affects one of us affects us all. Therefore, we should be good to everything and be tolerant of all beliefs and behavior (except that behavior which has been deemed politically incorrect).

A popular example is to think of life as a journey up a mountain. At the top of the mountain is our desire: call it "salvation" or "God," or "self-realization," or "nirvana," or whatever you want to call it. Many roads lead to the top. So it does not matter if we are Hindu, Buddhist, Muslim, Christian, nature worshipers, or Satan worshipers. If we are sincere, we will reach the top. For that reason, no person can claim that his or her road is best. We are all equal in our parallel journey to the top of the mountain.

Many of these New Age values have crept into the church. As a pastor, I have heard virtually all these ideas expressed by people who call themselves Christians:

- Many roads lead to God. It does not matter which one you take as long as you are sincere.
- We are saved if our good works outweigh our bad.
- Christianity is not superior to other religions.
- Jesus is not the only way to salvation.
- There is no such thing as absolute truth.
- Reincarnation is not incompatible with Christianity.
- What is sin for you may not be sin for me, regardless of what the Bible says.
- Being a Christian is a matter of what we believe, now how we live.

The collective understanding of historic Christian truth is being seriously eroded by the pervasive influence of the New Age movement. It is just as important today as it was in John's day for us to test the spirits, to see if they are of God. The tests that emerge from John's letter are:

- Doctrinal purity: we must acknowledge that Jesus has come in the flesh and is from God (4:2).

- Moral purity: we must live lives of holiness (3:4–6).
- Obedience: we must keep God's commands (3:21–24).
- Divine love: we must let the love of God live in us (4:12–13).
- Brotherly love: we must love our brother (4:21).
- Love of God: we must love God (5:2).

VII. TEACHING OUTLINE

A. INTRODUCTION

1. Lead Story: Canals on Mars
2. Context: In the church in Ephesus, false prophets taught such myths as the way to know God was not through Scripture, but through special inner insight, that you did not have to worry about sinning or being righteous, that Jesus was not really human and was not the Son of God. First John brings stern rebuttal of these ideas, setting the church straight on the truth, and calling us to be discerning and to live a life of love toward God and other Christians.
3. Transition: As we look into this chapter, we will see the apostle John telling us we must do three things: (1) test the spirits, (2) love one another, and (3) confess Christ.

B. COMMENTARY

1. Christians Must Exercise Discernment (vv. 1–6)
2. Christians Must Love One Another as God Has Loved Us (vv. 7–12)
3. Christians Must Acknowledge Jesus to Be the Son of God (vv. 14–21)

C. CONCLUSION: SPIRITUAL PICKPOCKETS

VIII. ISSUES FOR DISCUSSIONS

1. What false beliefs threaten the church? Where do they come from? How can we combat them?
2. What evidence does the world see that God lives in and through us?
3. In what way do we testify that God sent Jesus to be the Savior of the world?
4. In what ways do we show God's love to other people?
5. What attitude do we display as we realize that we must face Jesus at the final judgment some day?

1 John 5

Jesus Is Who God Says He Is

Q u o t e

"*A* man who was merely a man and said the sort of things Jesus said would not be a great moral teacher. He would either be a lunatic—on the level of a man who says he is a poached egg—or . . . the Devil . . . or . . . [our] Lord and God."

C . S . L e w i s

1 John

I N A N U T S H E L L

*W*e can have assurance of our salvation. A person who believes Jesus is the Son of God is born again. The Spirit testified that Jesus came by water and blood. Anyone born of God does not continue to sin. God keeps him safe, and the evil one cannot harm him.

Jesus Is Who
God Says He Is

I. INTRODUCTION

Hidden Rocks

Sara Orne Jewett, one of America's fine early writers, wrote *The Country of the Pointed Firs,* a novel about life in Maine. She described a woman walking up a path to the home of a retired sea captain named Elijah Tilley. On the way, the lady passed a number of wooden stakes driven, seemingly at random, into the ground. They were painted the same colors as the old sea captain's house.

The woman asked the captain about the colored stakes. He said the first time they plowed the ground, they hit a number of large rocks just under the surface. He put the stakes in the ground beside each of the large rocks so he wouldn't hit them in the future.

In a way, that is what God has done with the commandments in the Bible. They are stakes driven in the ground to show us where the danger is. Like the hidden rocks, we may not see the danger of disobedience; but when we heed the stakes, we avoid trouble.

God's love for us is what motivated him to drive the stakes into the ground. So, if we love God—if we want to please him and show him our gratitude for his gift to us—we keep his commandments. It only makes sense. It is for our benefit, and it pleases God when we obey him.

First John 5 emphasizes that if we love God, we will obey his commandments—and they are not burdensome to us.

II. COMMENTARY

Jesus Is Who God Says He Is

> **MAIN IDEA:** *We can be assured of our salvation. Only the person who believes that Jesus is the Son of God is born again. Jesus' baptism and crucifixion and the testimony of the Spirit agree that eternal life is in Jesus.*

A We Prove Our Love with Obedient Faith (5:1–5)

> **SUPPORTING IDEA:** *The true Christian overcomes the world by his faith and demonstrates his salvation by obeying God's commands—and they are not burdensome.*

5:1. We hear it again—one who believes in Jesus is born of God—but with a new twist: the person who loves the Father loves God's child as well. This is an appeal to the natural order of things. If we love our parents, we should also love his children, our siblings.

Conceivably, a person might love his parents and not love his brother or sister. For the Christian, this is a test of regenerate character: if you love God, you will love your brothers, too. These extreme and stark terms were demanded by the seriousness of the situation in Ephesus. The antichrists were apparently acting hatefully toward Christians, so the Ephesians needed the contrast of love with hate, not perfect love with imperfect love. We do not have to love our brothers perfectly to manifest a regenerate heart. We may love them imperfectly as we all do. If we hate them, as the antichrists did, we cannot have any confidence that we are born again.

5:2–3. These verses present the opposite of what we expect—that we know that we love the children of God **by loving God and carrying out his commands.** We expect to hear that we demonstrate our love for God by loving our brothers. The opposite appears. This demonstrates that love is a central characteristic. As a genuine mark of a born-again heart, it goes both ways: toward God and toward our brothers.

This love for God, then, is most clearly demonstrated by obeying him: "If you obey my commands, you will remain in my love" (John 15:10). Obedience does not always bring cheer to our hearts, so a profound statement follows: **his commands are not burdensome.** This stands contrary to what most people think. Certainly, God's commands are not always the path of least resistance in life. In that sense, it is often easier to disobey God than to obey him. If obeying a command of God is harder than disobeying, the consequences are easier.

For example, if it is harder to remain faithful to one's spouse (obeying the command not to commit adultery) than to give in to passion (disobeying a command), then the consequence of obeying (not committing adultery) will be much easier than the consequences of not obeying (committing adultery). In other words, sin has a price. When it is paid, we see it would have been easier not to have sinned. So in the long run, obeying God's commands is not burdensome. This is why Jesus could say his yoke is easy and his burden is light (Matt. 11:28–30).

5:4–5. Some Christians see their weakness regarding temptation and sin and decide their victory over the world is incomplete. They conclude that since they have not "overcome the world," they must not be truly Christian. This is not an accurate understanding of this verse.

As F. F. Bruce observed, the term *world* may mean (1) the false teachings of the antichrists who suggest that Jesus is not the Son of God and did not come in the flesh, or (2) the lure of the world (**lust of the flesh, lust of the** eyes, pride of life), or (c) the threat of open hostility that the world breathes toward those who follow Christ (*The Epistles of John,* 117). Regardless, John has already encouraged his readers that they are **from God and have overcome . . . because** [he] **who is in you is greater than the one who is in the world** (4:4). The victory is already won. We won it (past tense) with our union in Christ, and we win it (present tense) by our refusal to deny him.

As Simon Kistenmaker observes, "All who have their birth in God have overcome the world and therefore we can claim victory already" (*I–III John,* 350). Jesus said, "Take heart! I have overcome the world" (John 16:33). Jesus' victory has overcome the evil one and has set his people free from the power of Satan.

Faith is the basis of our victory. When we place our faith in Jesus, nothing can separate us from the love of God in Christ Jesus (Rom. 8:37–39; 1 Cor. 15:57). No forces of evil can conquer the person who trusts in Jesus. Instead, the believer is victorious over the world because of his faith in Christ.

Seen this way, this verse is not a matter of discouragement or fear that because we struggle with sin in our lives, we may not be Christians. Rather, it should be a matter of encouragement because in spite of our struggle with sin in our daily lives, the victory is already won. Our salvation is secure in Jesus.

James Boice supports this understanding: "Indeed, in the broadest view the faithfulness was not theirs, but rather his who . . . led them to faith in Christ, a pursuit of righteousness, and love for other Christians" (*The Epistles of John,* 158).

🅱 Jesus Gives Us Eternal Life (4:6–12)

SUPPORTING IDEA: *Jesus' baptism, his crucifixion, and the Holy Spirit—all three of these testify that Jesus is the Son of God. God's testimony is greater than human testimony, so anyone who does not accept it makes God a liar. The testimony is this: eternal life is in Jesus.*

5:6–8. The phrase **water and blood** automatically makes us think of the incident during the crucifixion of Jesus when the soldier pierced his side and water and blood came out (John 19:34). However, this is probably not a reference to that event, but to Jesus' baptism and crucifixion. Cerithus, a false teacher of that time, taught that Christ was a spiritual being who came down on the man Jesus when he was baptized, but left him before he was crucified. That way, Christ came through water (baptism) but not through blood (crucifixion). To correct this lie, John wrote that the one whom believers acknowledge to be the Son of God (v. 5) came not **by water only, but by water and blood.** The one who hung on the cross was the same person who was baptized in the Jordan River.

Our witness of what we have seen and heard (1:2, 4:14) is important, but there is a greater witness—the Holy Spirit (see John 15:26–27). The witness of the Spirit is joined to the witness of the water and blood, so that **the three are in agreement.**

The witness of the Spirit may be understood as the testimony of God (see v. 9) through the prophets (including John the Baptist) and the Scripture. All witnesses converge—the testimony of the Spirit through the prophets and Scripture, and the testimony of the historical facts of Jesus' life from the beginning of his ministry (baptism) to the end (crucifixion).

5:9–11. If human testimony is accepted on the basis of three witnesses, how much more should God's testimony be accepted. Two points are made before specifying God's testimony in verses 11–12. First, divine testimony should be accepted because it is greater than human testimony, which everyone accepts. Second, willful unbelief is sin. If we trust people to be true to their word, why would we not trust God, who is more trustworthy than humans?

If a person accepts the testimony of God, he has an internal (**in his heart**) assurance that what he has believed is actually true. Reformers called this the *testimonium Spiritus Sancti internum,* or the internal testimony of the Holy Spirit. It is given in addition to the historical evidence (Rom. 8:16). Anyone who rejects God's testimony **has made him out to be a liar.** There is no middle ground. You are either with God or against him.

5:11–12. So what is being testified to? That eternal life comes from God through his Son Jesus and through no other way. This statement is very likely directed at the antichrists who charged that the readers did not really have eternal life through Christ. Scripture makes it clear that we do have eternal life through Jesus. To deny this is to deny God's testimony and to call God a liar.

𝕮 Believers Are Assured of Eternal Life (5:13–15)

SUPPORTING IDEA: *You can be assured of eternal life, and with that assurance, have confidence with God in prayer.*

5:13. John clearly stated his purpose for writing the Gospel: "That you may believe that Jesus is the Christ, the Son of God, and that by believing you may have life in his name" (John 20:31). The Gospel was written to non-Christians to lead them to become Christians. In a parallel way, toward the end of his first epistle, John stated his purpose for writing it: **That you may know that you have eternal life.** First John is written to those who are Christians to give them assurance that they are saved.

5:14–15. Prayer was previously discussed in chapter 3. The Christian may have confidence in approaching God in prayer. Our confidence in prayer is a natural consequence of our assurance that we have eternal life (vv. 12–13). We may ask anything according to God's will, and we will receive it.

This leads many Christians to ask, How can I know what the will of God is? Sometimes Scripture will tell us what the will of God is, either explicitly or in principle. It may take spiritual maturation and discernment to learn which principles of Scripture should guide our prayers. Elsewhere, we are told that if we "abide (*remain,* NIV) in Jesus and God's Word abides in us, we may ask what we will and it will be given" (John 15:7–8,16).

Prayer must be viewed not as our attempt to get God to see things from our point of view but as our attempt to see things from God's point of view. When we grow, mature, study, and meditate on Scripture and seek the will of God, we try to ask ourselves not what *we* want, but what *God* wants. Then we make progress in prayer.

Ⓓ God's Children Do Not Continue to Sin (5:16–21)

SUPPORTING IDEA: *Pray for a brother who sins. No one who is born of God continues to sin. Jesus has come so we may know God and have eternal life.*

5:16–17. We are to pray for a brother who commits a sin that does *not* lead to death, but not to pray for a brother who commits a sin that *does* lead to death. What sin will **lead to death?** Several possibilities have been suggested by Bible teachers, but none is without difficulties, so we find ourselves with a variety of interpretations. Suggestions about the nature of the "sin to death" include the following:

1. A particularly bad sin which God will not pardon. Nothing else in the New Testament suggests that a sin can be so bad that God will not pardon it. Peter cursed and denied that he ever knew Jesus. This is about as bad a sin as we can imagine, but a number of days later this flamboyant sinner was eating breakfast with Jesus on the shores of the Sea of Galilee, in perfect fellowship with him. Peter went on to serve Jesus triumphantly.

2. This "sin to death" is identified by some as apostasy—to deliberately repudiate the Christian faith, after supposedly embracing it. First John 3:9 appears to teach that a true Christian cannot fall away from the faith. If someone does fall away, it indicates he or she was never a believer in the first place.

3. To others, this "sin to death" was blaspheming the Holy Spirit, a sin Matthew says will not be forgiven (12:31–32). But how could John call such a hardened sinner a brother?

4. Finally, some interpreters identify this "sin to death" as physical death. Some Christians in Scripture sinned so badly that God took their lives: Ananias and Sapphira (Acts 5:1–11); perhaps the man sinning with his stepmother in 1 Corinthians 5—who was delivered over to Satan for the destruction of his flesh but the salvation of his

soul—and the people who "fell asleep" in 1 Corinthians 11, perhaps because they were abusing the Lord's Supper. Some interpreters object to this view because we do not know what sin leads to death until the person dies, and then it is too late to pray for him or her. Other people counter that we can sometimes see the death coming, or fear that it may be coming because of an immoral or faithless life-style. Yet, the wayward person may be so hardened that he will not repent, and God takes his life. If a person is in that situation, it is not God's will to save his life, so we should not pray for it. We can always pray that the wayward person will repent, but if he does not repent, there is no value in praying for his life to be spared.

We cannot be sure of the correct interpretation of the "sin to death." Thus, we need to focus on the positive point: we are to pray for our sinning brothers. This is certainly in line with God's will. Jesus prayed for Peter on the night Peter betrayed him (Luke 22:32), and we should do the same for one another.

5:18–21. John brings his first epistle to a close by summarizing three final affirmations, each introduced with the phrase, "we know":

1. A person **born of God does not continue to sin** and is kept away from Satan's harm. Jesus keeps him safe. The believer is secure in the grace of God, and Satan cannot take his salvation from him.

2. **We are children of God**, not under Satan's control as the world is. This reinforces the distinction between the satanically-controlled world system and the Christ-controlled body of believers who have been delivered from its power.

3. The **Son of God has come** into this world to give us **understanding** which leads to salvation. This strikes a one-two blow against the false teachers, the antichrists who claimed to have special inner knowledge of God and salvation apart from Jesus. God can be known in only one way—through Jesus. Truth can be known in only one way—through Jesus.

Verse 20 presents a small problem with its last sentence. Does it make an affirmation about Jesus or about the Father? Bible students argue both ways. The Bible as a whole teaches both points. God is the only true God, and life in him is the only eternal life. Jesus is also equated with God and has provided eternal life through his death on the cross.

Anything which stands in opposition to the one true God is idolatry. "Keep yourselves from it," Scripture commands. "Worship only the true God and Jesus, whom we have heard and seen and touched and proclaimed to you."

MAIN IDEA REVIEW: *We can be assured of our salvation. Only the person who believes that Jesus is the Son of God is born again. Jesus' baptism and crucifixion and the testimony of the Spirit agree that eternal life is in Jesus.*

III. CONCLUSION

If I Were King

Obedience often seems hard because of all the people who have authority over us. They ask us to do things we don't want to do. *If I were king,* we think, *I could be happy.*

Yet, shortly after A.D. 1000, King Henry III of Bavaria grew tired of court life and the pressures of being a monarch. He decided to live the contemplative life of a monk, so he applied to a local monastery.

Richard, the prior or ranking member of the monastery, hesitated. "Your Majesty, do you understand that the pledge here is one of obedience? That will be hard for a king."

Henry replied, "I understand. The rest of my life I will be obedient to you, as Christ leads you."

"Then I will tell you what to do," said Prior Richard. "Go back to your throne and serve faithfully in the place where God has put you."

When Henry III died, it was said of him that "the king learned to rule by being obedient."

Whether you are a king or a pauper, you can serve Christ faithfully. If you are a teacher, a mother, or a construction worker, God expects you to be faithfully obedient where he puts you. When he returns, we'll rule together with him.

Christian faith rests on this truth: we prove our love to God with obedient faith. Jesus gives us eternal life, and we can rest assured that we have eternal life. God's children will not continue to live in sin. First John 5 reminds us to remember and to embrace these fundamental truths in the spirit of obedience.

PRINCIPLES

- God cares about our obedience.
- Love is manifested by obedience.
- Whoever has the love and Spirit of Jesus has eternal life.
- We may be confident before God in prayer.
- Christians should look out for one another.

APPLICATIONS

- Trust God, and obey his commandments.
- Rest in the assurance of eternal life that God gives you.
- Pray in the confidence that God hears you.
- If you see a brother sin, pray for him or her.

IV. LIFE APPLICATION

Sin Is a Boomerang

Following Christ can have a high price, particularly when persecution is involved. Fox's *Book of Martyrs* tells hair-raising stories of the persecution and suffering that Christians went through in the early days of the church. Yet today even more Christians are persecuted for their faith throughout the world.

In the less extreme environment of modern America we do not usually pay such a high price for being obedient to Christ. Our environment too often makes the reverse vividly clear—the high price of disobedience to Christ.

Sin is a boomerang. When someone throws out a sin, the consequences always come back to hurt—harming not only the sinner who threw it but other people as well. Dishonesty, for example, may ruin our reputation and cost us our job. That hurts us, but it also hurts our spouse and children. It embarrasses them and makes them suffer financially for our sin. Whatever the sin—dishonesty, immorality, anger, greed, pride, or gluttony—sin always boomerangs, hurting us and those we love.

Such pain extends beyond external circumstantial pain. Sin also brings the internal pain of guilt, broken relationships, frustration over lost potential, fear of the future, loneliness, and so forth.

We cannot break the laws of God. We can only break ourselves against them when we disobey. We think we can ignore the truth. We can't. We think we can sidestep obedience to God without paying a price. We can't. Sin always has a price.

Sometimes we reap the cause/effect consequences of sin. Consider the dishonest or lazy person who loses his job. It is part of the natural scheme of things: "A man reaps what he sows" (Gal. 6:7).

At other times God brings direct judgment upon sin. You might see this as a thunderbolt chastening us from heaven. Hebrews 12:5–6 reminds us: "My son, do not make light of the Lord's discipline, and do not lose heart when he rebukes you, because the Lord disciplines those he loves, and he punishes everyone he accepts as a son."

Perhaps we committed the "perfect crime" when we cheated on a business deal; yet the deal mysteriously fell apart, and we lost our money. An accident? A coincidence? Perhaps not. Maybe it was divine judgment as God chastened us to bring about our repentance.

Why does God require obedience from us? Everything God asks of us is because he wants to give something good to us and to keep us from harm. The straightest line between you and the life you long for is total obedience to Christ. The Bible clearly promises joy for obedience: "If you obey my commands, you will remain in my love, just as I have obeyed my Father's commands and remain in his love. I have told you this so that my joy may be in you and that your joy may be complete" (John 15:10).

Scripture, likewise, promises blessings to the person who is scrupulously obedient to God. We shouldn't ask, "How much can I get away with?" but "How obedient can I be?"

If we believe obedience is the shortest distance between us and the life we want, we will obey. When we disobey, it is because of a breakdown of our faith. We don't believe the course of obedience will bring joy. Or we don't believe a little disobedience will hurt all that much. Obedience is not nearly as hard if we become persuaded that it is not only for God's glory, but also for our good. Yes, obedience *sometimes* has a high cost, but disobedience *always* has a high cost.

V. PRAYER

Lord, help us to see that what you ask of us is for our own good. Help us believe that the shortest distance between us and the life we long for is total obedience to you. Help us be courageous and consistent in choosing to be obedient to you. Amen.

VI. DEEPER DISCOVERIES

A. Faith (v. 4)

Faith is a powerful motivator. When we believe that Jesus is who he says he is, that we are who he says we are, and that our destiny is what he says it will be, then committing our lives to Christ is the only reasonable course of action.

By faith, we overcome the world, in the sense that we are transferred out of the kingdom of darkness into the kingdom of light. Thus, we are destined to an eternity with God.

Faith is active in our everyday lives also. Faith determines our obedience to God. Obedience is the natural consequence of truly believing. If we believe the promises of God, obedience to his commands is a natural reaction. On the other hand, disobedience is a breakdown of faith.

Blaise Pascal, seventeenth-century philosopher, has articulated why this is so: "All men seek happiness. This is without exception. Whatever different means they employ, they all tend to this end. The cause of some going to war, and of others avoiding it, is the same desire in both, attending with different views. The 'will' never takes the least step but to this objective. This is the motive of every man, even of those who hang themselves."

This being the case, all people would chose to obey God in all things if they truly believed that such obedience brought joy, as the Scriptures say it will. This is why faith is so powerful. When we believe the promises of God and when we believe that obedience is the foundation for joy, we resist the pull of the world (**lust of the flesh, lust of the eyes, pride of life**, 1 John 2:16), and we resist the inclination to self-determination. Instead, we give ourselves wholly to God. Victory, then, is complete. Our eternal life is already won, and our abundant life is in the process of being won. Faith is, indeed, the victory that overcomes the world.

B. Blood (v. 6)

The Bible often uses blood as a metaphor for the crucifixion. As we get more and more sophisticated in our culture, we are less and less inclined to talk about blood or crosses. The crucifixion is a grisly execution that does not make for polite conversation. This results in a gravitational pull away from the cross. This pull we must resist. The Bible insists on certain fundamental absolute truths. If there is no cross, there is no Christianity; there is no salvation; there is no hope.

The simple fact is that humanity has sinned. That sin separated us from God. Jesus' death on the cross was the only means by which our sins could be forgiven and we could be reconciled to God. The grace of God comes to us stained with blood. Why would God leave the glories of heaven and come to earth? Why would he endure the humiliation of people who spat on him and beat him when he could have wiped them out with one word? Why would a holy God allow the sin of the world to be placed on him—an experience that surely aroused more revulsion and pain than any experience a human could have?

As Cornelius Plantiga asks in *Not the Way Things Are Supposed to Be,* "What had we thought the ripping and writhing on Golgotha were all about?" (p. 198). Would he have endured that for nothing? In the Garden of Gethsemane, Jesus prayed to the Father that if there were any other way to accomplish salvation for humanity, "let this cup pass from me." The cup did not pass from him. There was no other way. Do we think his pain and suffering were for nothing?

If the shedding of Jesus' blood on the cross was not necessary, then the gospel salvation by grace through faith becomes unnecessary, uninteresting, and ultimately offensive.

At a conference in Minneapolis in 1994, sponsored by the World Council of Churches, Christian soteriology (the doctrine of salvation) was attacked as promoting violence. A father (God) killing his son (Jesus) was a formula for child abuse. One speaker (Delores Williams) did not hide her agenda when she said, "I don't think we need a theory of atonement at all. I don't think we need folks hanging on crosses and blood dripping and weird stuff. We just need to listen to the god within." This is exactly what the antichrists were saying to the church in Ephesus in John's day.

Many people think we need only the gospel of self-esteem, or self-help, or good works, or humanitarianism. To speak of the blood of Christ becomes distasteful. If the cross were not necessary, then the crucifixion was merely a heroic example of sacrifice—a "cost" out of proportion to the "benefit."

It is popular now to speak of self-esteem and positive thinking as the heart of salvation. It is popular now for churches to provide "seeker-sensitive" services, so unbelievers are not turned off by our church services. Perhaps these things can be used to help create a receptive atmosphere if they are properly integrated with the rest of truth. However, for the Christian church to "ignore, euphemize, or otherwise mute the lethal reality of sin," Plantiga says insightfully, "is to cut the nerve of the gospel" (p. 199). To deny the necessity of the cross is to fall into the same error as the antichrists of Ephesus did in the apostle John's day.

VII. TEACHING OUTLINE

A. INTRODUCTION

1. Lead Story: Hidden Rocks
2. Context: The apostle John is wrapping up his letter to the church in Ephesus. In doing so, he reviews several themes he has already talked about earlier in the book. These summaries emphasize:
   a. The Christian should obey God's commands.
   b. Jesus is the Son of God.
   c. By believing in him, we can be assured of eternal life.
   d. God's children will not adopt a lifestyle of unrestrained sin.
3. Transition: As we conclude this study, we need to review our own situation. The review in Scripture can help us restate our own beliefs and gain new assurance of our place in God's kingdom. Let us see if we are sure we have eternal life. Let us see if we are sure we love God. Let us see what it takes to make us obedient to God.

B. COMMENTARY

1. We Prove Our Love with Obedient Faith (vv. 1–5)
2. Jesus Gives Us Eternal Life (vv. 6–12)
3. Believers Are Assured of Eternal Life (vv. 13–15)
4. God's Children Do Not Continue to Sin (vv. 16–21)

C. CONCLUSION: SIN IS A BOOMERANG

VIII. ISSUES FOR DISCUSSION

1. Describe the relationship between making the right doctrinal confession and living in love toward other people.
2. Describe the relationship between love and obedience.
3. Do you ever doubt your salvation? Why? What relieves your doubts?
4. How does 1 John define faith?
5. Do you expect every prayer you offer to God to be answered? Why or why not? How do you know if you are praying according to God's will?

2 John

Love and Resist

"*Faithfulness in little things is a big thing.*"

C h r y s o s t o m

BOOK PROFILE: 2 JOHN

- Sent to Christians near Ephesus, in Asia (western Turkey)
- The "chosen lady and her children" might refer to an actual family, or perhaps is a metaphor for a church, possibly near Ephesus, a sister church to the church that received 1 John
- Probably written approximately the same time as 1 John, perhaps slightly later
- Written to encourage and strengthen these Christians to walk in love toward one another and to resist false teaching. Very similar to 1 John
- Emphasizes the need to obey God's commands
- Refutes false teachers who denied that Jesus was truly God and truly man
- A highly personal letter reflecting John's affection for these believers and his deep concern for their welfare

AUTHOR PROFILE: JOHN

- Author is identified only as "the elder," traditionally identified as the apostle John. "Elder" probably does not refer to an office in the church, but rather is a term of endearment and veneration, similar to an "elder statesman"
- The apostle John, one of the original twelve disciples of Jesus, who also wrote the Gospel of John
- The disciple whom Jesus loved (John 21:20,24)
- One of the two sons of Zebedee, the brother of James
- Along with James, nicknamed the "Sons of Thunder" (Mark 3:17)
- Formerly a follower of John the Baptist
- Wrote this letter in his old age
- Known as the "Apostle of Love," since the theme of love is so prominent in his writings

 **I N   A   N U T S H E L L**

Many *deceivers are around, so I am glad to hear that some of you are walking in the truth, for God commanded that we walk in love. Be on guard against their teaching. Do not be taken in by them. Do not give them hospitality or aid in their damaging activity.*

Love and Resist

I. INTRODUCTION

Dependable as the Morning Mail

$\mathcal{H}$ow faithful do you have to be in order to be faithful? If your car starts two out of three times, do you think it's faithful? If your newspaper boy skips delivery once a week, is he faithful? What if you don't go to work twice a month? If you miss a couple of house payments a year, does the bank say, "Ten out of twelve isn't bad"?

No, a great deal more "faithfulness" is required in these areas. How faithful do we have to be in our Christian walk? Or how faithful do we have to be to the fundamentals of the faith? The apostle John wrote a letter to either a lady or a church (scholars are divided) commending them for their faithful Christian walk, and exhorting them to resist false teaching. He wanted his readers to be as dependable as the daily mail in both their actions and their beliefs. That's faithful.

II. COMMENTARY

Love and Resist

> **MAIN IDEA:** Christians are to walk in love toward one another, obey God's commandments, and be alert not to assist false teachers—those who deny Jesus.

A Salutation (vv. 1–3)

> **SUPPORTING IDEA:** May God's blessings be upon the people I love—people who let the truth live in them.

1–3. John writes to a **chosen lady and her children**. Bible scholars are divided as to whether this refers to an actual family whom John knew, or whether it refers to a church. The lack of any personal references in the letter, in contrast to 3 John, suggests to many that it is addressed to a church. In that case, it might be a sister church to the church John wrote to in his first epistle. This commentary will intentionally leave the question open.

John stated his love for the chosen lady, acknowledging that every person who loves truth loves her. This suggests the she was well known in Christian circles. **Chosen** means one of God's elect, a true Christian.

The relationship John had with her is founded on truth. That relationship is shared by all who know the truth, that is, all true believers. If it were not for Jesus, they would not have a relationship. Truth is the basis of all true love. It is not simply an intellectual property. It is that which lives in and directs life. Jesus is the truth that creates such love. This truth is eternal and must be guarded carefully.

John wished them **grace, mercy and peace**, common words in ancient Christian greetings. He also blessed them with the less common **truth and love**, two themes that form the foundation for the letter to follow.

B Christians Must Practice the Truth (vv. 4–6)

SUPPORTING IDEA: *It is a joy that some of you are walking in the truth. We are commanded to love one another and to walk in obedience to God's commands.*

4. When people we mentor and disciple are **walking in the truth** as God has commanded, we are filled with joy and pleasure. Pointing out some obedient people does not necessarily indicate that others were disobedient. Rather, John only knew about some of them.

5. This presents not a new command, but an old one, that we **love one another** (1 John 2:7–8). Followers of Jesus had this truth from the beginning of Jesus' ministry (John 13:34–35; 15:9–17).

6. What is love? It plays itself out in the real world in obedience. The essence of love is that we keep God's commandments. This glorifies God, is best for others, and is best for us. Everything God asks of us is intended to give something good to us or keep us from harm. First John presented the same emphasis on love and the same link between love and obedience.

C Christians Must Protect the Truth (vv. 7–11)

SUPPORTING IDEA: *We must not be led astray by the world's deceivers, those who do not acknowledge Jesus. Nor should we assist them in any way, thus participating in their evil.*

7. The deceivers going **out into the world** may refer to their leaving the church in Ephesus to found their own movement. Their very numbers, plus the magnitude of their error, made them dangerous people. They did not understand and believe correctly about Jesus. They denied that Jesus came in the flesh. Some people taught that he only appeared to be in the flesh. This strikes at the heart of true belief about Jesus (Col. 2:9; 1 John 4:2). It marks these people as antichrists, people who deny fundamental truth about Jesus (1 John 2:18,22; 4:3).

8. To heed the teachings of these antichrists results not in the loss of salvation but in the loss of spiritual reward. God would not forget what they had done for him: "God is not unjust; he will not forget your work and the love you have shown him as you have helped his people" (Heb. 6:10). Yet, to

depart from the rewardable path is to lose the full reward coming to those who do not follow such false teachers (1 Cor. 3:8,11–15).

9. The antichrists—the false teachers and false prophets talked about more thoroughly in 1 John—were running ahead, and were not continuing **in the teaching of Christ. Runs ahead** is also translated "goes too far" (NASB) or "transgresses" (NKJV). These give a more complete understanding of the danger. The teaching of Christ may refer to the teachings of Jesus or to teachings about Jesus. In either case, it refers to orthodox truth established and accepted in the church.

The text seems to center on defection from the truth by those who had once held to the truth. Some teachers believe this refers to Christians who depart from the faith. If this is the case, to deviate from the truth would be to leave God behind. In the sense of fellowship and blessing, the person who defects from the faith **does not have God.** According to this position, it does not suggest loss of salvation, but points to doctrinal deviation and disobedience.

Other Bible teachers believe the one who **runs ahead** is not a true Christian. He may have given every appearance of being a true Christian, but his defection from the faith proves he never was a true believer. This seems more in keeping with the teaching of 1 John.

Scripture seeks those who learn and practice the true teachings, those who have a full understanding of who Jesus is. Jesus is equal with God the Father. To have Jesus is to have the Father, and to have the Father is to have Jesus (see commentary on 1 John 5:20).

10–11. These verses seem harsh. Those who remain faithful to the teaching of Christ must resist those who do not. If a person did not teach truth about Jesus, these believers were not to practice hospitality toward him. This does not suggest that we are not to be cordial to false teachers, or that we cannot invite a member of a false sect into our home to talk with him. Rather, it refers to a level of hospitality that helps the false teacher spread his or her false doctrine.

In the first century, traveling was difficult. The traveler could not find hotels and restaurants. Traveling teachers and missionaries depended on others to house and feed them. John urged his readers not to "fund" these false teachers by housing and feeding them. To do so would be to share **in his wicked work.** In our day, when people of all sorts of religious belief use the media to plead for financial support, we need to be careful what kind of doctrine we fund.

D Farewell (vv. 12–13)

SUPPORTING IDEA: *Face-to-face fellowship often brings more joy than written correspondence.*

12–13. John had **much to write** to them, but he wanted to communicate with them **face to face.** He anticipated a **visit** to them soon and would say more then. This would make his **joy . . . complete.** We do not know what more he wanted to say, but we might speculate that he wanted to deal in greater detail with the problems at hand. Second John is a condensed version of the issue the apostle dealt with in 1 John, and we might imagine that he would cover the things in 1 John that we do not see in 2 John.

The unusual farewell can be understood as addressed either to a lady or a church. If it was to an individual lady, then the apostle had apparently met her sister's children, who sent their greetings. If the "lady" was a local church, then **your chosen sister** was also a local church. It suggests that the members of the church from which John wrote sent their greetings to the church to which the letter was addressed. It testifies to the interest and concern that different churches had for one another.

MAIN IDEA REVIEW: *Many deceivers are around, so I am glad to hear that some of you are walking in the truth, for God commanded that we walk in love. Be on guard against their teaching. Do not be taken in by them. Do not give them hospitality or aid in their damaging activity.*

III. CONCLUSION

Standing at Your Post

Excavations at the ancient city of Pompeii have revealed many historical insights and some stirring examples of faithfulness. When Mt. Vesuvius erupted and destroyed the city, many people were buried in the ruins. Some were found in cellars, as if they had gone there for safety. Some were found in the upper rooms of buildings, probably for the same reason. One Roman sentinel was found standing at the city gate where he had been placed by the captain, with his hand still grasping his weapon. There, while the earth shook beneath him—there while the floods of ashes and cinders covered him—he had stood at his post. There, after a thousand years, his faithfulness was revealed.

That is how faithful we are to be to Jesus and his truth. We are not to be deceived by those who would sway us from the truth. We are to stand firm, strong, and resolute. When Jesus comes, or when we go to meet him, we are to be found at our post with our weapons in our hands, believing the truth and living the truth.

John focused on faithfulness in his letter to the **lady and her children**. He commended them for faithfulness in their actions (walking in the truth) and exhorted them to be faithful in their belief (watch out for deceivers). He wanted them to stand, fixed, at their assigned post in life.

PRINCIPLES

- When we walk in truth, it makes other people happy. When others walk in the truth, it makes us happy.
- To love God is to obey him.
- Many deceivers in the world tempt the church in every age.
- Only alert believers are safe from deception.
- If we support evil workers in any way, we participate in their evil work.

APPLICATION

- Show your love for God not by warm, fuzzy feelings on Sunday morning, but in gritty obedience Monday through Saturday.
- Evaluate the television preacher, the author of the book you are reading, and the church you belong to and support by their faithfulness to who Jesus is and to their personal integrity.
- Give support to ministries that demonstrate integrity in character, holding to historic Christian truth.

IV. LIFE APPLICATION

The Liar's Club

I read once of a liar's club in Burlington, Wisconsin. You could join for one dollar—and a lie. Some of the stories people used to get into the liar's club were "doozies!" One man said his wife's feet were so cold that every time she took her shoes off the furnace kicked on. Another man said he was fishing one day where the fish were biting so well he had to stand behind a tree to bait his hook. Someone else said he cut a tree down on a day when it was so foggy that the tree didn't fall over until the fog lifted. One farmer said his wife was so lazy she fed the chickens popcorn so the eggs would turn themselves over when she was frying them in a pan.

A gentleman from Alabama looked over the national registry of the liar's club and discovered liars from every state in the country except Alabama. He wrote to the liar's club, pointed this out, and then added that this was because there were no liars in Alabama. The liar's club was so impressed that they gave him a free lifetime membership.

These aren't really lies, of course. They are tall tales. The difference is that no one is supposed to know that a lie is a lie, but everyone knows that a tall tale is not true. Lying is wrong. Tall tales are just fun.

While outrageous stories and tall tales are fun and harmless, lies are no fun—and they are very harmful. One of the pressing problems seen throughout the New Testament is false teachers. The faithful are warned about people going around trying to get others to believe their teaching, which is different from the teaching of Jesus or the apostles. Perhaps they could not be accused of lying, because they apparently believed what they were teaching. But their teaching certainly was not true, and we must treat their teaching as a lie.

The problem is not restricted to New Testament times. Lying is also with us today. Alan Bloom, in his masterful work, *The Closing of the American Mind,* states that the single most agreed-upon truth on the American college campus today is that truth is relative—that there is no such thing as absolute truth. Rather, each person is free to determine what is true for himself or herself. You may believe one thing is true, while another person believes the opposite. This is okay because each thing is true to the person who believes it.

This perspective is wreaking havoc with business, our education system, government, the family, morals and values, and everything else in American life. As a result, every person is doing what is right in their own eyes (see Judg. 21:25). When every individual does what is right in their own eyes, the social structure begins to break down. And this viewpoint is also creeping into the church, because all people in the church are influenced by society at large.

We are becoming sick because we are drinking from a polluted supply of truth. Into that supply have been dumped lies, inaccuracies, misconceptions, runaway individualism, the demand of rights without responsibilities, selfishness, sensuality, and a conviction that "my happiness is more important than yours." As we drink from this polluted supply, we are becoming morally ill, just as we would become physically ill if we were drinking water from a reservoir that contained filth, waste, and disease.

We may have little influence over what the world's values are, but we have great influence over the values in the church. There, we must raise the call for absolute truth. Truth is what God says it is, regardless of what we believe or what we feel. The church must stand firm on this point.

When we as believers make a skillful, pleasing defense of what we believe in and then back it up with good works, we create a wonderful message. We need to argue forcefully and candidly while demonstrating the love of Christ to the world. The world is so hardened to the Scriptures and so confused by the issue of truth that it cannot accept our message. When our message comes through the love of Christ, then people tend to accept the reality of what we say.

Like the readers of John's second epistle, we must practice the truth, and we must protect the truth. We must stand firm against the false teachers of our day, and we must live out our faith. In doing so, we remain strong; the church remains viable; and the lost are shown an accurate picture of Jesus.

V. PRAYER

Dear heavenly Father, help us to remain strong in our Christian walk, and help us to be alert to false teaching—to recognize it and to stand against it. Help us to pass on to future generations an accurate record of biblical truth and a good example to live by. Amen.

VI. DEEPER DISCOVERIES

A. Jesus Christ . . . in the Flesh (v. 7)

Scripture describes the devil as a deceiver and a destroyer. The many deceivers who have gone out into the world are playing into the hands of the great deceiver—Satan. His goal is to destroy. He wants to keep people from eternal salvation. He can encourage this in many ways. One way is to pervert the accurate picture of who Jesus is. If he can get people to accept an inaccurate understanding of Jesus, he can keep them from experiencing salvation. Therefore, distorting the accuracy of who Jesus is becomes a prime method of operation for the Evil One.

Two balanced truths about Jesus usually get distorted: he is fully God; he is fully human. It is critical to believe both these concepts, for two reasons. One is that Scripture teaches both truths. The second is that both are necessary for our salvation.

Jesus had a human body. He was born physically (Matt. 1:18) and he grew normally as humans do (Luke 2:52). He referred to himself as a man, and others recognized him as a man (John 8:40; 1 John 1:1). As all people do, he got hungry (Matt. 4:2), became thirsty (John 19:28), grew tired (John 4:6), felt love and compassion (Matt. 9:36), wept (John 11:35), and was tempted (Heb. 4:15).

He was also God. He existed before he was born as Jesus of Nazareth (John 8:58), was conceived by the Holy Spirit and born of the virgin Mary (Luke 1:31,34), claimed to be one with the Father (John 5:18), called himself the Son of God (Matt. 26:63–64), and performed miracles to prove that he could forgive sin (Mark 2:1–12). He was worshiped by men and angels (Matt. 14:33), and his name is mentioned with other members of the Trinity (2 Cor. 13:14). All the fullness of deity dwells in him (Col. 2:9). Philippians 2:1–11 refers to the relationship of his humanity and his deity and how these two facets of his being are related to each other.

Jesus brings salvation. If Jesus were not human, he could not have died for our sins. If he were not God, it would not have mattered if he had. He had to be sinless and human, or his death could not have counted for ours.

If we accept the clear testimony of Scripture, we must accept that Jesus was both fully human and fully divine. To deny either truth is to strike at the heart of the New Testament teaching, presenting a Christ who cannot save us from our sins.

B. May Be Rewarded Fully (v. 8)

First Corinthians gives us a picture of eternal rewards. We may work, but God provides the fruit. We are rewarded for our faithfulness, even though the results might be meager, because the results are up to God (3:6–8).

We may accrue rewardable works (gold, silver, costly stones) or unrewardable works (wood, hay, straw) (3:11–15). When we stand before the judgment seat of Christ (2 Cor. 5:10), our unrewardable works will be burned up, so to speak, but our rewardable works will remain.

The basis of rewards is our motives. At the judgment seat of Christ, Jesus will expose the motives of our hearts, and then each person will receive his or her praise from God (1 Cor. 4:5).

Because God rewards our faithfulness and our motives—not the results of our labors—the humble Christian whose work is obscure to the world can be rewarded as lavishly as the most prominent minister. Based on this understanding, we are urged to continue living faithfully and to hold fast to the truth of Christ.

VII. TEACHING OUTLINE

A. INTRODUCTION

1. Lead Story: Dependable as the Morning Mail
2. Context: John is writing to Christians in danger of being seduced by false teachers. He warns them not to trust their teaching and not to help sponsor their activities.
3. Transition: Let's look at John's powerful book; it helps us stand firm against false teaching and enables us to discern which ministries we should support and which ones we should not support.

B. COMMENTARY

1. Salutation (vv. 1–3)
2. Christians Must Practice the Truth (vv. 4–6)

3. Christians Must Protect the Truth (vv. 7–11)
4. Farewell (vv. 12–13)

C. CONCLUSION: THE LIAR'S CLUB

VIII. ISSUES FOR DISCUSSION

1. How faithful does God expect you to be? Are other people encouraged by your faithful walk?
2. Why should we keep God's commands? How do his commands relate to his love?
3. What so-called "preachers" and "witnesses" do you suspect of meeting the Bible's criteria for false teachers and antichrists? Are you supporting them in any way? Does your silence support them?
4. What are the basic biblical teachings about Jesus Christ? Do you have trouble believing any of these? Why or why not?

3 John

Practicing Hospitality

"*D*o not forget to entertain strangers, for by so doing some people have entertained angels without knowing it."

Hebrews 13:2

BOOK PROFILE: 3 JOHN

- Written to Gaius, a friend of the apostle John
- Probably written approximately the same time as 1 John and 2 John
- Written to commend Gaius and Demetrius to continue their hospitality toward Christian missionaries, and to rebuke Diotrephes, who forbade such hospitality
- Shortest book in the Bible
- A highly personal letter reflecting John's appreciation for Gaius and Demetrius because of their hospitality to other Christians

AUTHOR PROFILE: JOHN

- Author is "the elder," traditionally identified as the apostle John, one of the original twelve disciples of Jesus, who also wrote the Gospel of John
- The disciple whom Jesus loved (John 21:20,24)
- One of the two sons of Zebedee, the brother of James
- Along with James, nicknamed the "Sons of Thunder" (Mark 3:17)
- Formerly a follower of John the Baptist
- Wrote this letter in his old age
- Known as the "Apostle of Love," since the theme of love is so prominent in his writings

IN A NUTSHELL

*G*reetings, Gaius. I am overjoyed to hear that you are walking in the truth. I commend you for being hospitable to traveling missionaries. I am not happy with Diotrephes, who refuses to welcome brothers. Demetrius is a good man. I hope to see you soon.

Practicing Hospitality

I. INTRODUCTION

When Fish and Friends Stink

*B*enjamin Franklin once wrote that after three days fish and guests stink. This was a thinly veiled way of saying that no one should stay with someone else as a guest any longer than three days. Perhaps this statement reflected Franklin's limited capacity for hospitality rather than any great truth. The truth is that some guests "stink" before three days are up, and others never seem to overstay their welcome. We ought not to take our cue about hospitality from our own limited capacity. Rather, we ought to do what is right for other people.

When John wrote this epistle, travelers were dependent on the hospitality of other people, since hotels and restaurants were extremely rare. When Christian preachers traveled to spread the gospel, other Christians were expected to support their ministry by offering them hospitality. This was right, and it was also a rewardable practice. Those who offered hospitality participated in the travelers' ministries and received a reward for doing so (Matt. 10:41–42).

Our attitude toward visitors often determines when they begin to grate on our nerves. We ought to recognize the need to extend hospitality to others. And we are pleasing to God when we do so.

II. COMMENTARY

Practicing Hospitality

> **MAIN IDEA:** *Walking in truth and being hospitable toward traveling missionaries is good; refusing to do so is bad.*

A Gaius Is a Good Man (vv. 1–4)

> **SUPPORTING IDEA:** *When we are walking in the truth, we bring joy to Christian friends and mentors.*

1–2. The elder, the apostle John, wrote to **Gaius,** his dear friend whom he loved. This reveals an intimate, personal relationship between the author and the recipient. He loved him **in the truth,** a phrase identical with 2 John 1, perhaps meaning not only that he truly loved him, but that he loved him as a fellow believer, as one who believed the truth and was committed to it. John was pleased with the spiritual condition of Gaius, and he wished that he might do as well physically.

3–4. John greatly rejoiced to learn from **some brothers** about Gaius's faithful Christian life. Possibly the "brothers" who brought this testimony to John about Gaius had benefited from his hospitality.

John was overjoyed to hear that his **children** were **walking in the truth**. This wording is similar to 2 John 4. Perhaps Gaius was a convert of John's, or perhaps John just had a paternal perspective toward Gaius, a younger fellow believer.

B Gaius Is a Generous Man (vv. 5–8)

SUPPORTING IDEA: *Hospitality toward traveling missionaries brings God's commendation. We ought to help such people work together for the truth.*

5–6. In John's day, travelers generally depended on the hospitality of other people rather than commercial inns or eating places. Christian preachers and teachers often traveled to spread the gospel and so depended on the generosity of other Christians. Gaius was hospitable toward such traveling preachers. His conduct was praiseworthy because it was an act of faithfulness to the truth of God.

In Gaius's case, walking in truth was synonymous with walking in love. He showed visitors Christian love, and his reputation was well known. His example encouraged many others, and he was worthy of the God whom he served. His hospitality reflected God's own kindness. **You will do well** is idiomatic in Greek and equal to "please." To **send . . . on their way** suggests making adequate provision for guests at the time of departure, as well as during their stay. Nothing less than such open generosity would be **worthy of God**, who is ultimately generous to us, and who intends to meet the needs of others through us.

7–8. The traveling ministers went out to spread the message of the gospel. They were determined not to seek support from those who did not honor **the Name**. Perhaps this suggests a caution, even today, for ministries to seek money only from fellow believers—not from the unbelieving people to whom they preach God's free salvation. In this way, both minister and hospitable laity join together in spreading and living out God's truth.

Since the faithful preachers were limited in their source of support, Christians needed to be sure to help them. When they did this, they participated in their ministry. As Matthew wrote, "Whoever receives (shows hospitality to) a prophet . . . will receive a prophet's reward" (Matt. 10:41).

Ⓒ Diotrephes Is a Prideful Man (vv. 9–11)

SUPPORTING IDEA: *Prideful people who are malicious gossips oppose Christian hospitality.*

9. The reference to the church suggests that Gaius and **Diotrephes** might have been part of the same church. Perhaps John wrote a letter to the church, encouraging them to be hospitable toward traveling missionaries, but Diotrephes resisted it because of pride. He wanted to be **first** over them (note the NIV does not translate the Greek pronoun meaning "over them"). His lust for power and prestige meant he wanted to receive hospitality from others rather than stoop to serve others. He saw himself as too important to spend time preparing a house and meals for visitors who would be here today and gone tomorrow.

This letter to Gaius suggests, perhaps, that Gaius did not know about the original letter to the church. Perhaps Diotrephes used his leadership role to suppress knowledge of the letter. When John said that Diotrephes would **have nothing to do with us**, he was identifying with Diotrephes's refusal to be hospitable to the traveling brethren. Diotrephes may not have personally opposed John, but John interpreted his rejection of the traveling brethren as a personal rejection.

10. John determined to deal with the matter in person. Diotrephes was guilty of three things. First, he was **gossiping maliciously about us**. Literally, he was bringing false charges against other believers with evil words. Second, he refused **to welcome the brothers**. Gossip was bad enough, but he put his ungracious attitude into motion and refused to help the travelers. If that were not bad enough, his third sin was that he stopped **those who want to do so**. Using his self-proclaimed position, he forced other Christians to be inhospitable. If they weren't, he kicked them out of the church!

Apparently, Diotrephes wanted no outsiders coming to his church and finding out what was going on. He sought to ruin the reputation of any people who might question his authority and his way of running the church. He liked the way things were going, and he would go to any length to prevent change.

Gaius might already have known all this, and John was just reminding him of it. Gaius apparently had some status in the church and was able to stand against Diotrephes. Further, John would publicly deal with Diotrephes when he visited.

11. The apostle then declared moral judgment against Diotrephes. His conduct was evil. Gaius was not to imitate this behavior. **Anyone who does what is evil has not seen God**, John observed. It is not certain that John was questioning Diotrephes's salvation. At least he claimed that Diotrephes's behavior revealed a spiritual blind spot. His attitude and conduct certainly did not come from God. No one who shuts out his Christian brother could

claim to be practicing Christian love. Diotrephes was actually imitating the false teachers of 1 and 2 John.

D Demetrius Is a Good Man (v. 12)

> **SUPPORTING IDEA:** *You can recommend a person to other churches for hospitality and ministry when that person's life supports God's truth.*

12. John vouched for Demetrius's good reputation in the wider church family. Such recommendation came not just from what others said. John, whom Gaius trusted, put his own stamp of approval on Demetrius.

John might have been implicitly encouraging Gaius to extend hospitality to Demetrius. Some Bible teachers believe Demetrius was a traveling missionary. Perhaps he even delivered the letter from John to Gaius as a letter of introduction. Unlike Diotrephes, his life and character supported **the truth itself.** (Note: This Demetrius is probably not the same person in Acts 19:24 who is an enemy of the gospel. Demetrius was a very common name during the first century.)

E Farewell (vv. 13–14)

> **SUPPORTING IDEA:** *Personal friendship can be expressed through written benediction, but it is better expressed face to face.*

13–14. John still had much to say to Gaius, but he decided it would be better to do so in person. He closed the letter with a quick benediction of peace, wishing wholeness and completeness of life to believers (Hebrew, *shalom*).

> **MAIN IDEA REVIEW:** *Walking in truth and being hospitable toward traveling missionaries is good; refusing to do so is bad.*

III. CONCLUSION

Alter Your Course

When we set our navigational course according to pride, we are setting ourselves up for destruction. This truth is illustrated by the captain of a ship who looked ahead and saw a light in the distance. He told his signalman to send a message to the other vessel to alter its course ten degrees south. But a message was relayed back to the captain to alter *his* course ten degrees *north*.

The captain was angered. He sent another message saying, "Alter your course ten degrees south. I am the captain."

Soon a message came back, "Alter your course ten degrees north. I am seaman third class Jones."

Immediately, the captain sent a third message, mustering all the authority at his command: "Alter your course ten degrees south. I am a battleship."

A message came back, "Alter your course ten degrees north. I am a lighthouse!"

If the captain had remained on course, he would have destroyed himself, his ship, all aboard, and the lighthouse. When we refuse to alter our course of pride, we risk destroying ourselves and others. The apostle John warned Diotrephes to change his course, but Diotrephes refused. He risked destruction by his rebellious action. We would do well to learn from him and to live our lives as servants, showing love and hospitality toward others.

PRINCIPLES

- Christian hospitality is an important virtue.
- Those who minister are dependent upon those who support their ministry.
- Those who support a ministry are rewarded by God, just like those who minister.
- Pride and gossip are sins.
- Church leaders are just as capable of sin as other people.

APPLICATION

- Open your home to other people when circumstances enable you to do so.
- Assist other people in ministry when you are able to do so.
- Be grateful for the Lord's reward when you help others in ministry.
- Be discerning of the spiritual integrity of those in spiritual leadership.
- Beware of the insidious temptations to pride that come from positions of leadership and influence.

IV. LIFE APPLICATION

The Art of Being a Big Shot

In an article entitled "The Art of Being a Big Shot," prominent Texas businessman Howard E. Butt, an outstanding Christian layman, wrote:

> It is my pride that makes me independent of God. It's appealing to me to feel that I am the master of my fate, that I run my own life, call my own shots, go it alone. But that feeling is my basic dishonesty. I can't go it alone. I have to get help from other people, and I can't ultimately

rely on myself. I'm dependent on God for my next breath. It is dishonest of me to pretend that I'm anything but a man—small, weak, and limited. So living independent of God is a self-delusion. It is not just a matter of pride being an unfortunate little trait and humility being an attractive little virtue; it's my inner psychological integrity that's at stake. When I am conceited, I am lying to myself about what I am. I am pretending to be God, and not man. My pride is the idolatrous worship of myself. And that is the national religion of Hell!

Selfishness and pride are serious and damaging character flaws. All of us wrestle with them to some degree. C. S. Lewis once said, "Pride is the mother hen under which all other sins are hatched."

Satan sees to it that we are constantly tempted by selfishness and pride. It is not a problem we can get over; rather, it is a condition that must be monitored at all times.

Jesus said the person who would be first in his kingdom must be last, and the last would be first. "Whoever wants to be first must be slave of all. For even the Son of Man did not come to be served, but to serve, and to give his life as a ransom for many" (Mark 10:44–45). Paul echoed this truth in these words: "Do nothing out of selfish ambition for vain conceit, but in humility consider others better than yourselves. Each of you should look not only to your own interests, but also to the interests of others" (Phil. 2:3–4).

This is the standard we all fall short of. When we flagrantly disregard it, however, we can shipwreck our lives. James 3:13–16 warns us that if we have selfish ambition in our heart, it will produce wisdom that is "earthly, unspiritual, *of the devil*" (italics added). Where selfish ambition exists, there is "disorder and every evil practice."

When we do not look out for the needs of others, when we are governed by selfish ambition, bad things happen. We violate the commands of God; we disqualify ourselves from spiritual reward; we become vulnerable to demonic influence; and we set evil things in motion. This is what Diotrephes did. It is what John warns us not to do.

Pride is dishonest, self-destructive, harmful to others, and ultimately demonic. It is the sin of Diotrephes—and a sin that we must learn to turn from.

V. PRAYER

Dear heavenly Father, help us to see ourselves as you see us—people of infinite value but individuals of no more value than anyone else in your sight. Help us to be willing to serve others with our lives and in doing so, to honor you. May we have the power of the Holy Spirit, not demons, flowing through our actions. Amen.

VI. DEEPER DISCOVERIES

A. We Ought to Support Such Men (v. 8)

Hospitality is generally regarded as the practice of receiving someone into your home as a guest, providing food, shelter, and protection. It is not often perceived with as great a significance today as it has had in the past. Today, with hotels and restaurants within reach of nearly every place in the country, hospitality is considered more of an optional character trait than a necessary one. In Scripture, however, it is a highly praised character trait.

The Pentateuch specifically commanded hospitality for those in need. It instructed the Israelites to look out for the strangers among them (Lev. 19:33–34; Deut. 10:18–19; 24:17–22). The rationale for treating strangers kindly was that the Israelites were once strangers in Egypt. Rahab's act of hospitality was praised (Josh. 6:22–25; Heb. 11:31; Jas. 2:25), while a failure to be hospitable was condemned (Gen. 19:1–11; Judg. 19:10–25).

In the New Testament, hospitality was a qualification for a person who wished to serve as an elder (1 Tim. 3:2; Titus 1:8) and a general responsibility of all Christians (Rom. 12:13; 1 Pet. 4:9). Hebrews instructs believers to entertain strangers, for in doing so some people have entertained angels without knowing it (13:2).

But the issue goes beyond mere hospitality in 3 John. The main issue is support of those who are in the ministry. We should be hospitable when the circumstances call for it and when we are able, but even when the opening of our home is not required, we should be prepared to do what we can to support ministers to further the spread of the gospel (Luke 10:7; 1 Cor. 9:9).

Moreover, hospitality extends within the local church, not just to visiting strangers. Many college students, single parents, widows, senior citizens, and orphans seek hospitality, care, and love. Ministering to them brings abundant reward.

VII. TEACHING OUTLINE

A. INTRODUCTION

1. Lead Story: When Fish and Friends Stink
2. Context: John wrote his third epistle to a man named Gaius to encourage him to give support and hospitality, possibly to a man named Demetrius, who might have carried the letter to Gaius. John praised the hospitality of Gaius and condemned an inhospitable man, Diotrephes.
3. Transition: The apostle John commended Gaius, condemned Diotrephes, and commended Demetrius. He outlined a basic theology

of hospitality that guided the New Testament church and serves as an important guide for believers today.

B. COMMENTARY

1. Gaius Is a Good Man (vv. 1–4)
2. Gaius Is a Generous Man (vv. 5–8)
3. Diotrephes Is a Prideful Man (vv. 9–11)
4. Demetrius Is a Good Man (v. 12)
5. Farewell (vv. 13–14)

C. CONCLUSION: THE ART OF BEING A BIG SHOT

VIII. ISSUES FOR DISCUSSION

1. Define Christian hospitality in today's world. What opportunities do you and your church have to extend such hospitality?
2. What are the temptations of church leadership? How does a church leader fight against such temptations?
3. Is everyone in the church expected to exercise hospitality?
4. In what ways are you tempted by pride? What are you doing to resist such temptations?
5. How is your church tempted to resist outside influences so life can go on as usual with no threat to church leaders, church traditions, and church practices? Is your church resisting such temptations?

Jude

Defend the Faith

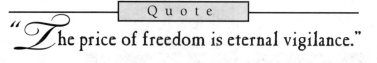

"*The* price of freedom is eternal vigilance."

Thomas Jefferson

BOOK PROFILE: JUDE

- The recipients of the letter are not known. References to Old Testament people, places, and events suggest that they were Christian Jews of Palestine (the land west of the Jordan River).
- The date of the epistle is uncertain. Most commentaries estimate the date to be between A.D. 67 and 80.
- Written to warn of false teachers and to encourage true believers to defend the faith
- Warns against denying Christ's lordship, following fleshly desires, rejecting authority, being divisive, and living for self
- Encourages the faithful to contend for the true faith against the false teachers who have crept into the church
- Refutes false teachers who perhaps suggested that spirit was good and flesh was bad (Gnosticism). Therefore, since the spirit and flesh were opposite, they—in a twisted turn of logic—felt free to indulge the desires of the flesh.
- An intense letter that, while brief, is important and powerful.

AUTHOR PROFILE: JUDE

- Three options as to who Jude might be:
  (1) a leader in the early church in Jerusalem
  (2) the apostle of Jesus
  (3) the half brother of Jesus
- Tradition most strongly supports the half brother of Jesus:
  (1) An apostle probably would have let his apostolic authority be known, since he was writing such an intense letter. Also, he referred to the apostles in verse 17, suggesting he was not one of them.
  (2) The "brother of Jesus" has strong support because he was the brother of James (also a half brother of Jesus). Jude the apostle was not the brother of James, but the son of James (Luke 6:16; Acts 1:13).
- Like his brothers, Jude did not believe in Jesus before the Resurrection (John 7:1–9).

- Wrote with a heart of love for his readers, but also an intense note of concern and warning
- Wrote with dynamic style, using brilliant figures of speech (clouds without rain, autumn trees without fruit, wild waves, wandering stars, etc.)

IN A NUTSHELL

Dear friends, earnestly contend for the faith against godless people who have slipped into the church, teaching false doctrine. God has dealt harshly with unbelief in the past and will do so again. The apostles have told us that false teachers will come. I tell you they are now here. Build yourselves up in the faith and help those who are weak. Jesus will help you if you turn to him.

Defend the Faith

I. INTRODUCTION

False Ceilings

*W*hen concerts and other special events are held in large auditoriums or arenas, "riggers" must work hundreds of feet above the floor hanging speakers and lights. Riggers will tell you they do not mind looking down a hundred feet to the floor. What they don't like is working in buildings that have false ceilings made of acoustical tile hung just a few feet below the ceiling on rafters and beams. It gives them a false sense of security. They feel as though they are working just a few feet above a floor; but if they stepped onto the tile, they would crash through and fall to their death many feet below. They don't like the deceptive look. It makes it easier to make a mistake.

Satan works like that. He makes dangerous things look safe. He gives us a false sense of security. He makes it easier for us to make a mistake. Satan tries not to scare us to death, but rather to make us think we face little danger of a spiritual fall.

The Epistle of Jude warns of the dangers of false teachers, whose end is destruction. We are to be alert for them, to strengthen ourselves against spiritual deception, and to be ready to help vulnerable believers. Christian friends must not be lulled into a false sense of security and take a disastrous spiritual fall.

II. COMMENTARY

Defend the Faith

MAIN IDEA: *Defend the faith against false teachers. Strengthen yourselves, and be merciful to those who are weak.*

A Jude States His Purpose for Writing (vv. 1–4)

SUPPORTING IDEA: *With God's mercy, peace, and love abiding on you, contend for the faith against false teachers who have slipped into the church.*

1–2. The author identified himself simply as **Jude** (a shortened form of Judas), **servant of Jesus Christ and a brother of James.** Jude was a common name at the time this letter was written. We take this to mean the half brother of Jesus (see Author Profile). Strikingly, if he was the half brother of Jesus, he showed a radical life change. Before the Resurrection he did not believe in Jesus. Now, he not only believed; he defended the faith. Yet in so doing, he still considered himself a servant—a willing slave—of his older half brother.

His readers are **called . . . loved by God the Father, and kept by Jesus Christ**. We take them to be Jewish Christians living in Palestine (see Book Profile). Jude was fond of presenting information in triads (threes). **Called** looks to the past (Rom. 1:6; 8:30; Eph. 4:4); **loved** looks to the present (1 John 4:8–10); while **kept** looks to the future (1 Thess. 5:23; 2 Tim. 1:12; 1 Pet. 1:5).

He wished **mercy, peace and love** (another triad) for his readers—a typical greeting of the culture and time. This greeting reflected a gracious concern for the welfare of his readers.

3–4. Jude's preference was to write a pleasant and encouraging letter on the subject of their common **salvation**. Circumstances pressed upon him, however, so that he wrote a brief but intense and potent warning against false teachers in the church. He jumped right to the point, urging them **to contend for the faith**. Why? Because false teachers, godless people, had **secretly slipped in among** them.

He described **the faith** as having been **once for all entrusted to the saints**. "The faith" is seen also in Galatians 1:23 and 1 Timothy 4:1. This refers to the body of information believed by the early church. It is the gospel, the message of truth that brings salvation to the person who believes it. "Faith" refers to a body of objective truth, not the subjective experience of believing something.

These **godless men** were not true believers. They were people **whose condemnation was written about long ago**. How long ago, we can't say for sure. Some interpreters think this refers to the prophecy of Peter in 2 Peter 2:3. Others look to the prophecies of Paul in Acts 20:29–30. Some think he refers to Jesus' teachings, such as Matthew 7:15; 13:24–25; or Mark 13:22. Still others take it back all the way to the Old Testament.

These godless people are charged by Jude with two serious sins. First, they **change the grace of our God into a license for immorality**. They were the forerunners of people called Gnostics (see Deeper Discoveries, 1 John 1), who believed that the spirit was good (created by God) while the flesh was bad (not created by God). The spirit was not touched by the flesh, or it would be contaminated. Therefore, they assumed that they could indulge every fantasy of the flesh, since their spirit was not affected. This theory resulted in flagrant immorality and perversion. They twisted the grace of God, claiming that God would overlook any sin, because sin was a product of the flesh.

The second sin they are charged with is denying **Jesus Christ our only Sovereign and Lord**. These false teachers might have taught that since the flesh is bad, Jesus could not be the Son of God. In their view, God could not assume human flesh without contaminating himself. They denied the true humanity of Christ and perverted the biblical truth of Jesus. "They claim to know God, but by their actions they deny him" (Titus 1:16). Like later Gnostics, they may have denied that the Creator God was the only or highest God, and they may have claimed that Jesus was a mere man on whom the Holy Spirit descended at his baptism but left before his crucifixion.

B Jude Describes False Teachers (vv. 5–16)

> **SUPPORTING IDEA:** *The past examples of Israel, angels, and pagan cities should persuade anyone that God is not to be trifled with. The sins of these godless men make them liable to God's judgment.*

5–7. Three examples from the past warn us of the danger of defecting from the faith. First, the Hebrew people were delivered under the leadership of Moses from slavery in **Egypt**. However, not all those Israelites were true believers. Some were rebellious against God. As a result, God destroyed them in the wilderness. Even some of the "chosen people" suffered judgment for their unbelief.

Second, angels rebelled against God. All angels were righteous in the beginning and had **positions of authority**. Apparently, Satan enticed some of these angels to follow him in rebellion against God. (Satan is called the "prince of demons" in Matt. 12:24.) When they abandoned their original position, God confined them **in darkness**, waiting eternal **judgment**. Some interpreters believe this may refer to Genesis 6:1–4 where the "sons of men" are interpreted to be angels who left their positions of authority and cohabited with human women ("daughters of earth"). As a result of the heinousness of this sin, God wiped them out immediately. The New Testament makes it clear that not all fallen angels (demons) are confined, but some are.

Other interpreters see these verses not as a reference to Genesis 6:1–4 but to a book called the Book of Enoch, which is not part of the Bible but is usually included in the Jewish writings known as the Pseudepigrapha. Since Jude did not tell us to what he was referring, we have to be content with ambiguity. Apparently, the common knowledge of the time did not make it necessary for Jude to explain himself further. His readers must have understood his reference easily. We do not.

Third, **Sodom and Gomorrah and the surrounding towns** were destroyed by God's judgment of fire. These towns gave themselves to sexual immorality and perversion (Gen. 19:1–29). Physical fire fell on them, destroying them and serving as an example to the false teachers, who will suffer the punishment of eternal fire in hell.

8–10. The godlessness of the false teachers can be described in four categories. First, they rejected authority. Apparently, they claimed divine revelation through dreams which gave them permission to participate in immoral acts. Thus, they let their dreams overrule biblical teaching and **pollute their own bodies.** Then, they rejected authority and slandered **celestial beings,** which Jude illustrated with the example of **the archangel Michael.** In an interesting peek behind the historical curtain that we do not get in the Old Testament, we learn that Michael was sent to bury the body of Moses when he died atop Mount Nebo (Deut. 34). According to Jewish tradition (supported by this passage), the devil argued with him about it, apparently claiming for himself the right to dispose of Moses' body. (For Jewish sources, see Bauckham, WBC 50, 65–76.) Michael, powerful as he was, **did not dare to bring a slanderous accusation** against the devil, but said instead, **The Lord rebuke you!**

The false teachers, on the other hand, spoke **abusively against whatever they do not understand.** We do not know what they did not understand. This abusive speech may refer to their slandering of angels mentioned in verse 8. Such slander may have included their claim that angels were messengers and guardians of the Law who envied and did not like humans, so they forced humans to obey the law. If so, they apparently had no respect for the authority of angels and slandered angels to escape the authority of the law. Their understanding only went as far as **unreasoning animals,** and as a result, they apparently engaged in self-destructive behavior. They followed fleshly instincts, unbridled by God's law, and thus would face judgment and eternal punishment at the last day.

Michael, on the other hand, had extreme respect. He would not even rebuke Satan, the fallen angel, but instead left such rebuke to God. Jude did the same. Obeying the law is not a matter of dismissing angelic authority. It goes much deeper. It rejects divine authority and dismisses threats of final judgment.

11. Second, these false teachers blundered around in sin. Jude turned to a triad of sins these godless people had committed and pronounced woe on them. They had **taken the way of Cain.** There is little agreement as to what this means, but there are several possibilities:

1. They were disobedient and unbelieving, charting their own course in life.
2. They worshiped God according to their own understanding, not according to God's revelation.
3. They were eaten up by envy of others.
4. They hated others and had a murderous spirit, as Cain did.
5. They taught heresy as some Jewish tradition attributed to Cain.

In addition to taking the way of Cain, they **rushed for profit into Balaam's error.** Balaam was hired by Balak to put a curse on the Israelites, who were wandering in the wilderness after their exodus from Egypt. Balaam did it for money (see Num. 22:21–31; 2 Pet. 2:15–16). Jude warned about opposing God for money.

Third, they have been **destroyed in Korah's rebellion**. Korah rebelled against the leadership of Moses and Aaron, refusing to acknowledge that God had placed them in authority over the Hebrews (Num. 16). Picturing the false teachers' destruction as a past event is probably a figure of speech designed to emphasize the certainty of their judgment, should they not repent.

12–13. Third, these godless people were deceptive leaders. Somehow they had gained positions as **shepherds** in the church, but they were serving for selfish reasons. They participated in **love feasts**—intimate, communal meals that Christians ate together for the purpose of fostering fellowship and unity (Acts 20:7–11; 1 Cor. 11:20–22). Originally, they may have been part of the Lord's Supper. Instead of participating in the spirit of the meal, they merely fed themselves. Perhaps the play on words is that, as shepherds, they were to feed their flock spiritually, but instead they were feeding themselves physically. They were seen as **blemishes** on the meal. This word for "blemish" is translated in some versions as "hidden rocks." The false teachers were seen by Jude as people who were about to cause shipwreck for the church. They blundered their way through these love feasts without the **slightest qualm**, seeing nothing wrong with what they did.

In vivid and colorful language, Jude strung together four word pictures to communicate the emptiness of their spiritual lives. They were **clouds without rain**. Travelers in desert lands know the disappointment of seeing clouds that they hope will contain water—but don't. They promise but do not perform. It is a form of deceit, if a cloud (shepherd) could rain (minister faithfully) but chooses not to. In addition, they were **autumn trees, without fruit**. Autumn is the time when fruit on trees is expected. The principle is the same as the clouds. The trees are not only without fruit, but they are also uprooted. This emphasizes their spiritual death.

Jude next spoke of **wild waves of the sea, foaming up their shame**. Perhaps their shame came from the pollution of their own bodies (v. 8). The picture is of the ocean surf washing up on the shore, bringing litter and garbage, fouling the beach with each successive wave.

Finally, these false teachers are described as **wandering stars**, destined for blackness. Since stars do not wander, this might be a reference to shooting stars that appear for a moment, then are lost in darkness. **Blackest darkness . . . forever** hints at the eternal destiny of these godless people. In verse 6, this darkness is mentioned in relationship to the fallen angels who suffer darkness as part of their punishment for rebelling against God.

These pictures are bleak, indeed, and would give pause to any heart that had a hint of life. If these godless people could withstand this intense verbal assault, it confirms the lifelessness of their hearts.

14–16. Finally, these godless people were self-serving; but before describing their self-serving ways, Jude mentioned a prophecy by Enoch about God's judgment on the ungodly. **Enoch** was the **seventh from Adam** (Gen. 4:17). His prophecy is either a general quote from the Book of Enoch, which is not part of the Bible, or perhaps, under divine inspiration, he recorded oral tradition (stories carefully memorized and passed down from one generation to the next). If Jude quoted generally from the Book of Enoch, it does not suggest that he considered the entire book inspired or that he approved of all the content of the book. It simply means that under the inspiration of the Holy Spirit, he accepted the prophecy as being true. The same is true with oral tradition. If Jude recorded oral tradition, it does not mean he accepted all oral tradition as being true—just this particular prophecy.

Jude declared that the godless people of his day were among the ones being referred to when Enoch prophesied. There is no new information in Enoch's revelation. When Christ returns, accompanied by **thousands upon thousands** of angels, he will judge the **ungodly acts** of these men, as well as the **harsh words** [they] **have spoken** against Jesus, whom they have denied.

Self-serving godlessness has four facets. First, they were **grumblers and faultfinders**. They saw flaws in others, but never in themselves. Such is the nature of pride.

Second, they followed **their own evil desires**, which might be the cause of their grumbling and fault finding. When someone determines to satisfy his or her own desires, grumbling and fault finding often follow, because evil desires are not easily satisfied. People and circumstances must cooperate. If they do not, complaining is a natural result.

Thirdly, these false teachers **boast about themselves** while they also **flatter others** in the hope that they may gain some advantage. The terms that appear here mean they used swollen and extravagant speech. This may refer to the godless people's habit of offering lofty, self-glorifying speeches in which they claimed superior knowledge of God.

On the other hand, these godless people were fawning and servile toward other people, smearing slimy, oily words around in the hope of getting others to think highly of them.

Ⓒ Jude's Defense Against False Teachers (vv. 17–23)

> **SUPPORTING IDEA:** Build yourselves up to resist ungodly people in the last times who will try to undermine you, and try to help others who might be taken in by them.

17–19. Warnings against false teachers and unscrupulous hucksters are common in the New Testament. They are "savage wolves" who would come in to destroy the flock and the truth (Acts 20:29–30). Against them we must uphold the truth of God and godly living (2 Tim. 3:1–17). Peter's second epistle sounds much like Jude in several places, as he warned his readers of the false prophets, reminded them of God's judgment on such people, and urged them to stand firm in their faith (2 Pet. 2:1–3:18).

We should remember the words of the **apostles** and be on guard against these people. These men were not Christians, and they moved among the congregation in an attempt to divide the people. As they taught their perverted heresy and lived their profligate lifestyles, some in the church might have followed them. Others would not. In this way, the believers could have been divided. No one should follow such false teachings. Consider their source—natural human instincts. This means their teaching was inherently selfish and wrong. Only teaching from the Spirit of God should be followed. These godless people certainly did not **have the Spirit**.

20–21. Knowing the reality of false teachers, how do we safeguard ourselves against them? The NIV seems to suggest three instructions, but the Greek gives us four participles: building, praying, keeping, and expecting. To arm ourselves against false teachers, we must (1) **build yourselves up in your most holy faith**, (2) **pray in the Holy Spirit**, (3) **keep yourselves in God's love**, and (4) **wait for the mercy of our Lord Jesus Christ to bring you to eternal life**.

To build oneself up in the most holy faith means to grow spiritually. Fundamental to such growth is to learn as much as possible of the truth of Scripture and to set one's life to believe and obey it. The **most holy faith** is that which was **once for all entrusted to the saints** (v. 3). It embodied the teaching of Jesus and the apostles and is now recorded in the Scriptures. "All Scripture is God-breathed and is useful for teaching, rebuking, correcting and training in righteousness, so that the man of God may be thoroughly equipped for every good work" (2 Tim. 3:16–17). If we want to be trained in righteousness and equipped for every good work, we must make the Scriptures a central part of our lives.

Praying **in the Holy Spirit** is not necessarily a reference to speaking in tongues but may include this as one part of prayer (see John 4:23–24; Rom. 8:15–16; Gal. 4:6; Eph. 6:18). Rather, it refers to praying under the direction and influence of the Holy Spirit, trusting him to intercede for us with "groans that words cannot express" (Rom. 8:26). The how of praying may not be so much in focus here as the need for life in the Spirit which the false teachers did not have (v. 19). They did not have the Spirit because they did not pray for the Spirit and did not let the Spirit guide them in their prayers. Those who build themselves up in faith do so not by mystic journeys to the heavens or by self-glorying speech but by spending time with the Holy Spirit.

Keeping oneself **in God's love** does not suggest that our salvation depends on our own effort, but rather that we live in faith and obedience to God.

Repeatedly in his Gospel and in his first epistle, John reminds us that if we love God, we keep his commandments (John 15:10; 1 John 3:24). So keeping ourselves in God's love must include keeping God's commandments from the heart (Rom. 6:17). Keeping those commandments finds its ultimate expression in love of the brothers (1 John 3:14; cf. 1 Thess. 4:10; 1 Pet. 1:22; 3:8).

To wait for the **mercy of our Lord . . . to bring eternal life** probably refers primarily to the hope of Christ's return. Jesus might come at any moment. Titus 2:13 captures the idea: the "blessed hope—the glorious appearing of our great God and Savior, Jesus Christ." Waiting in hope infuses all of life with expectancy and the desire to do all that Jesus expects of us so we will have no shame when he returns. This expectant waiting is a fourth means of building ourselves up.

Even if Jesus doesn't come in our lifetime, when we die and go into the presence of the Lord, we will receive his mercy and eternal life. That promise should be enough to motivate us to resist false teachers and to obey Christ by building ourselves up through prayer, love, and hope.

22–23. After we have safeguarded ourselves by building ourselves up in the faith, we are to look out for three groups of people. First, less mature Christians might begin to **doubt** their walk with the Lord because of the smooth and convincing false teaching they hear. Therefore, the more mature believers need to be **merciful** to them. Such mercy forgives the false steps of new believers and guides them to build up their own faith in Bible study, prayer, love, and hope.

Others probably refers to non-Christians, who do not doubt their faith (they have nothing yet to doubt), but who might be warned of coming judgment. If they repent, they will be snatched from the **fire** of hell.

The phrase **to others** refers to the godless people whose lives are so degenerate that their clothes smell like rotting flesh. To these people, we are to **show mercy**, but to do so with a very cautious attitude (**mixed with fear**), apparently so we do not become contaminated by their sin.

D Doxology (vv. 24–25)

SUPPORTING IDEA: *To God, who is able to keep us from falling into the snare of the godless ones, be great glory now and forever.*

24–25. The letter concludes with perhaps the loftiest doxology found in Scripture. It begins with the comforting affirmation that God is able to **keep you from falling** away from the faith. **Joy** permeates us when we grasp the power and glory of our Lord. False teachers, false doctrine, and false fears of failure cannot make us fall, for God keeps us. We affirm his **glory, majesty, power and authority**, which he works through Jesus, who will **present you before his glorious presence without fault**. Final judgment has no fear. God will be our representative there. His saving work in Jesus will speak for us.

We do not have to defend ourselves. Joy, indeed! Too good to be true! This greatness of God *has* always been true, *is* true now, and always *will* be true. With that triumphant note, this valuable letter ends.

MAIN IDEA REVIEW: *Defend the faith against false teachers. Strengthen yourselves, and be merciful to those who are weak.*

III. CONCLUSION

Loss of Hope

In his book *Man's Search for Meaning*, psychiatrist Victor Frankl observed that "the loss of hope and courage can have a deadly effect on man." As a result of his own experiences in a Nazi concentration camp, Frankl contended that when a person no longer possesses a reason for living . . . no future to look forward to, he shrivels up and dies. "Any attempt to restore a man's inner strength in camp," he wrote, "had first to succeed in showing him some future goal." ("Man's Search for Meaning" by Victor Frankl, quoted in *Illustrations for Biblical Preaching*, ed. Michael Green, [Grand Rapids: Baker Books, 1989], p. 194.)

So it is with life. Life is a concentration camp, in the sense that none of us gets out alive. Yet, we can all have something to look forward to. We do not have to shrivel up and die.

After warning his readers about the dangers of false teachers and the need to resist them, Jude concluded his letter by presenting a resounding doxology of hope. "God is able to keep you from stumbling now," he declared, "and to present you before his glorious presence without fault and with great joy!" What a hope. What a day to look forward to. What a reason to keep going. Scripture calls it the "blessed hope" (Titus 2:13), and so it is.

PRINCIPLES

- False teachers are a danger to Christianity.
- False teachers are persuasive and convincing.
- Spiritual maturity is our protection against false teachers.
- Immature people may need help in resisting false teaching.
- The hope of heaven is a great motivator for life on earth.

APPLICATION

- Pay close attention to Bible teachers. They may be 95 percent accurate and 5 percent heresy.
- Commit yourself to spiritual maturity through Bible study, prayer, love, and hope.

- Be on the lookout for others in danger so you can show them mercy and help.
- Focus on your hope in heaven for strength for the present journey.

IV. LIFE APPLICATION

The Light in the Window

When John Todd, a nineteenth-century clergyman, was six years old, both his parents died. A kindhearted aunt raised him until he left home to study for the ministry. Later, this aunt became seriously ill. In distress she wrote Todd a letter. Would death mean the end of everything, or could she hope for something beyond? Here, condensed from *The Autobiography of John Todd,* is the letter he sent in reply:

> It is now thirty-five years since I, as a boy of six, was left quite alone in the world. You sent me word you would give me a home and be a kind mother to me. I have never forgotten the day I made the long journey to your house. I can still recall my disappointment when, instead of coming for me yourself, you sent your servant, Caesar, to fetch me.
>
> I remember my tears and anxiety as, perched high on your horse and clinging tight to Caesar, I rode off to my new home. Night fell before we finished the journey, and I became lonely and afraid. "Do you think she'll go to bed before we get there?" I asked Caesar.
>
> "Oh, no!" he said reassuringly. "She'll stay up for you. When we get out o' these here woods, you'll see her candle shinin' in the window."
>
> Presently, we did ride out into the clearing, and there, sure enough, was your candle. I remember you were waiting at the door, that you put your arms close about me—a scared and bewildered little boy. You had a fire burning on the hearth, a hot supper waiting on the stove. After supper you took me to my new room, heard me say my prayers, and then sat beside me till I fell asleep.
>
> Some day soon God will send for you, and take you to a new home. Don't fear the summons, the strange journey, or the messenger of death. God can be trusted to do as much for you as you were kind enough to do for me so many years ago. At the end of the road you will find love and a welcome awaiting, and you will be safe in God's care (*Illustrations for Preaching and Teaching*, ed. Brian Larson, [Grand Rapids: Baker Books, 1993], p. 55).

The forces of evil are aligned against the kingdom of God, so that life itself can begin to seem like a battle. When it does, hope for peace at the end can be a tremendous encouragement. Hope can give strength and courage for the trials of the day.

The marvelous picture of hope and security painted by the skillful writing of John Todd gives comfort, consolation, encouragement, and hope. All's well that ends well, and to have light in the window at the end of life's dark night is a profound encouragement.

It is that very encouragement that Jude's concluding doxology gives to the battle-weary warrior for Christ. We may feel weary and uncertain of our stamina. But Jesus will see us through to the end. He is able, Jude says, to keep us from falling. He is able to present us without fault before his glorious presence. He is able to give us reason for great joy! Like a light in the window of life, Jesus gives us hope, comfort, encouragement, and strength to see us through to the end.

V. PRAYER

Dear heavenly Father, grant to us the wisdom and strength to recognize and stand against false teaching ourselves, and help us to help those who are vulnerable. Father, thank you for the glorious hope of heaven and the profound promise that Jesus will see us through until then. May you receive all due glory and praise for eternity. Amen.

VI. DEEPER DISCOVERIES

A. Sodom and Gomorrah (v. 7)

Sodom and Gomorrah are so well known that they have become a synonym for evil and debauchery. They were sister cities in the time of Abraham, possibly located in the Valley of Siddim (Gen. 14:3,8,10–11) near the southern end of the Dead Sea.

The city of Sodom was renowned for homosexuality, so much so that our modern term *sodomy* has come from its name. Even though Abraham pleaded for the city, not even ten righteous men could be found in it (Gen. 18:22–32). The cities were destroyed by fire and brimstone as a direct judgment of God. The memory of their destruction is often invoked as a metaphor of God's divine judgment on wickedness (see Isa. 13:19; Jer. 49:18; Matt. 10:14–15).

B. Celestial Beings (v. 8)

Jude introduces an interesting glimpse into the world of angels and demons. The godless men slandered celestial beings and spoke abusively against things they didn't understand. Many of us, however, have a shallow understanding of angels.

The term *angel* means "messenger." God created angels before he created the world. They have remarkable power. One angel was all God was going to use to destroy the entire city of Jerusalem (2 Sam. 24:16). In Revelation, though the language is highly symbolic, angels carry out monumental tasks requiring unimaginable power.

Some angels rebelled against God and followed Satan. Some scholars believe that a third of them were lost to Satan (Rev. 12:4), and that, as demons, they are now organized in a hierarchical system, doing the bidding of Satan and resisting the will of God (Eph. 6:12). Some scholars suggest that angels are also arraigned in a hierarchy, including archangels (1 Thess. 4:16; Jude 9), an honored class of cherubim and seraphim that minister in the presence of God (Isa. 6:2–6), guardian angels (Heb. 2:14), and others with specific rank and responsibility.

How much of this is the case, we do not know. We do know that celestial beings are immensely powerful and that any person would be foolish, indeed, to slander or speak abusively against them, whether angels or demons.

C. Enoch, the Seventh from Adam (v. 14)

This reference to Enoch has a couple of problems associated with it. First, Enoch is not the seventh generation from Adam. He is the sixth. The generations from Adam are Seth, Enosh, Kenan, Mahalalel, Jared, and Enoch. However, the Jewish custom in such circumstances was to count the first generation. Counted in this fashion, Enoch would be the seventh generation from Adam.

Second, Jude's reference to Enoch's prophecy is a near quote from a passage in the Book of Enoch. This has led to speculation that Jude was quoting from the Book of Enoch. This may not be the case, however. He may have been quoting a prophecy that was passed down through oral tradition (carefully memorized stories passed down from one generation to the next).

Does this quotation in Jude have an adverse effect on the doctrine of inspiration? The doctrine of inspiration states that God oversaw the human authors so that, using their own individual personalities, they composed and recorded without error his revelation to man in the words of the original manuscripts. Using this definition, regardless of where the prophecy came from (oral tradition or the Book of Enoch), God still inspired Jude to record the prophecy as part of Scripture.

The fact that Jude recorded the prophecy in his letter does not mean that he holds all the oral tradition to be true (if he took it from oral tradition) or that he holds all of the Book of Enoch to be true (if he took it from the Book of Enoch). It just means that he considered the prophecy itself to be true, a fact later confirmed by the inspiration of the Holy Spirit.

Quoting from a non-biblical source is not unheard of in the Bible. For example, the apostle Paul quoted a Cretan poet in Titus 1:12: "Even one of their own prophets has said, 'Cretans are always liars, evil brutes, lazy gluttons.'" This did not mean that Paul thought everything the Cretan poet said was true. But he thought the quote was true.

These quotes from sources outside the Scripture do not cast doubt in any way upon the doctrine of inspiration.

VII. TEACHING OUTLINE

A. INTRODUCTION

1. Lead Story: False Ceilings
2. Context: Jude warns Christians of godless false teachers, urging us to be on the lookout for them, to strengthen ourselves against false teaching, and to be ready to help other believers who are vulnerable to these false teachings.
3. Transition: Jude tells us first to be aware of the deception of false teachers, and then he gives us a defense against them. We will find how we can build up our faith and strengthen our hope in the face of teachers who make fun of our faith and claim to have an easier way to heaven.

B. COMMENTARY

1. Jude States His Purpose for Writing (vv. 1–4)
2. Jude Describes False Teachers (vv. 5–16)
3. Jude's Defense Against False Teachers (vv. 17–23)
4. Jude's Doxology (vv. 24–25)

C. CONCLUSION: THE LIGHT IN THE WINDOW

VIII. ISSUES FOR DISCUSSION

1. Describe the relationship Jude says we as Christian believers have with God.
2. How can we recognize false teachers?
3. How can we prepare ourselves to oppose false teachers?
4. Contrast the hope we have with the hope of false teachers.
5. How does Jude's quotation of Enoch contribute to our understanding of the inspiration of Scripture?

Glossary

Aaron—Moses' brother; the first high priest of Israel.

Ananias and Sapphira—A Christian couple in the early church at Jerusalem who sold a piece of property and brought only a portion of the proceeds from its sale, claiming they were bringing the total amount, and were struck dead for lying to the Holy Spirit.

antichrist—Anyone who opposes God or Christ; especially the evil leader at the end of the age that Christ will defeat at his Second Coming.

apostles—Men chosen by Jesus as his official messengers.

archangel—A chief angel; a celestial being highest in rank among the angelic hosts of heaven.

atonement—Reconciliation between God and humans effected by the death, burial, and resurrection of Jesus Christ; associated in the Old Testament with sacrificial offerings and, especially, the Day of Atonement ritual.

atoning sacrifice—A sacrifice offered as an atonement for a person's or a nation's sins; particularly the blood sacrifice and burnt offerings of animals offered during Old Testament times.

Babylon—The name of an evil city and empire in the sixth century B.C.; a code name for Rome.

Balaam—A soothsayer or magician who was hired by the king of Moab to curse the Israelites; instead, he blessed the people of Israel.

Calvary—A hill just outside Jerusalem on which Jesus was crucified; the name means, "place of the skull."

carnality—The opposite of spirituality; giving in to the desires and appetites of the flesh, or the body.

Christological—Of or pertaining to Christ; the nature and work of Jesus Christ.

confess—To admit one's sin and to acknowledge Jesus as Lord.

conversion—The experience of an individual in which a person turns from sin and trusts in Jesus Christ for salvation, resulting in an outward change in daily life.

Cretan—A native or citizen of Crete, an island in the Mediterranean Sea.

Day of the Lord—God's time of decisive intervention in history.

Demetrius—A Christian commended by the apostle John because he was "well spoken of by everyone" (3 John 12).

Diana (Artemis)—Roman (Greek) goddess of the moon; daughter of Zeus; cared for nature; mother goddess; fertility goddess; identified with Ephesus (see Acts 19:28).

Diaspora/Dispersion—Jews scattered in lands outside of Palestine as a result of the fall of Samaria in 722 B.C. and of Jerusalem in 586 B.C.; gave rise to Jewish communities and Jewish synagogues in which Paul began his ministry in cities he visited.

Diotrephes—An early believer who was reprimanded by the apostle John (3 John 9–10).

divine chastening—God's punishment, or discipline, designed to guide believers in making correct choices and following his divine will.

docetism—A heretical belief which taught that God did not take on human flesh in the form of Jesus and that Jesus only *seemed* to have a physical body.

doctrine—Carefully formulated statements of belief about the Christian gospel based on the teachings of Jesus and God's Word.

doxology—A brief hymn which expresses God's glory and power; a declaration of praise to God.

elders—In the church, spiritual leaders and ministers, usually equated with bishops and pastors; a decision-making council.

elect—Those whom God has chosen to follow him and obey his commandments.

Enoch—The father of Methuselah; taken directly into God's presence without experiencing death.

Enoch, Book of—A book of the Pseudepigrapha.

excommunicate—To expel a member from the church; to withdraw fellowship because of divisiveness, heretical beliefs, or moral lapse.

expiation—An action directed toward nullifying the effects of sin that breaks the relationship between a person and God; emphasizes the saving event of the atonement of Christ rather than the penalty or punishment endured.

familial forgiveness—Forgiveness practiced by persons toward one another in the give and take of human relationships.

fellowship—Shared encouragement and support among Christians.

foreknowledge—God's eternal knowledge of the future.

Gaius—The person to whom the apostle John addressed his third epistle (3 John 1, 5); may be the same Gaius who was baptized under Paul's ministry (1 Cor. 1:14).

glory—A quality of God's character that emphasizes his authority.

Gnosticism—A view fully developed after A.D. 100 that emphasized salvation through a secret knowledge and a dualistic worldview with equal powers of good and evil.

Gnostics—Adherents or followers of Gnosticism.

heresy/heretical—Opinion or doctrine not in line with the accepted teaching of a church; opposite of orthodoxy.

holy—Set apart from ordinary use for God's use; set apart from sin.

hospitality—The practice of welcoming and entertaining strangers graciously and in the spirit of Christ.

incarnation—God becoming human; the union of divinity and humanity in Jesus of Nazareth, qualifying him to be the agent of God's saving plan for humanity.

inheritance—Humanly, a legal transmission of property after death; theologically, the rewards God gives his children who are saved through Jesus Christ.

judgment seat of Christ—The divine tribunal before which believers will stand in the end time.

judicial forgiveness—Forgiveness of God directed toward humans in his role as divine judge.

justification—The act/event by which God credits a sinner who has faith as being right with him through the blood of Jesus (Rom. 3:21–26; 4:18–25; 5:10–21; 1 Pet. 3:18).

Lord's Supper—A church ordinance or observance with breaking of bread and drinking of wine helping Christians (1) remember the last meal Jesus ate and his death on the cross making salvation possible, (2) examine their own lives in light of Christ's demands, and (3) anticipate Christ's return (Mark 14:22–25; 1 Cor. 11:23–26).

love feasts—A meal shared by the early Christians when they met to observe the Lord's Supper and to fellowship together.

man of lawlessness—Another name for the Antichrist.

Mark—Author of the Gospel of Mark; called "my son" by the apostle Peter (1 Pet. 5:13).

martyr—A person who witnesses for Christ by dying rather than deny Christ.

Michael—An archangel who disputed with Satan over the body of Moses (Jude 9).

Moses—The leader that God used to bring the Israelites out of slavery in Egypt.

Nero—An evil emperor of Rome who persecuted Christians in the A.D. 60s.

New Age movement—A modern philosophy which teaches that God is all things and that all things are God; a belief that humans should tap into the divine potential within themselves and achieve their full potential.

new birth—God's work in the believer at conversion to create a new person empowered by the Holy Spirit.

nirvana—A New Age teaching in which persons find permanent bliss and an end to reincarnation and human suffering.

orthodoxy—Holding right beliefs as opposed to heretical beliefs.

paraclete—Greek word for Helper and Counselor as promised by Jesus; looking to the coming of the Holy Spirit.

Pentateuch—First five books of Hebrew Bible (Genesis, Exodus, Leviticus, Numbers, Deuteronomy); only Scriptures recognized by the Samaritans and the Sadducees.

Pentecost—Israel's feast of weeks at the time of wheat harvest; celebrated fifty days after Passover; time of year when the Holy Spirit came in power for the first time on Christ's disciples (Acts 2).

Philo—A Jewish historian who recorded the events surrounding the fall of Jerusalem in A.D. 70.

preexistence—Existing always and before the creation of the universe; a characteristic of the trinitarian God alone.

propitiation—An action directed toward God seeking to change his wrath to favor; one way of explaining Christ's atonement.

Pseudepigrapha—A collection of Jewish writings which included wisdom literature and questions on the suffering of the righteous; many of the books are named for notable figures in Jewish history, such as Adam, Moses, and Solomon.

Rahab—A prostitute of Jericho who hid two Hebrew spies and helped them escape from the city.

reconciliation—The bringing together of alienated persons; the saving work of Christ and a ministry given to believers.

red heifer—A calf without blemish offered as a sacrifice to bring about purification from uncleanness.

redeem—To release something or someone by paying a price.

regeneration—Radical spiritual change in which God brings an individual from a condition of spiritual death to a condition of faith and responsiveness to God.

righteousness—The actions and positive results of a sound relationship within a local community; the right relationship created by God between himself and a person of faith.

saint—Literally "holy one," but used for each person who believes in and follows Jesus.

sanctification—The process by which God conforms the believer's life and character to the life and character of Jesus Christ through the Holy Spirit.

Satan—Name for the devil, emphasizing that he is the adversary of God.

Septuagint—The oldest translation of the Hebrew Old Testament into Greek; often quoted in the New Testament.

Silas—A prominent member of the early church at Jerusalem; a missionary who accompanied the apostle Paul on some of his journeys.

Sodom and Gomorrah—Two cities near the Dead Sea destroyed by God because of their wickedness.

spirits in prison—Those to whom Jesus preached in connection with his death and resurrection.

Tartarus—The name in classical mythology for the subterranean abyss in which rebellious gods and other such beings as the Titans were punished.

transfiguration—Transformation of the outward appearance of Jesus in the company of Moses and Elijah; witnessed by Peter, James, and John (Matt. 17:1–13; Mark 9:1–13; Luke 9:28–36; cf. 2 Pet. 1:16–18).

trinity—God's revelation of himself as Father, Son, and Holy Spirit unified as one in the Godhead and yet distinct in person and function.

Uriah—A Hittite warrior sent to his death on orders of King David so that David's adulterous relationship with Uriah's wife Bathsheba would not be discovered.

worldliness—An affection for that which is unlike God, opposed to his nature, and contrary to his will and desire.

Yahweh—The Hebrew personal name of God revealed to Moses; came to be thought too holy to be pronounced by Jews; often translated LORD or Jehovah.

Zion—Another name for Jerusalem.

Bibliography

1 and 2 Peter, Jude

Archer, Gleason L. *Encyclopedia of Bible Difficulties*. Grand Rapids: Zondervan Publishing House, 1982.

Barclay, William. *The Letters of James and Peter*. Toronto: G. R. Welch Co. Ltd., 1976.

Bauckham, Richard J. "Jude, 2 Peter." In *The Word Biblical Commentary*, vol. 50. Waco, Tex.: Word Books, 1983.

Bruce, F. F., gen. ed. *The International Bible Commentary*. Grand Rapids: Zondervan Publishing House, 1986.

Carson, D. A., Douglas J. Moo, and Leon Morris. *An Introduction to the New Testament*. Grand Rapids: Zondervan Publishing House, 1992.

Carson, D. A., R. T. France, J. A. Motyer, and G. J. Wenham. *New Bible Commentary, 21st Century Edition*. Downer's Grove, Ill.: InterVarsity Press, 1994.

Cedar, Paul A. "James, 1, 2 Peter, Jude." In *The Communicator's Commentary*, vol. 11. Waco, Tex.: Word Books, 1984.

Clowney, Edmund P. *The Message of 1 Peter*. Downers Grove, Ill.: InterVarsity Press, 1988.

Craddock, Fred B. *First and Second Peter and Jude*. Louisville: Westminster John Knox Press, 1995.

Davids, Peter H. *The First Epistle of Peter*. Grand Rapids: William B. Eerdmans Publishing Company, 1990.

Elwell, Walter A. *Evangelical Dictionary of Theology*. Grand Rapids: Baker Book House, 1984.

————.*Evangelical Commentary on the Bible*. Grand Rapids: Baker Book House, 1986.

————.*Evangelical Dictionary of Biblical Theology*. Grand Rapids: Baker Book House, 1996.

Enns, Paul P. *The Moody Handbook of Theology*. Chicago: Moody Press, 1989.

Ferguson, Sinclair B., and David F. Wright, eds. *New Dictionary of Theology*. Downers Grove, Ill.: InterVarsity Press, 1988.

Gaebelein, Frank E., ed. *The Expositor's Bible Commentary*, vol. 12. Grand Rapids: Zondervan Publishing House, 1981.

Geisler, Norman, and Thomas Howe. *When Critics Ask*. Wheaton, Ill.: Victor Books, 1992.

Green, Michael. *The Second Epistle General of Peter and the General Epistle of Jude*. Grand Rapids: William B. Eerdmans Publishing Company, 1989.

Grenz, Stanley J. *Theology for the Community of God*. Nashville: Broadman & Holman Publishers, 1994.

Grudem, Wayne A. *The First Epistle of Peter*. Grand Rapids: William B. Eerdmans Publishing Company, 1989.

Gundry, Robert H. *A Survey of the New Testament*. Grand Rapids: Zondervan Publishing House, 1994.

Guthrie, Donald. *New Testament Introduction*. Downers Grove, Ill.: InterVarsity Press, 1973.

Hiebert, D. Edmond. *Second Peter and Jude*. Greenville, S.C.: Unusual Publications, 1989.

Hillyer, Norman. "1 and 2 Peter, Jude." In *The New International Biblical Commentary Series*, vol. 16. Peabody, Mass.: Hendrickson Publishers, Inc., 1992

House, H. Wayne. *Charts of Christian Theology and Doctrine*. Grand Rapids: Zondervan Publishing House, 1992.

Keeley, Robin, ed. *Eerdmans Handbook to Christian Belief*. Grand Rapids: William B. Eerdmans Publishing Company, 1982.

Kistemaker, Simon J. *Exposition of the Epistles of Peter and of the Epistle of Jude.* Grand Rapids: Baker Book House, 1987.

Lucas, Dick, and Christopher Green. *The Message of 2 Peter and Jude.* Downers Grove, Ill.: InterVarsity Press, 1995.

Marshall, I. Howard. "1 Peter." In *The IVP New Testament Commentary Series.* Downers Grove, Ill.: InterVarsity Press, 1991.

McHenry, Raymond. *The Best of In Other Words.* Houston, Tex.: Raymond McHenry, Publisher, 1996.

McKnight, Scott. "1 Peter." In *The NIV Application Commentary.* Grand Rapids: Zondervan Publishing House, 1996.

Michaels, J. Ramsey. "1 Peter." In *Word Biblical Themes.* Dallas, Tex.: Word Publishing, 1989.

"1 Peter." In *Word Biblical Commentary,* vol. 49. Waco, Tex.: Word Books, 1988.

Motyer, Stephen. "1 Peter." In *The Evangelical Commentary on the Bible,* edited by Walter A. Elwell. Grand Rapids: Baker Book House, 1994.

Perkins, Pheme. *First and Second Peter, James and Jude.* Louisville: John Knox Press, 1995.

Richards, Larry. *Bible Difficulties Solved.* Grand Rapids: Fleming H. Revell, 1993.

Rienecker, Fritz, and Cleon Roger. *Linguistic Key to the Greek New Testament.* Grand Rapids: Zondervan Publishing House, 1980.

Selwyn, Edward Gordon. *The First Epistle of St. Peter.* Grand Rapids: Baker Book House, 1981.

Stanley, Charles. *The Glorious Journey.* Nashville: Thomas Nelson Publishers, 1996.

Tripp, Rhoda Thomas. *The International Thesaurus of Quotations.* New York: Harper and Row, Publishers, 1970.

Walvoord, John F., and Roy B. Zuck, eds. *The Bible Knowledge Commentary, New Testament Edition.* Wheaton, Ill.: Victor Books, 1983.

Wilson, Neil S., ed. *The Handbook of Bible Application.* Wheaton, Ill.: Tyndale House Publishers, Inc., 1992.

Wolff, Richard. *A Commentary on the Epistle of Jude.* Grand Rapids: Zondervan, 1960.

Youngblood, Ronald F., gen. ed. *Nelson's New Illustrated Bible Dictionary.* Nashville: Thomas Nelson Publishers, 1995.

1, 2, 3 John

Barker, Glen W. *1, 2, 3 John.* Expositor's Bible Commentary. Grand Rapids: Zondervan, 1981.

Blaney, Harvey J. S. *1, 2, 3 John.* Beacon Bible Commentary. Kansas City: Beacon Hill Press, 1967.

Brown, Raymond E. *The Epistles of John.* The Anchor Bible. Garden City, N.Y.: Doubleday, 1982.

Bruce, F. F. *The Epistles of John: Introduction, Exposition, and Notes.* Old Tappan, N.J.: Revell, 1970.

Dodd, C. H. *The Johannine Epistles.* New York: Harper & Brothers, 1946.

Drummond, R., and Leon Morris. *Epistles of John.* New Bible Commentary. Grand Rapids: Eerdmans, 1954.

King, Guy. *The Fellowship: An Expositional and Devotional Study of 1 John.* London: Marshall, Morgan, and Scott, 1963.

Kistemaker, Simon J. *Exposition of the Epistle of James and the Epistles of John.* Grand Rapids: Baker, 1986.

Marshall, I. Howard. *The Johannine Epistles.* New International Commentary on the New Testament. Grand Rapids: Eerdmans, 1978.

Palmer, Earl E. *1, 2, 3 John, Revelation.* The Communicator's Commentary. Waco, Tex.: Word Books, 1982.

Smalley, Stephen S. *1, 2, 3 John.* Word Biblical Commentary. Waco, Tex.: Word Books, 1984.

Smith, D. Moody. *1, 2, and 3 John.* Interpretation Commentary. Louisville: John Knox Press, 1991.

Stott, John R. W. *The Epistles of John.* Tyndale New Testament Commentaries. Grand Rapids: Eerdmans, 1964.

Vine, W. E. *The Epistles of John: Light, Love, Life.* Grand Rapids: Zondervan, 1965.

Westcott, B. F. *The Epistles of St. John.* 3rd ed. Grand Rapids: Eerdmans, 1966 reprint.